AF600351

THE CATHOLIC UNIVERSITY OF AMERICA
CANON LAW STUDIES
No. 358

Guardians of the Mentally Ill in Ecclesiastical Trials

A CANONICAL COMMENTARY WITH HISTORICAL NOTES

A DISSERTATION

SUBMITTED TO THE FACULTY OF THE SCHOOL OF CANON LAW OF THE CATHOLIC UNIVERSITY OF AMERICA IN PARTIAL FULFILLMENT OF THE REQUIREMENTS FOR THE DEGREE OF DOCTOR OF CANON LAW

BY

REV. GENNARO J. SESTO, S.D.B., A.B., S.T.L., J.C.L.
PRIEST OF THE PROVINCE OF SAINT PHILIP THE APOSTLE

THE CATHOLIC UNIVERSITY OF AMERICA PRESS
WASHINGTON, D. C.
1956

IMPRIMI POTEST:

Ernestus Giovannini, S.D.B.
Superior Provincialis

Novae Rupellae, die 16 iulii, 1955

NIHIL OBSTAT:

Joannes Rogg Schmidt, A.B., J.C.D.
Censor Deputatatus

Washingtonii, D.C., die 2 septembris, 1955

IMPRIMATUR:

✠ Jacobus A. McNulty, D.D.
Episcopus Patersonensis

Patersonii, die 6 septembris, 1955

Printed by Theo. Gaus' Sons, Inc., Brooklyn 1, N. Y., U. S. A.

TO MY MOTHER AND FATHER

TABLE OF CONTENTS

PAGE

Foreword ix

CHAPTER I

The Historical Development and Function of Guardianship of the Mentally Ill 3

Article I. In Roman Law and Doctrine 3

Article II. In Ecclesiastical Law and Doctrine 15

Concluding Remarks 26

CHAPTER II

The Mentally Ill and their Processual Disability in Ecclesiastical Trials 31

Historical Note 31

Article I. The Mentally Ill 35

Article II. The Processual Disability of the Mentally Ill .. 43

CHAPTER III

The Qualifications of Guardians 52

Article I. In the Roman Law 52

Article II. In the Law of the Code 54

CHAPTER IV

The Manner of Appointment of Guardians for the Mentally Ill 62

Preliminary Considerations 62

Article I. The Manner of Appointment in Roman Law and Doctrine 62

Article II. The Manner of Appointment in Subsequent Civil Legislation and Doctrine 67

Article III. The Manner of Appointment in the Law of the Code and Canonical Doctrine 69

CHAPTER V

THE ECCLESIASTICAL AUTHORITIES COMPETENT TO APPOINT GUARDIANS 82

Article I. Approval of the Civil Law Guardian 82

Article II. Appointment of Guardians by the Ordinary 89

Article III. Appointment by the Ecclesiastical Judge 97

CHAPTER VI

THE GUARDIAN'S RIGHT TO STAND IN ECCLESIASTICAL TRIALS 102

Preliminary Considerations 102

Article I. The Ward's Freedom from Canonical Disqualifications 109

A. Disqualifications of Infidels 109

B. Disqualifications of Excommunicated Catholics 114

C. Disqualifications of Baptized Non-Catholics 118

D. Disqualifications of Religious 119

Article II. The Mandate of the Guardian 123

CHAPTER VII

THE RIGHTS AND DUTIES OF GUARDIANS AT THE VARIOUS PERIODS OF THE CANONICAL TRIAL 131

Article I. The Guardian in the Introductory Period 131

A. The Formulation of the Bill of Complaint 131

B. The Formal Summons 133
C. The Joining of Issues 134
Article II. The Guardian in the Probatory Stage of the Process 136
A. Judicial Interrogations 136
B. The Testimony of Witnesses 138
C. Documents 141
D. Judicial Experts 142
E. Judicial Access and Inspection 143
F. Presumptions 143
G. Probatory Oaths 145
Article III. The Guardian in the Definitive Stage of the Trial 147
A. The Publication of the Process 147
B. The Conclusion of the Process 148
C. The Discussion of the Case 149
D. The Formulation and Publication of the Sentence ... 150
Article IV. The Guardian and Legal Redress against the Sentence 152
A. The Correction of Material Errors 152
B. The Right of Appeal 152
C. The Complaint of Nullity 156
D. *Restitutio in Integrum* 159

CONCLUSIONS 161

BIBLIOGRAPHY 163

ABREVIATIONS 173

ALPHABETICAL INDEX 174

CANON LAW STUDIES 177

BIOGRAPHICAL NOTE 179

FOREWORD

This study is concerned with and limited to the subject of guardians of the mentally ill in ecclesiastical trials. No attempt has been made in the historical notes or in the canonical commentary to give a description of the entire institute of guardianship.

No detailed historical conspectus has been given, nor is it necessary, since guardianship, as it is found in modern legislations, does not present any essential departures from the kindred institutes of *tutela* and *cura* as described in classical and post-classical Roman Law and doctrine. The historical notes included in this work are derived almost exclusively from that law and doctrine. References, however, to subsequent civil and canonical law and jurisprudence are also included. The references made to civil legislation are intended to inform the reader of particulars which are not contemplated by the Code but which may serve as guides in the application of the institute of guardianship in the ecclesiastical forum. For, although the civil institute of guardianship has not been canonized by the ecclesiastical legislator, Church Law does recognize both the institute and its civil effects, as outlined by the law of the various civil jurisdictions.

This work discusses the guardian-ward relation as it functions in ecclesiastical trials of the mentally ill; it is not directly concerned with the duties and rights of guardians in the administration of their wards' patrimony or in their general well-being. In a well-ordered society the state concerns itself competently and satisfactorily with problems arising from the guardian-ward relation in the order of administration and general supervision.

The legitimate representation of a mentally ill person by a guardian is of particular importance in matrimonial cases tried in countries whose courts recognize decisions of ecclesiastical tribunals. In those countries provisions of the inferior ecclesiastical courts and the related definitive sentence are forwarded to the Supreme Tribunal of the Apostolic Signatura, which examines whether the canonical norms relative to competence, citation, representation, and contumacy have been observed and then sends on the provisions and sentence with its own decrees to the civil court of appeal[1] or to the Supreme Court of the respective country.[2]

The guardianship of the mentally ill finds application, too, in the other contentious causes which the Church Tribunals are competent to judge.

To the writer's knowledge, there has been no detailed study published on this particular point. He hopes that his effort will satisfy the desire expressed by recent commentators that a study on guardianship in the ecclesiastical forum be undertaken.

The writer wishes to express his gratitude to his religious superiors for the opportunity to pursue advanced studies in Canon Law; to the Faculty of the School of Canon Law of the Pontificium Athenaeum Salesianum, Turin, Italy; to the Faculty of the School of Canon Law of the Catholic University of America; to all others who have aided in any way in making this work possible; and especially to our Lady under whose protection this work was begun and concluded.

---

[1] Cf. *Conventiones cum Italia seu Pacta Lateranensia* (11 *Febr.* 1929 *inita; 7 Iunii* 1929 *confirmata*), art. 34—A. Perugini, *Concordata Vigentia, Notis Historicis et Iuridicis Declarata* (Romae: Apud Custodiam Librariam Pont. Instituti Utriusque Iuris, 1934), p. 135.

[2] Cf. *Concordatum cum Austria* (5 *Iunii* 1933 *initum; 1 Maii confirmatum*), art. vii, 4—Perugini, *op. cit.*, p. 278.

CHAPTER I

The Historical Development and Function of Guardianship of the Mentally Ill

Article I. In Roman Law and Doctrine

Primitive times showed but little sympathy towards the mentally ill. Indeed, it is commonly stated that the ancients destroyed their mentally defective children,[1] as they were considered a burden, heavy to bear in proportion to their mental affliction. Relatives and friends looked after them; but should they become dangerous to society, they were thrown into prison, as asylums for lunatics did not exist in primitive society.[2] As a matter of fact, not until the idea that the insane were ill and not wicked had penetrated into the public consciousness did the humanitarian movement in treating the insane begin.[3]

However, legal protection was afforded one general class of mental cases, the *furiosi,* by the most important early enactment of Roman legislation, the Twelve Tables (451-450 B.C.).[4] The text, assigned by scholars to Table V. 7a and 7b, reads:

a. SI FURIOSUS ESCIT, ADGNATUM GENTILIUMQUE IN EO PECUNIAQUE EIUS POTESTAS ESTO. . . .

---

[1] H. H. Goddard—X (anonymous contributor), "Feeble-Mindedness," *Encyclopaedia Britannica* (Chicago: Encyclopaedia Britannica, Inc., 1944), Vol. IX, p. 141.

[2] Cf. F. Schulz, *Classical Roman Law* (Oxford: Clarendon Press, 1951), p. 197.

[3] Philippe Pinel (1745-1826), director of the Bicêtre and, later, of the Salpêtrière, two insane asylums in Paris, achieved that change in public opinion. "Upon his instigation and under his direction jails were changed into hospitals and jailers into nurses, shackles were removed from the patients, and physicians were trained." Cf. J. H. Van der Veldt—R. P. Odenwald, *Psychiatry and Catholicism* (New York: McGraw—Hill Book Company, Inc., 1952), p. 38.

[4] This celebrated code was the foundation of Roman Law and, though

b. AST EI CUSTOS NEC ESCIT.[5]

According to this enactment, both the person (*in eo*) and the property (*pecunia*) of a *furiosus* were in *potestate* of the *proximus adgnatus* or of the *gens,* in cases in which the *furiosus* had neither father nor *tutor* (*ast ei custos nec escit*).[6] Insane persons who were *in potestate patris* or *in tutela,* for instance, did not fall under the provisions of this enactment, as the *paterfamilias* or the *tutor* had the right and duty of looking after them. As a matter of fact, there was never any question of guardianship of any sort except where the person concerned was *sui iuris*: a person who was *in potestate, in manu,* or *in mancipio* needed no guardian.[7]

This elementary ruling illustrates the remarkable antiquity of legal enactments embodying the cause of the insane.[8] Indeed, the text reveals that the *gens* was in the habit of taking charge in some way of lunatics and insane persons.[9] For one of the main purposes of the decemviral code was to give all the citizens equal private rights whether they happened to be members of a gentile association

---

greatly improved and modified, it was never wholly superseded by subsequent enactments, interpretations, and praetorian remedies. It continued to be, in theory, the ancient statutory source from which all civil law in the strict sense flowed until the time of Justinian himself (A. D. 527-565). For reconstructions of the law of the Twelve Tables see: C. G. Bruns, *Fontes Iuris Romani Antiqui* (Tubingae: Mohr, 1910); S. Riccobono, J. Baviera, C. Ferrini, J. Furlani, V. Arangio-Ruiz, *Fontes Iuris Romani Antejustiniani* (Florentiae: Barbera, 1940-1943), *Pars Prima*: *Leges* (Riccobono, 1941).

[5] Cf. Bruns, *Fontes Iuris Romani Antiqui,* p. 23; Riccobono, *Fontes Iuris Romani Antejustiniani,* p. 39.

[6] Cf. S. Perozzi, *Istituzioni di Diritto Romano* (2. ed., 2 vols., Roma: Athenaeum, 1928), I, 524.

[7] Cf. H. F. Jolowicz, *Historical Introduction to the Study of Roman Law* (2. ed., Cambridge: University Press, 1952), p. 120 (hereafter cited *Historical Introduction*).

[8] Cf. R. C. Pickett, *Mental Affliction and Church Law* (Ottawa, Ontario: The University of Ottawa Press, 1952), p. 11.

[9] Cf. Edward Poste, *Gai Institutiones or Institutes of Roman Law by Gaius,* 4. ed., revised and enlarged by E. A. Whittuck (Oxford: Clarendon Press, 1904), p. 112 (hereafter cited *Gai Institutiones*); J. Muirhead, *Roman Law* (London, 1899), §§26, 28.

or not.[10] So it was—one may safely conjecture—with regard to the institution of guardianship. The *gens* had provided for the guardianship of its pupil, female, and imbecile members, and charged itself with the surveillance of their guardians;[11] but the Twelve Tables dealt with the whole subject in the interests of non-gentilitial as well as for gentilitial citizens,[12] and it did so incidentally and not in detail. For of the institutions of the family, of the fundamental rules of succession, of testaments, and so forth, a general knowledge was presumed, and the *decemviri legibus scribundis* thought it unnecessary to go into detail. So was it with guardianship, of which, too, it may be said: "nothing of the customary law, therefore, or next to nothing, was introduced into the Tables that was already universally recognized as law, and not complained of as either unequal, indefinite, defective, or oppressive."[13]

The institution of guardianship matured greatly in the centuries to follow. It was under the celebrated jurists of the classical age that the most important development took place. As a matter of fact, writings and treatises of Labeo, Julianus, Gaius,[14] Scaevola, Celsus, Papinianus, Ulpianus, and Paulus form the major part of Justinian's *Digest,*[15] while his *Institutes* follow closely the *Insti-*

---

[10] Cf. Tacitus, *Annales,* III, 27: "Duodecim tabulae finis aequi iuris."

[11] Cf. J. Muirhead, *Historical Introduction to the Private Law of Rome,* revised and edited by H. Goudy, 3. ed. revised and edited by A. Grant (London: Black, 1916), pp. 31, 104.

[12] Muirhead, *op. cit.,* p. 104; Poste, *Gai Institutiones,* p. 112.

[13] Muirhead, *op. cit.,* p. 91.

[14] The earliest extant systematic treatment of the subject of guardianship is found in the Institutes of Gaius, whose production performed for more than three centuries the same service for Roman Law students as Blackstone's Commentaries did for generations of English lawyers. The exact date of Gaius' birth and death are unknown. He himself mentions that he lived under Hadrian (A.D. 117-138); and from the fact that he wrote upon an enactment of the Senate passed under Commodus (A.D. 180-193), it may be inferred that he lived up to that time. From internal evidence it is argued that his Institutes were written partly in the reign of Antoninus Pius (A.D. 138-161) and partly in that of Marcus Aurelius (A.D. 177-180). Cf. Poste, *Gai Institutiones,* p. lii.

[15] Cf. L. Wenger, *Die Quellen des Römischen Rechts* (Wien: Druck und Verlag Adolf Holzhausens NFG, 1953), p. 591.

tutes of Gaius.[16] The extensive treatment of the subject of guardianship found in the *Corpus Iuris Civilis*[17] is indeed a fusion of the cited authors' exposition of the law of guardianship. They had subjected the powers, duties, responsibilities, manner of appointment of guardians to careful and elaborate definition and regulation,[18] and consequently, Justinian's production reveals itself very thorough in the protection accorded the person and estate of individuals who because of age or peculiar conditions required the special consideration of the law.[19]

Roman legal language had no general term for *guardian* and *guardianship*,[20] but distinguished between *tutor* and *tutela* on the one hand and *curator* and *cura* on the other.[21]

---

[16] Cf. C. Longo—G. Scherillo, *Storia del Diritto Romano* (Milano: Giuffrè, 1944), p. 63.

[17] Cf. Inst. (1, 13-26); D. (26, 1-10), (27, 1-10); C. (5, 28-75).

[18] Cf. Muirhead, *Historical Introduction*, p. 315.

[19] Cf. Inst. (1, 13-26); D. (26, 1-10), (27, 1-10); C. (5, 28-75). See also: Pickett, *Mental Affliction and Church Law*, p. 24.

[20] With regard to the connotation of the term "guardian" in English law, Black remarks: "This term might be appropriately used to designate the person charged with the care and control of idiots, lunatics, habitual drunkards, spendthrifts, and the like; but such person is, under many of the statutory systems authorizing the appointment, styled 'committee,' and in common usage the name 'guardian' is applied only to one having the care and management of a minor." H. C. Black, *A Law Dictionary* (2. ed., St. Paul, Minn.: West Publishing Co., 1910), p. 861, sub. v. *guardian;* cf. also p. 364, sub v. *committee.*

[21] In a general manner these two terms connoted the authority (*ius, vis, potestas*) of the guardian over the person subjected to guardianship. "The chief distinction between *tutela* and *cura* appears in the relation of *tutores* and *curatores* to the property of their respective wards: *tutores* represent constantly the personality of their wards in all proprietary relations . . . Additional *tutores* or *curatores* may be appointed for a single transaction or for a special purpose only (e.g. *ad litem.*). The essence of *tutela* is the duty of supplying the deficiency in the ward's capacity to perform legal acts; this is called the *auctoritatis interpositio* . . . . the tutor cured (*augebat*) the inability of his *pupillus* to understand the meaning of legal transactions. The essence of *cura* was the administration of property (*gestio, administratio*) and, though in some cases the *curator* was concerned with the personal welfare of his ward, he was in the main charged with the duty of preventing pecuniary damage or loss to him. In this sense the

Guardianship necessitated by extreme youth or sex was termed *tutela;* that occasioned by immaturity, incompetency, or mental deficiency was known as *cura.*[22] Roman law contemplated two forms of *tutela*: one for *sui iuris* persons,[23] both male and female, under the age of puberty;[24] and another for women *sui iuris* above the age of puberty. The first form was known as the *tutela impuberum,* while the second was styled *tutela mulierum.* The form

---

maxim, *tutor personae datur, curator rei,* is true, but not as commonly stated, that the tutor is given to the person of the pupil and the curator to the management of his property. . . . The tutor may have the *gestio* of his pupil's property, as in *tutela impuberum;* or he may lack it, as is *tutela mulierum;* to the office of *curator,* however, *gestio* is essential."—J. J. Robinson, *Selections from the Public and Private Law of the Romans* (New York: American Book Company, 1905), p. 141. (hereafter cited *Selections*).

For similar observations cf. A. Butera, *Il Codice Civile Italiano commentato secondo l'ordine degli articoli* (Torino: Unione Tipografico—Editrice Torinese, 1939), p. 429 (hereafter cited *Il Codice Civile Italiano*); B. Brugi, *Istituzioni di Diritto Romano* (Diritto Privato Giustinianeo) (3 ed., Torino: Unione Tipografico—Editrice Torinese, 1926), 122, 125; S. Perozzi, *Istituzioni di Diritto Romano,* pp. 429, 492, 525; R. W. Leage, *Roman Private Law Founded on the 'Institutes' of Gaius and Justinian* (2. ed., by C. H. Ziegler, London: MacMillan and Co., 1948), p. 114 (hereafter cited *Roman Private Law*).

The term *curatela* is not found in Justinian's work in the meaning of *cura, curatio.* Its use in this meaning is of late medieval origin. Cf. Muirhead, *Roman Law,* p. 111, note 1.

[22] Inst. (1. 13), (1. 23). Cf. C. P. Sherman, *Roman Law in the Modern World* (2. ed., 3 vols., New York: Baker, Voorhis and Co., 1924), II, p. 101.

[23] A person was *sui iuris* when he was not subject to a family head. Cf. Leage, *Roman Private Law,* p. 52, III.

[24] *Pubertas* was originally determined by physical development but was later fixed by the jurists at fourteen for males and twelve for females. Accordingly, those persons under the completed twelfth and fourteenth years respectively were *impuberes. Impuberes* were further divided into *infantes,* or children under seven years of age, and *infantia maiores,* children between the completed seventh and fourteenth years of age. *Maior aetas* (*perfecta aetas, legitima aetas*) was fixed by the *lex Plaetoria* (about 204 B.C.) at the completed twenty-fifth year. Hence the distinction *maiores* and *minores XXV annis.* Cf. Robinson, *Selections,* pp. 120-121. The *lex Plaetoria* is also referred to as *lex Laetoria.* Cf. Schulz, *op. cit.,* p. 191.

of guardianship under which the *furiosi* fell was designated by the classical lawyers as the *cura furiosi.* It is interesting to note that, whereas the word *tutela* appears on a fragment of the Twelve Tables,[25] the words *curare, curator, cura, curatio* are not found on any preserved portion of that law. It is under the term *potestas* that the Twelve Tables designate the function, or the sum-total of rights, of the *adgnati* or the *gentiles* in respect to the person and the patrimony of the *furiosus.*[26]

The Roman Law of guardianship grew out of the family organization; and the power of a guardian, whether *tutor* or *curator,* was originally a form of family power that substituted the power (*potestas*) of the *paterfamilias*[27] over persons *sui iuris* who because of extreme youth, sex, immaturity, incompetency, or mental deficiency could not act with full legal effects.[28] Since guardianship (*tutela legitima*) was originally regarded as a complement or substitute of the *potestas* that bound together the members of a Roman *familia,* Justinian's Institutes present the doctrine of

[25] Cf. Table V. 3: "Uti legascit super pecunia tutelave suae rei, ita ius esto."

[26] Cf. F. De Visscher, "'Potestas' et 'Cura,'" *Studi Perozzi* (1925), p. 400 ff., where the author adds: "Il est vrai qu'Ulpien, paraphrasant les dispositions légales relatives au 'furiosus' . . ., parle expressément d'une mise sous curatelle des agnats: 'Lex duodecim tabularum furiosum . . . in curatione iubet esse agnatorum' mais cette terminologie est démentie par nos sources en ce qui concerne la disposition relative au 'furiosus'. . . . C'est sous le nom de 'potestas' que cette loi (the Twelve Tables) désigne les droits dont elle investit les agnats et les gentils sur la personne et le patrimonie du 'furiosus'. . . ."

[27] Cf. Brugi, *Istituzioni di Diritto Romano,* 122; Sherman, *Roman Law in the Modern World,* II, p. 101; C. Sanfilippo, *Istituzioni di Diritto Romano* (2. ed., Napoli: Humus, 1946), n. 144; Robinson, *Selections,* p. 139. The term *paterfamilias* applied to every male who was *sui iuris,* no matter what his age was and whether he had or had not any children *in potestate.* Though time effected a diminution of his practically unlimited authority, even to the last day of the Roman system the *paterfamilias* possessed great power over all those subject to him. For further details, cf. Leage, *Roman Private Law,* p. 90 ff.; Burdick, *The Principles of Roman Law and Their Relation to Modern Law* (Rochester: The Lawyers Co-operative Publishing Co., 1938), p. 254 ff.

[28] Cf. Brugi, *loc. cit,;* Sherman, *loc. cit.;* Sanfilippo, *op. cit.,* n. 144.

guardianship immediately after explaining the legal conception of the Roman *familia*;[29] and his Digest offers ample space to the subject of guardianship between the important topics of *familia* and heredity.[30]

The *tutela perpetua mulierum* was almost obsolete at the time of *Gaius,* who attributed the institution of *tutela perpetua mulierum* to the conviction of ancient lawyers that women were fickle-minded.[31] Later, jurists sought to justify the perpetual guardianship of women on grounds of feminine frailty (*fragilitas sexus*), lack of business experience (*forensium rerum ignorantia*), unsound judgment (*infirmitas consilii*), and intellectual weakness (*animi levitas*). The real reason of the *perpetua tutela,* however, seems to be that a woman could not found a *potestas* and consequently could not have *sui heredes.*[32]

Gradually the lifelong guardianship of women passed into disuse and disappeared entirely about the beginning of the fourth century.[33]

When a Roman boy reached the age of puberty, *tutela* would normally cease and he would attain full juridic capacity—i.e., he would be endowed with both capacity of right and capacity of disposition. According to law he became fully competent to administer his own property and to dispose of it at will. Such was

---

[29] Cf. Inst. (1. 13-26) ; Brugi, *loc. cit.;* Sherman, *loc. cit.*

[30] Cf. D. (26. 1-10), (27. 1-10) ; Brugi, *loc. cit.;* Sherman, *loc. cit.*

[31] Gaius, Inst. (1. 144-145) : "Veteres voluerunt feminas, etiamsi perfectae aetatis sint, propter animi levitatem in tutela esse; . . . exceptis virginibus Vestalibus, quas liberas esse voluerunt." In another context, this celebrated jurist voices his own opinion: "Feminae vero perfectae aetatis in tutela esse fere nulla pretiosa ratio suasisse videtur; nam quae vulgo creditur, quia levitate animi plerumque decipiuntur et aequum erat eas tutorum auctoritate regi, magis speciosa videtur quam vera. . . ."

[32] A *suus heres* was a person who was in the *potestas* of the *testator* at the latter's death, and who by this event became *sui iuris.* He became heir, without any need for assent, from the moment of his ancestor's death and originally was liable for the latter's debts out of his own property. Cf. Leage, *Roman Private Law,* p. 220.

[33] Cf. Poste, *Gai Institutiones,* p. 111; Robinson, *Selections,* p. 155, offers a brief presentation of the evolution from guardianship to complete emancipation.

the normal event. The law of the Twelve Tables, however, limited the capacity of the *furiosus* and of the *prodigus,* placing them under the control of their *adgnati* and *gentiles,* or, as the classical lawyers designated this control, under the *cura furiosi* and the *cura prodigi.*[34] Subsequently, other forms of *cura* evolved—namely, the *cura minorum*[35] and the *cura debilium,*[36] as well as the *cura*

[34] D. (27, 10) 1: "Lege duodecim tabularum prodigo interdicitur bonorum suorum administratio, quod moribus quidem ab initio introductum est. Sed solent hodie praetores vel praesides, si talem hominem invenerint, qui neque tempus neque finem expensarum habet, sed bona sua dilacerando et dissipando profudit, curatorem ei dare exemplo furiosi." On petition of relatives, the magistrate might subject the administration of the spendthrift's affairs to some person whom he appointed *curator,* at the same time prohibiting the *prodigus* the management of his own property. Cf. *Epit. Ulp.* (12.1-3), (20.13); *Sententiae Pauli,* 3.4a.7; Schulz, *Classical Roman Law,* pp. 200-201, discusses these texts. Jolowicz remarks: "The whole question of the treatment of *prodigi* at the time of the XII Tables is much disputed"—Jolowicz, *Historical Introduction,* p. 121, note 7.

[35] After the *lex Laetoria* (*lex Plaetoria*) granted special protection to minors (*minores viginti fuinque annis,* or *adulescentes*), it is possible that the praetor, when requested by an interested party, occasionally granted the minor a *curator,* but it was only by a constitution of the Emperor Marcus Aurelius (161-180 A.D.) that *cura minorum* became a legal institution. Cf. Muirhead, *op. cit.* p. 315-316: "The guardianship or curatory (*cura*) of minors above pupillarity owed its institution to Marcus Aurelius . . ."; Schulz, *Classical Roman Law,* n. 331, pp. 192-193. In n. 332, this author offers a text from the so-called *Scriptores Historiae Augustae* (*Capitolinus, Marcus Antoninus Philosophus* 10.12) to support his statement. The text reads: ". . . de curatoribus vero, cum ante non nisi ex lege Laetoria, vel propter lasciviam vel propter dementiam darentur, ita statuit, ut omnes adulti curatores acciperent non redditis causis." Schulz interprets the passage thus: "Whereas before Marcus a *curator* was given only on the strength of the *lex Laetoria,* namely, where he was either a lunatic or a spendthrift, according to Marcus' constitution a *curator* had to be given to the minor in any case, if requested, *non redditis causis,* viz, even if the applicant did not allege lunacy or prodigality." Then he goes on to comment: "The author is in error in so far as he believes that a *curator furiosi* and *prodigi* were given *e lege Laetoria;* but apart from that his account is right: before Marcus a *curator* was only given to a minor if he was either a lunatic or a spendthrift, whereas Marcus ordered a *curator* to be given in other cases as well. Any other interpretation on the text is evidently in conflict with the wording."

[36] This was an extension or application of the *cura furiosi* and *cura*

ventris,[37] the *cura bonorum,*[38] and *cura ad certam rem* (e.g. *curator ad litem*).[39]

In order to discover the function of guardianship we must consider a person's position before the law, with respect to his private rights.[40] Whatever may have been the original meaning of *caput,*[41] it came to mean his personality or jural capacity, passive and active, in public and private life. The measure of that capacity depended on the individual's *status,* which modern students of Roman Law subdivide into *status libertatis, status civitatis,* and *status familiae.* The *status libertatis* denoted whether an individual was a free man or a slave; the *status civitatis* denoted whether, being free, he was a citizen or a non-citizen; the *status familiae* denoted what, being a citizen, was his position with regard to his family.[42]

According to the theory of the *jus civile* and of the *jus gentium* alike, a man had no rights unless he was free.[43] Being free, a person had capacity according as to whether he was a citizen or not: were he not a citizen, only exceptionally could he enjoy any of the public rights of a citizen, while his private rights included those accorded him by the *ius gentium* and such civil rights as had been specially conceded to non-citizens.

---

prodigi to persons of weak mind, or deaf, dumb, or subject to an incurable malady. Cf. Inst. (1,23) 3: "Sed et mente captis et surdis et mutis et qui morbo perpetuo laborant, quia rebus suis superesse non possunt, curatores dandi sunt." See also: D. (3,1)2; (26,5)8; (27.10)2; C. (5,4)25. "*Curatores* were appointed at the request of such persons and had the administration of their affairs. *Debiles* were capable of acquiring, alienating, binding themselves and making a testament."—Robinson, *Selections,* p. 156.

[37] Cf. D. (26,7)48.

[38] Cf. D. (26,7)48.

[39] Cf. Inst. (1,23)2.

[40] Modern legal science distinguishes between capacity of right (*capacitas iuridica*) and capacity of disposition (*capacitas agendi*).

[41] Cf. Schulz, *op. cit.,* p. 72-73; V. Arangio-Ruiz, *Istituzioni di Diritto Romano,* (10. ed., Napoli, 1949), pp. 44-45.

[42] Cf. Schulz, *op. cit.,* p. 72; Arangio-Ruiz, *op. cit.,* p. 45; Muirhead, *Historical Introduction,* p. 116.

[43] Cf. D. (4,5)3: "Servile caput nullum ius habet."; Inst. (1,16)4: "servus . . . nullum caput habuit."

The position of an individual in his family was also of great importance with regard to his private life; the *paterfamilias* alone enjoyed full jural capacity; those subject to him had a more limited personality.[44] From the birth of Rome down through the Republic, all the members of the Roman *familia* were under the absolute power of the *paterfamilias*. He answered for all wrongs done by any member of the *familia,* and he alone sued for compensation due to any of his dependents.

When *patria potestas* came to cease and the dependents of the *paterfamilias* became *sui iuris,*[45] they became independent subjects of rights and obligations and enjoyed full capacity of right. However, Roman Law did not automatically recognize in these independent persons the capacity to act with full legal effect. This prerogative was limited by law for reasons of age, sex, and mental stability.[46]

The *furiosus,* for instance, entirely lacked legal capacity to act, since the capacity to act with legal effect required certain qualities of reason and will which were completely wanting in such a person.[47] Any *negotium* effected by him was void *iure civili,* even if the other party was ignorant of his state.[48] Should he commit delicts, he was not held liable to a fine or damages.[49]

Since the *sui iuris furiosus* and those persons who came in legal

---

[44] In public life, however, a citizen's supremacy or subjection in his family was immaterial.

[45] The termination of *patria potestas* did not necessarily imply that the family head's dependents became *sui iuris,* since they could fall under another's *potestas*—e.g., at the death of their grandfather, grandchildren fell under their father's *potestas* and did not become *sui iuris.* Cf. Gaius, 1. 146: "Nepotibus autem neptibusque ita demum possumus testamento tutores dare, si post mortem nostram in patris sui potestatem [iure] recasuri non sint. Itaque si filius meus mortis meae tempore in potestate mea sit, nepotes ex eo non poterunt ex testamento meo habere tutorem, quamvis in potestate mea fuerint; *scilicet quia mortuo me in patris sui potestate futuri sunt.*"

[46] Cf. Jolowicz, *Historical Introduction,* p. 120.

[47] D. (50,17)40: "Furiosi vel eius, cui bonis interdictum sit, nulla voluntas est."

[48] Cf. D. (44,7) (1.12); (44,4)16.

[49] Cf. D. (9,2)(5.2); (1,18)14.

contact or conflict with him needed protection, the mentally afflicted person fell, by law, under the custody of a *curator,* who had to care for the lunatic's person as well as for his property.[50] The *furiosus* remained the owner of the property; he still possessed full capacity of right. But he could not dispose of his property or burden it with obligations; his capacity of disposition was curtailed. His guardian, the *curator,* was *vice domini,* and it was the latter's right and obligation to dispose of and watch over his ward's patrimony.[51] Poste observes: "The diminution of rights in a lapse from independence to curatel was less than the least *capitis minutio,* and accordingly a prodigal who was interdicted from the administration of his estate and subjected to the control of a curator was not said to undergo a *status mutatio*: his patrimony still rested in him, though he was deprived of its administration; whereas *adrogatio* and *in manum conventio* divested a person of the capacity of ownership and active obligation: inferior status, in a word, is incapacity of right; wardship and curatel are only incapacities of disposition."[52]

Guardianship was assigned by the Twelve Tables to the presumptive male successors on intestacy, those very persons who would benefit should the ward die without having attained testamentary capacity.[53] Thus it appears that guardianship was originally designed to safeguard the interests of the heirs, or, at any rate, to look to the advantage of the *familia,* rather than shield the incapable person from the ill effects of his inexperience, mental disease, or folly.[54] The whole institution aimed to keep the property

[50] Cf. Schulz, *op. cit.*, p. 197; E. Renier: "Observations de la terminologie de l'aliénation mentale," *Revue Internationale des Droits de l'Antiquité,* V (1950), 435-436.

[51] Cf. D. (47,2) (57.4).

[52] Poste, *Gai Institutiones,* p. 90.

[53] Testamentary capacity was attained by reaching puberty in the case of a boy or in the case of a lunatic or a *prodigus* by recovering his senses or having the interdiction removed respectively. Cf. Jolowicz, *Historical Introduction,* p. 122, note 2.

[54] Cf. Jolowicz, *op. cit.*, pp. 121-122; Poste, *op. cit.*, p. 112. Writing of *tutela mulierum,* Poste remarks: "It is transparent that the wardship of women after full age was not designed to protect their own interests, but those of their heirs apparent, their agnates."—*Op. cit.*, p. 110.

in the agnatic family[55] of the incapable person.

In the developed law, guardianship became an institution designed to shield incapable persons from the consequences of their peculiar disability.[56] Protection of the needy members of society was already the main purpose of guardianship at the time of Servius Sulpicius (106-43 B.C.).[57] His definition of *tutela* was accepted centuries later by the compilers of Justinian's Institutes: *"Est autem tutela ut Servius definivit, ius (vis) ac potestas in capite libero ad tuendum eum, qui propter aetatem se defendere nequit, iure civili data ac permissa. Tutores autem sunt, qui eam vim ac potestatem habent, ex qua re ipsa nomen ceperunt. Itaque appellantur tutores quasi tuitores atque defensores, sicut aeditui dicuntur qui aedes tuentur."*[58] The purpose of the chief forms of *cura,* too, was the protection of the persons subject to the *curator,*[59] so that Servius' definition applies, *mutatis mutandis,* to these types of guardianship. In fact, Justinian's Digest states clearly the function of the guardians of the insane: *"Consilio et opera curatoris tueri debet non solum patrimonium, sed et corpus ac salus furiosi."*[60] Moreover, the same source furnishes a text which implies that the curator is more than a mere administrator.[61] Survival

---

[55] Jolowicz, *op. cit.,* p. 122; Perozzi, *Istituzioni di Diritto Romano,* p. 460: "Esula così dalla tutela romana primitiva l'idea odierna della tutela, che essa sia un ufficio stabilito a solo vantaggio del pupillo, che conferisce al tutore certi diritti. Essa è invece un diritto, a cui si accompagnano certi doveri."

[56] Cf. below, p. 65.

[57] In the estimation of the writers of the Digest, Servius was the greatest lawyer of the Republic. Cf. H. J. Roby, *An Introduction to the Study of Justinian's Digest* (Cambridge: Cambridge University Press, 1886), pp. cx-cxiii. Cicero extolled Servius for his dialectical jurisprudence. Cf. Cicero, *Brutus,* 41. 152; Schulz, *op. cit.,* pp. 68, 336-337, note m.

[58] Inst. (1,13)1; cf. also, D. (26, 1)1.

[59] Cf. Jolowicz, *op. cit.,* p. 121; Bonfante, *Corso di Diritto Romano,* pp. 445, 494-496; Schulz, *Classical Roman Law,* pp. 197-198; Brugi, *Istituzioni di Diritto Romano,* n. 122.d.

[60] D. (27,10)7.

[61] D. (26,1) 13: "Solet etiam curator dari aliquando tutorem habenti propter adversam tutoris valetudinem vel senium aetatis: qui magis administrator rerum, quam curator esse intelligitur."

of the guardianship of insane and incapable persons is world-wide. These persons are protected in modern law by guardians, as in Roman Law.[62] Indeed, in the civil codes of today only slight departures from the Roman Law of guardianship are evident. Substantially the institute has remained intact.[63]

Article II. In Ecclesiastical Law and Doctrine

Prior to the norms of the Code of Canon Law, nothing existed in the form of canonical legislation touching the guardianship of the mentally ill.[64] For, though the guardian is entrusted with the

---

[62] Cf. Civil Codes of France (e.g., arts. 489, 502, 936 . . .), of Italy (e.g., arts. 409, 410, 412), of Spain (e.g., arts. 213, 220, 221), of Japan (e.g., arts. 900, 911, 912), and of the various jurisdictions in the United States. Rivier remarks: "La tutelle de l'insensé . . . ne paraît pas dans les lois des barbares; en France, les curatelles romaines sont en usage, même dans les pays coutumiers, dès le XIVe siècle . . . Les curatelles romaines du furieux et du prodigue ont de bonne heure été introduites dans l'empire allemand."—A. Rivier, *Précis du Droit de Famille Romain* (Paris: Rousseau, 1891), p. 364, note 1.

[63] ". . . ove noi, prendendo le mosse dalle norme del nostro codice civile risalissimo lungo il corso dei secoli, noi vedremo che—salvo lievi modificazioni, che però non intaccano la fisionomia caratteristica dell'istituto—la tutela rimane, sostanzialmente, quella stessa che noi possiamo studiare nel Corpus Civilis."—E. Bussi, *La Formazione dei Dogmi di Diritto Privato nel Diritto Comune* (*Contratti, Successioni, Diritto di Famiglia*) (Padova: Cedam, 1939), p. 303. (hereafter cited *La Formazione dei Dogmi*). Cf. also D. Staffa, "De Constitutione Curatoris pro mente Infirmis in Jure Canonico," *Apollinaris,* XVI (1943) (66-67 (hereafter cited "De Constitutione Curatoris").

[64] Cf. Staffa, "De Constitutione Curatoris," p. 68. The absence of pre-Code legislation regarding guardianship of the mentally ill can be concluded from observing that the present canons which refer to this subject—viz., canons 1648, §§1 and 2, 1650, 1651—bear no references to such legislation. Cf. A. Pugliese, "La Necessità del Curatore Canonico e dell'Avvocato d'Ufficio per le Persone Deboli di Mente nelle Cause Matrimoniali Ecclesiastiche," *Salesianum,* VI (1944), p. 184, n. 2 (hereafter cited "La Necessità del Curatore"). The sources cited in reference to canon 1648, §1, refer to the guardianship of minors: (1) Gratian, c.14. C.II, 9. 1, concerns "Qui ab accusatione prohibeantur, et qui recipiantur." The Master declares: "Prohibentur accusare alii propter sexum vel etatem, ut mulier et pupillus . . .",

supervision and control both of his ward and his estate, the main object of guardianship is the protection of property.[65] Consequently, guardianship was considered an institution of principal concern to Civil Law;[66] and the Church never felt the need of enacting extensive norms concerning the institution of guardianship in general, although ecclesiastical legislation as well as the doctrine of theologians, moralists, and canonists often dealt with the mentally ill and their capacity to receive the sacraments, to incur penalties, to make wills and vows, and to appear in trials.[67] Moreover, the principles of law governing the institute of guardianship were well established in the Roman Law, to which the Church could turn confidently to regulate, according to that law, situations which the Divine Positive Law had left untouched. Bouix expressly affirms that the law of Justinian regarding the representation of the mentally ill was accepted by the Church in her forum: Writing *de infantibus, furiosis et amentibus,* he declares: *"Isti, utpote qui nequeunt sua jura recte prosequi aut defendere, per seipsos in judicio stare nequeunt, neque tamquam Actores neque tamquam*

---

no mention being made of the feeble-minded or insane. (2) C.3. *de iudiciis,* II, I, in VI° refers to minors: "Si vero infra XIV annum exsistas, per te agere aut defendere non poteris super ipsis [id est super causis spiritualibus vel cum spiritualibus connexis]; sed vel per tuum Episcopum vel per officialem ejusdem tibi curator dabitur ad lites hujusmodi exercendas: aut tu ipse, si major infante fueris, cum auctoritate alterius eorundem procuratorem ad eas poteris deputare. Delegatus etiam Apostolicae Sedis et subdelegatus ab eo, tibi, si non habeas, curatorem dare valeant, vel auctoritatem constituendi procuratorem praestare, ad illas causas vel lites dumtaxat, quae coram ipsis fuerint ventilandae. In hujusmodi quoque litibus sive causis. quanquam in potestate patris existas. nec alias absque ipsius assensu in judicio regulariter esse possis, ejus, quum de iis se intromittere non habeat, nequaquam requiri debebit assensus." (3) Finally, c. 14, X. *de restitutione spoliatorum.* II, 13. declares that a woman of minor age may appoint a procurator to represent her in marriage cases.

65 Cf. 25 Am. Jur., *Guardian and Ward,* § 17; Jolowicz, *Historical Introduction,* p. 120.

66 Cf. *Glossa in Sextum* ad c. 3, II, 1 *ad verbum "debebis"*: "De tutelis et curis non posuerunt tamquam de materia nobis non multum necessaria." Cf. Staffa, "De Constitutione Curatoris," p. 68, note 38.

67 Cf. Pickett, *Mental Affliction and Church Law,* pp. 29-97, for abundant references.

Rei; sed ipsis dantur tutores vel curatores, qui id muneris ipsorum loco expleant. Id vero non tantum jure Justinianeo, in foro Ecclesiae quoad hanc dispositionem recepto, praescriptum reperitur, sed ad jus etiam naturale referendum est, ut patet."[68]

Ecclesiastical literature, however, and early councils of the Church were not silent about the civil institution of guardianship, especially with reference to clerics.

The Apostle of the Gentiles himself alludes to the *tutela impuberum*: "*Quanto tempore heres parvulus est, nihil differt a servo, cum sit dominus omnium; sed sub tutoribus et actoribus est usque ad praefinitum tempus a patre.*"[69] Then he delves into one of his favorite teachings: in the fullness of time, the Son of God freed man from the bondage of the law and elevated him to the status of an adopted son of God.[70] The same Apostle's words to Timothy—"*Nemo militans Deo implicat se negotiis saecularibus*"[71] —were taken up by Christian writers and early Councils to forbid secular transactions to clerics. Saint Ambrose, for instance, was very explicit in this regard; and in his exhortation to his clergy not to engage in unnecessary secular transactions and in judicial matters, one may include the function of guardianship: "*Non te implices negotiis saecularibus, quoniam Deo militas. Etenim si is qui imperatori militat, a susceptione litium, actu negotiorum forensium, venditione mercium prohibetur humanis legibus, quanto magis, qui fidei exercet militiam, ab omni usu negotiationis abstinere debet.*"[72] The Fathers were but voicing the mind of the Church as clearly set forth in canon 15 of the III Council of Carthage (398): "*Placuit ut episcopi et presbyteri, et diaconi, vel clerici non sint conductores, neque procuratores, neque ullo turpi vel in-*

---

[68] M. D. Bouix, *Tractatus de Judiciis Ecclesiasticis* (3. ed., 2 vols., Parisiis, 1883), I, 168. Cf. also M. Lega, *Praelectiones de Iudiciis Ecclesiasticis* (4 vols., Romae, 1896-1901), I, 89.

[69] Galatians, IV, 1-2.

[70] *Ibid.*, IV, 3 ff.

[71] II Timothy, II, 4.

[72] *De Officiis*, Lib. I, cap. 36—*MPL*, XVI, 78. See also St. Jerome, *Epist. 52, Ad Nepotianum*, cap. 16—*CSEL*, LIV, 439; and St. Augustine, *De Opere Monachorum*, cap. 15—*CSEL*, XLI, 556.

honesto negotio victum quaerant. Quia respicere debent scriptum esse: 'Nemo militans Deo, implicat se negotiis saecularibus.' "[73]

More explicit, in so far as it expressly mentions *cura,* though not as absolute in its prohibition as the above, is canon 3 of the IV Council of Chalcedon (451): *"Decrevit . . . concilium, nullum deinceps, non episcopum, non clericum, vel monachum, aut possessiones conducere, aut negotiis saecularibus se immiscere, praeter pupillorum (si forte leges imponant) inexcusabilem curam, aut civitatis episcopus ecclesiasticarum rerum solicitudinem habere praecipiat, aut orphanorum et viduarum, earum quae sine ulla defensione sunt, ac personae quae maxime ecclesiastico indigent adjutorio, et propter timorem domini causa deposcat. Si quis autem de coetero transgredi haec statuta tentaverit; qui est hujusmodi, ecclesiasticis increpationibus subjacebit."*[74]

The civil authority, on its part, relieved clerics and monks of every sort of guardianship.[75]

In a letter to Anastasius, Pope Gelasius I (492-496) strongly urged that bishop to provide for the guardianship of two minor children destitute of the assistance of parents and relatives.[76]

---

[73] Mansi, III, 883; III, 147; Nov. 123, 6.

[74] Mansi, VII, 374. For an English version and brief comment, see H. J. Schroeder, *Disciplinary Decrees of the General Councils* (St. Louis: Herder, 1937), p. 90. Similar to this decree is the injunction contained in canon 13 of the IV Council of Orleans (511)—*MGH, Leges,* I, p. 231, n. 4.

[75] Cf. Leo Augustus, C.(51, 1) 3: "Generaliter sanccimus, omnes uiros reuerentissimos episcopos, nec non presbiteros seu diaconos et subdiaconos, et precipue monachos, licet non sint clerici, immunitatem ipso iure omnis habere tutelae, siue testamentariae siue legitimae, siue datiuae, et non solum tutelae esse eos expertes, sed etiam curae, non solum pupillorum et adultorum, sed furiosi, et muti, et surdi, et aliarum personarum, quibus tutores uel curatores a ueteribus legibus dantur. §1. Eos tamen clericos et monachos huiusmodi habere beneficium sanccimus, qui ad sacrosanctas ecclesias uel monasteria permanent, non deuagantes, neque circa ministeria diuina desides, cum propter hoc ipsum beneficium eis indulgemus, ut, aliis omnibus derelictis, Dei omnipotentis inhereant ministeriis. §2. Et hoc non solum in ueteri Roma uel in hac regia ciuitate, sed in omni terra, ubicumque Christianorum colitur nomen, obtinere sanccimus." This text was later cited by Gratian under the heading *Omnes clerici vel monachi tutelae immunitatem habere debent,* C. XVI, q.1, c. 40.

[76] "Desolatis propriae defensionis auxilio, et qui suis actibus prodesse

Bishops, however, were not to exercise personally the function of guardian in the civil forum, but were to act through an archpriest or archdeacon.[77] Canon 23 of the IV Council of Toledo (633) decreed that clerics who, because of their age, stood in need of protection should be placed under the guardianship (*tutela*) of priests.[78]

It is during the period from about the middle of the twelfth century to the middle of the sixteenth that the development of canonical jurisprudence made its greatest strides. It is the period of the *jus novum*. The first two centuries of this era, in particular, form the golden age of Canon Law, during which the gradual development of the Church's legal institutions along well defined lines is to be seen, a development that received a decided impetus with the advent of the printing press in the middle of the fifteenth century. However, although this period witnessed a pronounced development in canonical legislation in general, the law of guardianship remained out of the orbit of ecclesiastical law. In fact, not one of the collections offers special treatment to the institute of guardianship.

The adherence of canonical doctrine to the institute of guardianship as presented by the Roman sources is exemplified in the *Speculum Iuris* of Guilelmus Durantis (c. 1237-1296), whose

---

pro etatis infirmitate non possunt, exoratum decet pontificem subuenire, quia pupillis tuicionem etiam divinitas iussit impendi. Et ideo Maximo et Ianuario clericalis offitii (qui se solatiis parentum vel propinquorum asserunt destitutos) auxilium ex nostra delegatione prestabis, ut adversus inprobitates aduersariorum suorum protecti tuae executionis annisu noxia commenta non sentiant."— P. Jaffé, *Regesta Pontificum Romanorum ab condita Ecclesia ad annum post Christum natum 1198* (2. ed. correctam et auctam auspiciis Gulielmi Wattenbach curaverunt F. Kaltenbrunner, P. Ewald, S. Toewenfeld], 2 vols., Lipsiae, 1885-1888), n. 726 (hereafter referred to as Jaffé with the corresponding number of the document).

[77] Cf. a letter from Pope Gregory to Romanus Defensor (anno 599)— Jaffé, n. 1293; *Statuta Ecclesiae Antiqua*, canons 17, 18—H.Th. Bruns, *Canones Apostolorum et Conciliorum Saeculorum IV-VII* (2 vols., Berolini, Reimeri, 1839), I, p. 143.

[78] "Quod si aliqui ex his pupilli existunt, sacerdotali tutela foveantur, ut et vita eorum a criminibus intacta sit, et res ab iniuria impiorum."— Bruns, *op. cit.*, I, 231.

production was regarded the most outstanding treatise on processes throughout the Middle Ages.[79] Besides, neither the text nor the annotations to the text composed by Joannes Andreae (c. 1270-1348) and Baldus de Ubaldis (c. 1327-1440) reveal any substantial departures from the Roman Law on guardianship.[80]

The acceptance by canonists of the Roman institute of guardianship is not difficult to explain. Down the centuries to the promulgation of the *Codex Iuris Canonici,* Roman Law was a supplementary source for the law of the Church, in the sense that, when the ecclesiastical authorities had made no specific disposition to cover a particular point, then the norm for action was the one that obtained in the civil law.[81] From the law of Rome the Church drew heavily to develop her own institutes; and canonists cited Roman Law and jurisprudence to explain ecclesiastical norms.[82] Indeed, the relation between the *Ius Canonicum* and the *Ius Civile* was so intimate, that it was universally held that the one law could not

---

[79] Cf. F. Roberti, *De Processibus* (2 vols., Vol. I, 2. ed., Romae: Apud Custodiam Librariam Pontificii Instituti Utriusque Iuris, 1941), p. 33: "*Speculum iuridiciale*: complectitur totam tunc temporis doctrinam de processu canonico et civili . . . Nullus tractatus canonicus tantam assecutus est auctoritatem quantam habuit Speculatoris opus." See also A. Van Hove, *Commentarium Lovaniense in Codicem Iuris Canonici,* Vol. I, Tom. I, *Prologomena* (2. ed., Mechliniae—Romae: Dessain, 1945), pp. 491-492, G. Falletti, "Guillaume Durand," *Dictionnaire de Droit Canonique,* V (1953) 1014-75.

[80] Cf. G. Durandus, *Speculum Iuris* (ed. by G. Bindonus, Venice: 1577), Lib. I, partic. III, *de Tutore* (pp. 241-252), *de Curatore* (pp. 252-259). That Durandus meant to summarize the Roman Law treatment of guardianship may be inferred from his *additio* to the title *de Tutore*: "Ad materiam istius rubricae, et rubricae sequentis non sufficiunt volumina, nam de ea occupati sunt duo libri Digest. scilicet 26 et 27 in C. cod. tit."—Cf. *op. cit.*, p. 241.

[81] Cf. e.g., Pope Gregory I (590-604), who enjoined that the rules of Roman Law procedure be followed in points which were not contemplated by Church Law.—*Gregorii I Papae Registrum Epistolarum, Ep. XIII—Monumenta Germaniae Historica, Epistolarum Tomus I et II* (edd. P. Ewald et L. Hartmann, Berolini: Apud Weidmannos, 1891-1899), I, 47.

[82] Cf. A. M. Stickler, *Historia Iuris Canonici Latini, I, Historia Fontium* (Augustae Taurinorum: Apud Custodiam Librariam Pontif. Athenaei Salesiani, 1950), p. 427.

properly be understood without a sufficient knowledge of the other.. *"Canonista sine legibus nihil valet. Legista sine canonibus parum valet"* was the pithy manner of expressing the necessity of being versed in both canon and civil law.

The reason for this phenomenon is not difficult to find. The Church was born and grew in the Roman Empire, rich in a system of law that was called the *ratio scripta,* so firmly was it founded on principles of natural justice and equity. The technical perfection of the Roman system of law commanded respect and admiration; and Pope John VIII (872-882) voiced the general opinion when he stated in a letter to King Louis: *"Romanae leges divinitus per ora principum promulgatae . . ."*[83]

From Justinian to Gratian, we may say that in the spheres of private and procedural law:[84] *Ecclesia vivit lege Romana.*[85] For, in the East, the ecclesiastical legislation of the Emperors was received and then fused into the *Nomocanones* which lay at the bottom of subsequent canonical doctrine in the Eastern Churches. In the West, at the fall of the Roman Empire, the Church preserved for posterity the fruit of Rome's juridical genius.[86]

In Gratian's *Decretum* are found side by side texts derived from both canonical and Roman Law sources. The principle that guided the Master in his choice of civil law is expresed in the *dictum*: *"Constitutiones Principum Ecclesiasticis legibus postponendae sunt. Ubi autem evangelicis atque canonicis decretis non obviarint, omni reverentia dignae habeantur."*[87]

With respect to this reliance of the Church on the secular law,

---

[83] C. 16, q. 3, c. 17.—Jaffé, n. 2970 (2247).

[84] Cf. O. Cassola, *La Recezione del Diritto Civile nel Diritto Canonico* (Tortona, 1941), p. 5; Bussi, *La Formazione dei Dogmi,* p. 303; Roberti, *De Processibus,* I, p. 2; C. Augustine, *A Commentary on the New Code of Canon Law* (8 vols., St. Louis: Herder & Co., Vol. VII, *Ecclesiastical Trials,* 1923), VII, 1 (hereafter cited *Ecclesiastical Trials*).

[85] Lex Ripuaria, tit. 58. 1. Cf. K. A. Eckhardt, *Die Gesetze des Karolingerreiches,* 714-911. I. *Salische und ribuarische Franken* (Weimar, 1934).

[86] For documentary proof of these statements, see Cassola, *op. cit.,* pp. 6-11.

[87] D. (10, 6).

we have a letter of Pope Lucius II (1181-1185) in which he said that when in judicial matters the laws of the Church were deficient or incomplete, the civil law could be followed to determine the case in question.[88] Accordingly, the works of the early canonists, decretists, and decretalists alike, as well as the productions of commentators up to the time of the Code, abound in clear references to Roman Law, to which they resorted for guiding principles and norms when the Church Law did not cover a particular situation.[89] Canonical doctrine regarding the subject of guardianship is conspicuously based on Roman Law and doctrine.[90] In fact, in the commentaries of canon lawyers down to the Codex, no substantial change can be found in the Roman doctrine of guardianship, though it must be admitted that some modifications were introduced in regard to the method of appointment and the obligation of undertaking guardianship, for example. Such adaptations, however, did not give rise to new principles of law regarding the function of guardianship. which remained substantially similar to the Roman institution as we find it delineated in the *Corpus Iuris Civilis.*[91]

At this point, one may ask whether it is permissible to appeal to the Roman Law in order to supply the *lacunae* which exist in the Code of Canon Law. Authors agree that the Roman Law no longer serves as a supplementary source of the present Canon Law; for, in canon 20, the lawgiver makes no mention of the Roman Law. Moreover, since the Church even refuses to recognize

---

[88]. C.1, X, *de novi operis nunciatione,* V, 32: "Sicut leges non dedignantur sacros canones imitari, ita et sacrorum statuta canonum principum constitutionibus adiuvantur." The glossa to the word *adiuvantur* adds: "Et ita in causa ecclesiastica, leges possumus allegare, ut etiamsi canones deficiunt. possit iudicari secundum leges." Cf. Jaffé, n. 151 8 9 (9673); Van Hove, *Prologomena,* pp. 461ff, 523ff. For an interesting treatment of the controversy concerning the influence of Christianity on Roman law, see M. Roberti, "Cristianesimo e Collezioni Giustinianee," *Cristianesimo e Diritto Romano* (Milano, Univ. S. Cuore: Scienze Giuridiche) 43 (1935), pp. 4-64.

[89] Cf. Cassola, *op. cit.,* pp. 15, 16, 19-21, 30, 67.

[90] Augustine, *Ecclesiastical Trials,* p. 1.

[91] Cf. Bussi, *op. cit.,* pp. 302-303.

as a subsidiary source her own former law which is not expressly contained in the Code, it may be argued that for a greater reason should she refuse such honor to the law of Rome.[92] Thus, even though the Roman Law treated at great length, for example, the appointment of tutors and curators, and clearly outlined their rights and duties, and accurately determined the extent of their power, it cannot serve as a supplementary source in this matter for the existing Canon Law.[93]

In the existing law of the Church guardianship in general has received more frequent mention than in previous legislation. Canon 89 declares that minors remain subject to their parents or guardians in the exercise of their rights, except in matters in which the law holds them exempt from parental power.[94] By virtue of canon 93, § 1, insane persons share the domicile of their guardians, while minors share the domicile of their parents or guardians.[95] Children who have not reached the age of puberty may not freely

---

[92] Cf. I. Chelodi, *Ius Canonicum de Personis* (3. ed., curavit P. Ciprotti, Trento: Libreria Moderna Editrice, 1942), p. 121; G. Michiels, *Normae Generales Juris Canonici* (2 vols., 2. ed., Tournai: Desclée & Co., 1949), vol. I, pp. 478-479; A. Crnica, "De Lacunis Legis Supplendis ad Normam Codicis J.C.." *Jus Pontificium* XVI (1936). 193-196.

[93] Cf. C. F. O'Donnell, *The Marriage of Minors,* The Catholic University of America Canon Law Studies, n. 221 (Washington, D. C.: The Catholic University of America Press, 1945), pp. 89-90.

[94] Canon 89. Persona maior plenum habet suorum iurium exercitium; minor in exercitio suorum iurium potestati parentum vel tutorum obnoxia manet, iis exceptis in quibus ius minores a patria potestate exemptos habet. The last section of this canon mentions parental power, omitting any reference to the powers of guardians. O'Donnell explains: "The reason for such an omission is evident, because if the law exempts the minor from the authority of the parents then for a much greater reason should it also remove him from the authority of the guardian. For if the law denies this authority even to parents, who from the natural law are constituted guardians of their children, then it would not be right to expect a legal guardian to possess such power, since the power of parents over their children is far more extensive than the authority enjoyed by tutors and curators."—O'Donnell, *op. cit.,* pp. 82-83.

[95] Canon 93, § 1. Uxor, a viro legitime non separata, necessario retinet domicilium viri sui; amens, domicilium curatoris; minor, domicilium illius cuius potestati subiicitur.

choose a church or a cemetery for their funeral, but their parents or guardians may even after the death of these children make the choice.[96] Again, it is through their parents or guardians that minors may exercise the right of patronage.[97]

A judge should not accept for trial a case in which he is interested by reason of guardianship; nor should the Promoter of Justice or the Defender of the Bond act in a case under the same circumstances.[98]

Parents and guardians are bound to plead or defend the cases of minors and persons without the use of reason. If the judge thinks that the rights of such persons are in conflict with the rights of the parents or guardians or that they live at so great a distance from the parents or guardians that the latter cannot at all, or can only with great difficulty represent their charges in court, a guardian *ad litem* is to be appointed by the judge. In spiritual cases, however, or in cases connected with spiritual affairs, minors who have attained the use of reason can sue and defend without the consent of the parent or guardian; if they are fourteen years of age, they can in person plead their case, but otherwise they must plead through a guardian appointed by the Ordinary, or by a guardian chosen by the minor with the approval of the Ordinary.[99]

---

[96] Canon 1224. Ecclesiam funeris aut sepulturae coemeterium eligere prohibentur: 1.° Impuberes; verum pro filio aut filia impubere, etiam post eorum mortem, hanc electionem facere possunt parentes vel tutor.

[97] Canon 1456. Uxor per seipsam ius patronatus exercet, minores per parentes aut per tutores; quod si parentes vel tutores acatholici sint, ius patronatus interim suspensum manet.

[98] Canon 1613, § 1. Iudex cognoscendam ne suscipiat causam in qua . . . ratione tutelae et curatelae . . . aliquid ipsius intersit. . . .

§ 2. In iisdem rerum adiunctis ab officio suo abstinere debent iustitiae promotor et defensor vinculi. Cf. also S.C. de Sacramentis, *Instructio Servanda a Tribunalibus Diocessanis in Pertractandis Causis de Nullitate Matrimoniorum*, 15 aug. 1936—*AAS*, XXVIII (1936), 313-361, art. 30 (hereafter this Instruction will be referred to simply as *Instructio*); *Regulae Servandae*. art. 16; *Normae S. R. Rotae*, art. 33, § 1; *Regulae Servandae in Processibus Sacrae Ordinationis*, art. 8.

[99] Canon 1648. § 1. Pro minoribus et iis qui rationis usu destituti sunt, agere et respondere tenentur eorum parentes aut tutores vel curatores.

§ 2. Si iudex existimet ipsorum iura esse in conflictu cum iuribus

Persons who because of their spendthrift habits have been deprived of the administration of their goods, and weak-minded persons can appear personally in court only to answer for their offenses, or at the order of the judge; otherwise they must sue and be sued through their guardians.[100]

Before a guardian assigned to a person by the civil authority can be admitted by the judge into court, the consent of the proper Ordinary of that person is required. The Ordinary may also appoint another guardian for the ecclesiastical forum, if after mature reflection he thinks such appointment prudent.[101]

Minors and other persons who enjoy the privileges of minors, when gravely injured, as well as their heirs and successors, may in addition to the ordinary means of getting redress apply to the court for the extraordinary relief of the *restitutio in integrum,* if they were injured in an affair or valid act which can be rescinded.[102] This remedy may be granted to the persons mentioned above even *ex officio* by the judge, after consultation with, or at the instance of, the Promoter of Justice.[103]

---

parentum vel tutorum vel curatorum, aut ipsos tam longe distare a parentibus aut tutoribus vel curatoribus, ut hisce uti aut minime aut difficulter liceat, tunc stent in iudicio per curatorem a iudice datum.

§ 3. Sed in causis spiritualibus et cum spiritualibus connexis, si minores usum rationis assecuti sint, agere et respondere queunt sine patris vel tutoris consensu; et quidem, si aetatem quatuordecim annorum expleverint, etiam per seipsos; secus per tutorem ab Ordinario datum, vel etiam per procuratorem a se, Ordinarii auctoritate, constitutum.

[100] Canon 1650. Bonis interdicti, et ii qui minus firmae mentis sunt, stare in iudicio per se ipsi possunt tantummodo ut de propriis delictis respondeant, aut ad praescriptum iudicis: in ceteris agere et respondere debent per suos curatores.

[101] Canon 1651 § 1. Ut curator ab auctoritate civili alicui datus a iudice ecclesiastico admittatur, debet accedere consensus Ordinarii proprii illius cui datus est.

§ 2. Ordinarius potest quoque alium curatorem constituere pro foro ecclesiastico, si, omnibus mature perpensis, id statuendum esse prudenter censuerit.

[102] Canon 1687. § 1. Minoribus vel minorum iure fruentibus graviter laesis eorumque heredibus et successoribus, ad laesionem reparandam ex negotio seu actu valido rescindibili, praeter alia ordinaria remedia, suppetit remedium extraordinarium restitutionis in integrum.

[103] Canon 1688. § 2. Minoribus vel minorum iure fruentibus restitutio

If a guardian ceases to act for his ward, the lawsuit remains interrupted until a new guardian has been appointed or the ward has been permitted to pursue personally the trial of the case.[104]

Guardians are disqualified from testifying as witnesses in the cases of their wards. The juridical reason for this disqualification is that they really take the place of their wards in a trial,[105] so that they testify as persons taking the place of the parties, enjoying the prerogatives of the parties, and bound by the restrictions binding the parties.[106] Finally guardians may not serve as experts in the cases of their wards.[107]

Concluding Remarks

The scattered norms and references to guardianship in ecclesiastical writings indicate that guardianship has always been regarded as an institute of particular concern to the civil forum,[108] whose statutes were to be observed in this matter. They reveal also the interest of the Church in the legal protection of the immature, of the weak, and of the incapacitated.[109] Worthy of note is the fact

---

concedi potest a iudice etiam ex officio, audito vel instante promotore iustitiae.

[104] Canon 1735. Procuratore aut curatore a munere cessante, tandiu interrupta manet instantia, quandiu pars aut ii ad quos pertinet novum procuratorem vel curatorem nominaverint aut per se ipsi in posterum agere se velle professi fuerint.

[105] Canon 1757, § 1. Ut non idonei repelluntur a testimonio ferendo impuberes et mente debiles.

§ 3. Ut incapaces: 1.° Qui partes sunt in causa, aut partium vice funguntur, veluti tutor in causa pupilli . . . Cf. *Instructio,* art. 119, § 1, § 3, n. 1.

[106] Cf. Doheny, *Canonical Procedure in Matrimonial Cases,* pp. 352-353.

[107] Canon 1795, § 2. Qui a testimonio ferendo excluduntur ad normam can. 1757, ne ad peritorum quidem officium assumi possunt. Cf. *Instructio,* art. 142, § 2.

[108] The Code of Civil Procedure promulgated by Pius VII on November 22, 1817, as well as the *Regolamento Legislativo e Giudiziario* promulgated by Gregory XVI on November 10, 1834, contains lengthy and detailed norms on the institute of guardianship. The first Code dedicates titles VIII and IX to the guardianship of the mentally ill, while the second considers in detail the disqualification of the mentally ill (*interdizione per vizio di mente*) in Section X, Chapter I, Articles 1584-1596.

[109] Stitt remarks: "Semper in Ecclesia sacrum fuit tutelam peculiarem

that the Synod of Pavia (850) advised the ecclesiastical authorities to seek the defense of persons neglected by their civil law guardians.[110] From this fact one may infer that the Church exercised a certain degree of vigilance over the activity of guardians.

The solicitude of the Church for the incapacitated and for the good of society is manifest more than ever in her present day legislation. Valid baptism renders a person a full-fledged member of the Church of Christ with all the rights and duties of a Christian.[111] Since, however, the exercise of rights supposes certain necessary personal faculties of intelligence and will, the law provides for cases involving persons who are either not fully developed, such as infants and minors,[112] or who are affected with mental deficiency,[113] either depriving these subjects altogether of the exercise of a particular right or confiding its exercise to a person of mature judgment.[114] Accordingly, only a person of major

---

praestare juribus eorum qui sese nullatenus vel vix adaequate defendere possent . . . Ratio hujusmodi tutelae invenitur in eo quod, nisi societas ipsa provideret, complurium subditorum jura semper essent in periculo violationis et revera violarentur, quin haberent vindicatorem; et inde sequeretur ordini sociali damnum minime parvum."—A. M. Stitt, *De Promotore Justitiae Ejusque Munere in Curia Dioecesana,* Dissertatio ad Lauream in Facultate Juris Canonici Pontificiae Universitatis Gregorianae (Romae: Ed. Scientifica Internazionale, 1939), n. 102. See also, *op. cit.*, n. 130.

[110] Canon 20. Comperimus, quod ab his, qui secundum mundanas leges viduarum et orfanorum tutelam sibi vindicant, non solum neglegantur, verum etiam aliquotiens opprimantur; quibus ecclesiastica sollicitudine succurrendum censemus. Et si huiusmodi oppressores ad episcopalem admonitionem corrigi voluerint, gratulandum his est; si autem in opstinationis impietate duraverint, suggerendum clementissimo imperatori, quatenus ipse efficacem tutorem eis tribuat, ut et illi remuneratio reddatur a Deo et de inutili silentio sacerdotalis ordo non dampnetur.—*MGH, Leges,* II, 122.

[111] Canon 87.

[112] Cf. canons 89, 167, § 1, n. 2, 854, § 1, 940, § 1, 1067, 1309, 1456, 1648, § 1, 1757, § 1.

[113] Cf. canons 88, § 3, 93, § 1, 167, § 1, n. 1, 1648, 1650.

[114] Pickett writes: "Insanity does not deprive one of personality in the Church acquired by Baptism, nor of the rights consequent upon the same, even though such rights may necessarily be exercised through others, e.g., parents or guardians. This is true of all rights legitimately acquired before the appearance of the insanity. Such rights and privileges are not

age[115] is entitled to the full exercise of his rights.[116] Minors[117] remain subject to their parents or guardians in the exercise of their rights,[118] those matters excepted in which the law holds them exempt from that subjection.[119] Persons habitually devoid of the use of reason are regarded by the law as in a class with infants;[120] they are not held responsible for their actions, and the exercise of their rights is confided to their parents and guardians.[121] Spendthrifts (*bonis interdicti*) may not perform acts of administration without the consent of their guardians.[122] Moreover, their legal

---

forfeited on that account."—*Mental Affliction and Church Law,* p. 109. In like terms write B. Ojetti, *Commentarium in Codicem Juris Canonici* (4 vols., Romae: Apud Aedes Universitatis Gregorianae, 1927-1931), Vol. I, n. 5, and G. Michiels, *Principia Generalia de Personis in Ecclesia* (Lublin: Universitas Catholica, 1932), p. 52.

115 Cf. canon 88, § 1.

116 Cf. canon 89.

117 Cf. canon 88, § 1.

118 Cf. canons 89, 1648, § 1.

119 Cf. canons 89, 1648, § 3.

120 Cf. canon 88, § 3.

121 Cf. canon 89, which applies *a fortiori* to infants and those *usu rationis habitu destituti,* and canon 1648, § 1.

122 This is a prescription, found in Civil Law codes, which must be observed also in ecclesiastical matters regarding contracts and payments, according to the general norm found in canon 1529: Quae ius civile in territorio statuit de contractibus tam in genere, quam in specie, sive nominatis, sive innominatis, et de solutionibus, eadem iure canonico in materia ecclesiastica iisdem cum effectibus serventur, nisi iuri divino contraria sint aut aliud iure canonico caveatur. The reader is therefore referred to the law of his jurisdiction. When considering the civil law, he should bear in mind canon 1513, which places charitable bequests in a special way under ecclesiastical jurisdiction. Cf. J. D. Hannan, *The Canon Law of Wills,* The Catholic University of America Canon Law Studies, n. 86 (Washington, D. C.: The Catholic University of America, 1934), p. 124, note 175: "According to this canon (1513), when there is question of bequests in favor of the Church, the formalities of Civil Law should be complied with if possible, but if they are not, the heirs are to be admonished, nevertheless, to fulfill the wish of the testator. These principles are to be applied when considering bequests made by the mentally ill and spendthrifts, although there is no specific legislation in the Code referring to such persons."

capacity personally to sue and be sued in court is also limited: they may appear personally in court only to answer for their offenses or at the order of the judge; otherwise, their guardians must handle their case.[123] Weak-minded persons[124] suffer limitations in the exercise of their procedural rights;[125] excepting cases in which such persons must answer for their offenses[126] and those in which the judge orders them to appear personally, these persons must plead and defend their causes through their guardians.[127]

The guardian and ward relation is designed to integrate the limited capacity of certain persons personally to exercise their rights.[128] In cases in which the ward is wholly incapable of exercising his rights—viz., infants and the insane—the guardian supplies for the complete want of capacity to act.[129] The limitation in the exercise of one's rights because of his abnormal condition of mind and judgment is a measure taken by the legislator in view of the importance of the rights involved and the consequences of the defective exercise of these rights to both the individual and society. The purpose of the legislator in so restricting the mentally ill in the exercise of their rights is not to punish but to help them. The restriction is not a penalty inflicted upon them, but rather it is a privilege conceded to them. In enacting this limitation, the legislator has also in mind the common good of society; for the free and complete exercise of some rights by irresponsible persons might serve at times to jeopardize and even harm the public good.

---

[123] Canon 1650.

[124] Weak-minded persons (canon 1650: *ii qui minus firmae mentis sunt*) are in a category distinct from the insane (canons 89, 1648, § 1). The distinction will be dealt with at length in a subsequent chapter of this dissertation.

[125] The Code does not consider other limitations, as does the Civil Law.

[126] Mental weakness diminishes but does not destroy imputability (canon 2201, § 4). Logically, therefore, is it ordained that weak-minded persons appear personally in court to answer for their offenses (canon 1650).

[127] Canon 1650.

[128] Staffa remarks: "Curatoris ergo constitutio pro mente infirmis eamdem naturam in iure canonico hodierno servat quam habebat in veteri, id est actus quo infirmi capacitas agendi integra fit, actus nempe in eius favorem non contra eum."—"De Constitutione Curatoris," p. 77, note 78.

[129] Cf. Pugliese, "La Necessità del Curatore," p. 184, note 3.

It must always, however, be borne in mind that the personal exercise of one's procedural rights is the rule in the ecclesiastical forum;[130] the assignment of guardians to act for the mentally ill may be called an emergency measure taken by the law to supply for natural incapacity to act found in a particular subject.

Finally, the two terms, *tutor* and *curator,* employed by the Code to denote guardians, do not imply, in the law of the Code, any difference in the functions they are to perform; they both represent their wards. In fact, the latter are said to act *per tutorem* or *per curatorem* when under the control of one or the other. The different terms are used to indicate that different persons are being represented. The Code generally employs the term *tutor* when referring to the guardian of a minor, sane or insane, and uses the term *curator* to designate the guardian of majors under disability. Ecclesiastical documents, however, frequently interchange the terms so that their use in their proper meaning is not constant.

---

[130] Cf. canon 1646.

CHAPTER II

The Mentally Ill and Their Processual Disability in Ecclesiastical Trials

Historical Note

Although Greek doctors of classical times already possessed a considerable stock of knowledge about mental diseases[1] and their writings were certainly known in Rome,[2] the Roman jurists paid little attention to them. *Quid sit furor? Quid sit dementia?* The problems connected with determining the nature and cause of insanity was a source of discussion in the schools of rhetoric. The jurisconsults, however, remained true to the general principle expressed by Aquilius Gallus[3] in regard to answering *quid aut sit aut evenerit aut futurum sit aut quid omnino fieri possit*: "*'Nihil hoc ad ius; ad Ciceronem,' inquiebat Gallus noster, si quis ad eum quid tale rettulerat, ut de facto quaereretur.*"[4] "Cicero"—i.e., the judicial orators might discuss those problems. Those whose task it was to declare the validity of juridical acts, to confirm in office the *curator legitimus*, or to appoint a guardian themselves, were not concerned with the nature and cause of insanity. These magistrates had only to proceed with caution and prudence to ascertain the fact (*factum*) and thus avoid being deceived by parties who might simulate mental disease, in order to be placed under *cura* and shirk responsibility for their acts.[5]

In the *Corpus Iuris Civilis* several terms were employed to denote mental disease and the afflicted persons, e.g., *furor, furiosus*

---

[1] Cf. Van der Veldt—Odenwald, *Psychiatry and Catholicism*, pp. 36-37; Schulz, *Classical Roman Law*, p. 198, n. 345.

[2] Cf. Renier, "Observations de la Terminologie de l'aliénation mentale," p. 453; Schulz, *loc. cit.*

[3] Gaius Aquilius Gallus, a distinguished jurist, was praetor with Cicero in 66 B.C.

[4] Cf. Cicero, *Topica*, 11.50; 12.51.

[5] Cf. D. (27, 10) 6.

(*-a*); *dementia, demens; mente captus* (*-a*), *fatuus* (*-a*).[6] The word *furiosus* had been used in the Twelve Tables[7] to designate an insane person.[8] In the rhetorical writings occur the terms *dementia* and *demens* together with, or instead of, *furor* and *furiosus.* At the time of Ulpian's legal activity, this double terminology made its way into the classical legal writings and the imperial constitutions.[9] A person was considered *furiosus* when he had lost completely the use of reason,[10] while a person afflicted by a mild form of mental disease, e.g., *monomania, dementia senilis, imbecility,* was regarded as *demens.*[11]

It may be noted here that the insane were likened, at different

---

[6] Cf. Inst. (1,23) 4; D. (3,1) 2; D. (26,5) 8; D. (27,10) 6,7,14; C. (5,4) 25; etc.

[7] V. 7. Cf. p. 3, above.

[8] The mentally ill, the ancients believed, were under the influence of gods or demons who manifested their power over them by throwing them into trances, transports of ecstasy, violent convulsions, and fits of queer, unreasonable behavior—all evident manifestations of mental infirmity. Cf. Van der Veldt—Odenwald, *Psychiatry and Catholicism,* p. 36; Perozzi, *Istituzioni di Diritto Romano,* I, p. 525, note 2.

[9] Cf. Renier, "art. cit.," pp. 431, 454. The indiscriminate usage of the terms in classical legal writings gave rise to the belief that the classical lawyers knew two sorts of insanity. As a matter of fact, they used the terms *furor* and *furiosus* only, and they also avoided using the term *mente captus.* Cf. Schulz, *Classical Roman Law,* p. 199, who adds: "In lawbooks outside the *Corpus iuris* the terms *dementia* and *demens* occur only in C.Th. (9,43) I (only metaphorically they are used in a few other texts); in the C. Iust. they occur only in Justinian's enactments. This is in itself a powerful argument against the classicality of the few passages in the *Digest* in which these terms occur. In some of them the interpolation can be proved: I think that is as much proof as can reasonably be required."

[10] Cf. Schulz, *op. cit.,* p. 197; Renier, "art. cit.," p. 431; Perozzi, *op. cit.,* p. 525.

[11] Cf. Renier, *loc. cit.* "A côté de 'furor' qui désigne toute folie complète, 'dementia,' qui s'en distingue nettement à l'époque d'Ulpien, va désigner toutes les formes secondaires d'insanité d'esprit que les médecins du temps étudient et définissent, depuis les monomanies jusqu' à la démence sénile en passant par l'imbecillité. Et si la comprehension du terme 'dementia' reste imprécise, c'est qu'une discrimination plus rigoureuse était inutile aux juristes dans la pratique." Cf. also Perozzi, *op. cit.,* p. 526.

times and by different jurists, to the absent,[12] to the sleeping,[13] and even to the dead.[14]

"Furiosi . . . nulla voluntas est"[15] was a general principle of Roman Law. Insanity automatically produced incapacity to act juridically;[16] a magistrate's decree of interdiction was not required to disqualify the unsound of mind.[17] On the other hand, a person regained fully his capacity to posit juridical acts as soon as he recovered from his mental infirmity. Insanity and recovery from insanity could be proved as any other fact; no special proofs were necessary, neither was a decree or any sort of declaration by a person in authority.[18] "There appears to have been no procedure outlined by the law for the solution of doubts and disputes, that might arise from time to time, as to the presence or absence of that degree of mental capacity necessary for the placing of juridical acts in those persons whose insanity was intermittent or partial. We can hardly presume that experts in the sphere of health and sanity were resorted to, as they are today, for there is no intimation of such a procedure in the law. Moreover, experts in such a highly specialized field as the one under consideration would scarcely be available in Roman times. It seems more probable that the magistrate was invested with absolute power in this respect, as in so many others, and that he made the necessary decision, rightly or

---

12 Cf. D. (29,7) 2; (50, 17) 124.1.

13 Cf. D. (41,2) 1.3.

14 Cf. D. (39,5) 2.

15 D. (50,17) 40. Cf. also D. (9,2) 5.2: "quae enim in eo (furioso) culpa sit, cum suae mentis non sit?"

16 "A *furiosus* entirely lacked legal capacity, whether he had or had not a *curator*. Any *negotium* effected by him was void *iure civili* even if the other party was ignorant of his state. Delicts committed by him did not render him liable to a fine or damages, though this rule was only reluctantly acknowledged in the classical period."—Cf. Schulz, *op. cit.*, p. 198.

17 The spendthrift (*prodigus*), however, had to be expressly interdicted: cf. D. (12,6) 29; (18,1) 26; (27,10) 1.; and the restriction had to be expressly lifted before he regained the free exercise of his rights. Cf. Bonfante, *Corso di Diritto Romano*, I, 483-486.

18 Cf. D. (1,18) 14; C. (4,38) 2; (6,22) 9.

wrongly, in doubtful cases."[19] Thus, the magistrate who placed a mentally infirm person under guardianship or delivered him from guardianship did not declare judicially the fact of insanity or of return to sanity, but simply verified that fact. Moreover, the incapacity to act validly could very well precede the magistrate's confirmation of a guardian, as could the reacquisition of complete capacity the revocation of guardianship.[20]

The doctors knew well that the *furiosi* could possibly enjoy lucid intervals;[21] and though the classical lawyers did not discuss the subject in their writings, legal practice did not disregard them.[22] In fact, the acts which the *furiosus* performed in a lucid interval were considered valid and imputable.[23] Though he could, however, personally act validly when enjoying the temporary use of reason, the habitually insane person was not released from the control of his lawful guardian.[24]

---

[19] Cf. Pickett, *Mental Affliction and Church Law*, pp. 14-15.

[20] Cf. C. (5,70) 6; Staffa, "De Constitutione Curatoris," p. 65.

[21] Cf. Caelius Aurelianus, *De Morbis Chronicis*, 1.5.151: "Est autem insania sive furor nunc iugis nunc temporis interiecti requie levigatus."

[22] Cf. Schulz, *op. cit.*, p. 199.

[23] Cf. e.g., D. (1,18) 14; (28,1) 20.4; Robinson, *Selections*, pp. 155-156; P. A. D'Avack, *Cause di Nullità e di Divorzio nel Diritto Matrimoniale Canonico* (Firenze: Casa Editrice del Dott. Carlo Cya, 1952), I, p. 144 (hereafter cited *Cause di Nullità*).

[24] Cf. C. (5,70) 6: "Cum aliis quidem hominibus continuum furoris infortunium accidit, alios autem morbus non sine laxamento ingreditur, sed in quibusdam temporibus quaedam eis intermissio pervenit, et in hoc ipso multa est differentia, ut quibusdam breves indutiae, aliis maiores ab huiusmodi vitio inducantur, antiquitas disputabat, utrumne in mediis furoris intervallis permanent eis curatoris intercessio, an cum furore quiescente finita iterum morbo adveniente redintegratur. Nos itaque eius ambiguitatem decidentes sancimus, cum incertum est in huiusmodi furiosis hominibus, quando resipuerint, sive ex longo sive in propinquo spatio, et impossibile est et in confinio furoris et sanitatis eum saepius constitui et per longum tempus sub eadem esse varietate, ut quibusdam videatur etiam paene furor esse remotus, curatoris creationem non esse finiendam, sed manere quidem eum, donec talis furiosus vivit, quia non est paene tempus in quo huiusmodi morbus desperatur: Sed per intervalla, quae perfectissima sunt, nihil curatorem agere, sed ipsum posse furiosum, dum sapit, et hereditatem adire et omnia alia facere, quae sanis hominibus competunt: sin autem furor

The attitude of the Roman jurists towards mental disease was adopted by subsequent jurists down to our own day. The jurist is not chiefly concerned with the causes, the nature, the distinctive characteristics, and similar problems connected with mental illness. The law considers the fact, the existence of mental disease in a particular case, and its consequences as to the performance of juridical acts.[25] "In no age have legislators followed or felt the need to follow the lead of medicists in the use of a multiformity of division or a variation of nomenclature in the matter of insanity. A few clearly defined distinctions have always sufficed to cover the field of mental incompetence from the point of view of law."[26]

Article I. The Mentally Ill

The Code of Canon Law considers mental illness in relation to a person's general juridical capacity,[27] to his processual capacity,[28] and to his responsibility and liability.[29] Canon 2201, which treats of delictual liability, suggests the division of mental illness into *amentia habitualis* (§ 2), *mentis perturbatio* (§ 3), and *mentis debilitas* (§ 4); and it refers also to the possibility of lucid intervals (§ 2). Now, with regard to unsoundness of mind, that which has importance and bearing in law, and in moral theology, is not so much the singling out of the *species morbi* as rather the determination of the *gradus morbi* in relation to the *discretio judicii* of the subject affected.[30] There may be numerous variations in the

stimulis suis iterum eum accenderit, curatorem in contractus vocari, ut nomen quidem curatoris in omne tempus habeat, effectum autem, quotiens morbus redierit, ne crebra vel quasi ludibriosa fiat curatoris creatio et frequenter tam nascatur quam desinere videatur." This decision eliminated what could have become a nuisance of repeated appointments to the office of guardian.

25 Cf. 28 Am. Jur., *Insane and Other Incompetent Persons*, § 2; D'Avack, *op. cit.*, pp. 143,185.

26 Cf. Pickett, *Mental Affliction and Church Law*, p. 2.

27 Canons 12; 88, § 3.

28 Canons 1648, § 1; 1650.

29 Canons 2201, § 1; 2218, § 2; 2229, § 3, n. 2.

30 Cf. D'Avack, *op. cit.*, p. 185.

definitions and tests of mental illnesses, but from the standpoint of the juridic capacity of a person, the concern of the law, both civil and canonical, is with the effect of mental disease, rather than with the cause that produced it.[31]

Canon Law, however, does not offer any simple rules or norms applicable to determine when insufficient maturity of judgment and discretion exists.[32] Since each individual case must be studied in particular, it is obvious that the ecclesiastical authorities should have such knowledge of mental conditions as to enable them to perform their office intelligently and competently, aided by capable and trustworthy experts whenever the law or circumstances require their assistance and intervention.[33]

Mental infirmity is a broad concept which admits of a wide variety of conditions and involves varying degrees of severity, depending upon the individual case.[34] Courts have not attempted to define precisely or to classify the numberless forms of insanity and incompetency, though they have been impelled to give judicial recognition to their general effects.[35] Neither do psychiatrists venture to offer a real definition of mental illness. Indeed, it is generally felt that no satisfactory definition of mental deficiency can be arrived at, since it would first be necessary to define what is meant by sanity, which involves one in equal difficulties.[36]

---

[31] Cf. 28 Am. Jur., *Insane and Other Incompetent Persons,* § 2; D'Avack, *op. cit.,* pp. 143, 185. As Pickett states it: "Varieties of legal insanity are varieties in degree; varieties of medical insanity are varieties in kind. The physician is primarily interested in the various types of insanity and their causes. These points are only of secondary interest to the jurist who is concerned chiefly with the degree of juridical incapacity engendered by insanity in any given case." *Op. cit.,* pp. 2-3.

[32] Cf. W. J. Doheny, *Canonical Procedure in Matrimonial Cases,* Vol. I, *Formal Judicial Procedure* (Milwaukee: The Bruce Publishing Co., 1948), p. 784.

[33] Cf. canons 1792, 1808, 1982.

[34] Cf. 28 Am. Jur., *Insane and Other Incompetent Persons,* § 3; C. S. Read, "Insanity," *Encyclopaedia Britannica* (Chicago: Encyclopaedia Britannica, Inc., 1944), Vol. XII, p. 383; V. M. Palmieri, *Medicina Legale Canonistica* (Bari, 1946), p. 33.

[35] Cf. 28 Am. Jur., *loc. cit.*

[36] Cf. Read, *loc. cit.* Two modern authors write: "Where is the demar-

In his description of *dementia,* Zacchia, whose production on forensic medicine is cited by ecclesiastical courts today, reveals the wide comprehension of mental illness: "*Quocumque modo ac in quocumque tempore aut morbo rationalis animae functiones non bene ac naturaliter celebrantur, sed vel nullo modo, vel debiliter, vel depravate, tunc dementia fit, quod tamen multis modis contingere potest non solum pro earumdem cerebri animaeque facultatum diversitate, sed pro modo et ratione diversa, qua eaedem facultates male et non naturaliter operari possunt.*"[37]

Examination of the works of psychiatrists leads to the following practical description of mental disease: mental disease is a malfunctioning of the cognitive or appetitive faculties, whose origin may be somatic, psychic, or both somatic and psychic, and which results in the diminution or complete loss of the use of reason.[38]

With reference to guardianship, the Code considers two classes of persons affected by mental disorder—viz., the *rationis usu destituti*[39] and the *minus firmae mentis.*[40]

The *rationis usu destituti* are persons without the use of reason or individuals habitually afflicted with one form or other of mental derangement that deprives them of the use of their higher faculties. They are the insane, the *usu rationis habitu destituti* of canon 88, § 3, the *habitualiter amentes* of canon 2201, § 2.[41]

---

cation land between normality and abnormality? The psychiatrists will admit that there is none, because there is a gradual and imperceptible transition from what is certainly normal to what is certainly abnormal. . . ." —Van der Veldt-Odenwald, *Psychiatry and Catholicism,* p. 34.

[37] Cf. P. Zacchia, *Quaestiones Medico-Legales,* II, tit. 1, q.1, p. 103.

[38] Cf. Van der Veldt-Odenwald, *op. cit.,* p. 39 ff; T. M. Moore, *The Nature and Treatment of Mental Disorders* (New York: Grune and Stratton, 1944), pp. 1-32; E. A. Strecker, *Fundamentals of Psychiatry* (4. ed., Philadelphia: Lippincott, 1947), pp. 50-83.

[39] Cf. canon 1648, § 1.

[40] Cf. canon 1650.

[41] Cf. A. Pugliese, "La Necessità del Curatore," pp. 183, 185; G. Michiels, *Principia Generalia de Personis in Ecclesia* (Lublin-Polonia: Universitas Catholica, 1932), p. 49, has this to say about the *usu rationis habitu destituti*: "Quacumque demum ex causa proveniat amentia stabilis supradicta sive ex vitio corpori congenito sive ex vitio postea orto, omnes qui ea de facto laborant, in jure nostro dicuntur 'usu rationis habitu

According to the Rotal jurisprudence, the habitually insane are classified into *amentes,* or the *insanientes quoad omnia,* and the *dementes,* or the *insanientes quoad unum vel alterum punctum,* the *monomaniaci.*[42] The latter were and remain a source of discussion, especially with reference to their capacity to contract a valid marriage, since persons suffering from this type of mental disease seem normal in their mental approach to the generality of subjects but are quite clearly abnormal with regard to one and at times with regard to several particular subjects.

Sanchez (1550-1610) declared that during his time authors did not agree on whether there were really such persons as monomaniacs. The negative view argued thus: the intellectual faculty and the spirit of man, as the basis of activity of both the intellect and the will, is one; if it is deranged at all, it must be *ex toto,* even though the manifestation of abnormality and illness is not on a general plane. Sanchez, however, accepted the opinion common among older authors that monomaniacs could and did exist.[43] If, however, marriage was the matter in regard to which they were deranged, they were considered as being subject to the general norms on insanity.[44]

---

destituti' (can. 82, § 2), etsi aliquando lucida intervalla habeant." (Hereafter this work is cited *De Personis*).

[42] Cf. S. R. R., *Decisiones,* XIV (1922), dec. XXI, n. 3, p. 210; S. R. R., *Decisiones,* XIX (1931), dec. XIX, n. 5, p. 152; S. R. R. *Decisiones,* XXIII (1940), dec. VIII, n. 3, p. 83. See also, "Aliénation Mentale en Matière de Consentement Matrimonial"—*Dictionnaire de Droit Canonique,* I, p. 415, n. I: In the language of scientific psychiatry, however, *amentia* denotes a special type of mental disease and *dementia* a particular species of organic insanity characterized by a gradual destruction and shrinking of the brain tissue. Cf. R. Allers, "Annulment of Marriage by Lack of Consent because of Insanity," *The Ecclesiastical Review,* CI (1939), 330, 340. The term *demens* is also used generically to denote individuals lacking normal mental stability. Cf. the *Responsum* of Jan. 25, 1943, in *AAS,* XXXV (1943), 58, which bears the title "De Curatore Dementis" and includes under the term both the *rationis usu destituti* and the *minus firmae mentis.* Cf. Aguirre "De Curatore Dementis," p. 294.

[43] T. Sanchez, *Disputationum de Sancto Matrimonii Sacramento Tomi Tres* (*Antverpiae,* 1607), Lib. I, disp. VIII, nn. 22-23. (Hereafter cited *De Matrimonio*).

[44] The theory defended by Sanchez is still accepted by ecclesiastical

D'Annibale noted that some medical experts of his day were equating *amentia*, or total insanity, with *dementia*, implying that the so-called *monomania* was merely the most extreme manifestation of a latent general insanity.[45] Noting that the question was a matter of dispute, Gasparri did not decide definitely in favor of either opinion, although he did observe that the civil law made no distinction as regards responsibility between the *amens* and the *demens*.[46] More recent authors tend to discountenance the possibility of partial insanity properly-so-called.[47] Van der Veldt and Odenwald affirm: "modern psychiatry rejects the older opinion that a mental patient can be ill only in one particular point; rather, it considers a mental disorder as affecting the whole personality. That does not imply, however, that the individual's reason and will are always so affected that he is freed from all responsibility. The majority of the mentally ill combine relative responsibility with relative lack of responsibility."[48]

It may be observed in passing that the Penal Law of the State

jurisprudence. Cf. S. R. R., *Decisiones*, XXVII (1935), dec. LXXXIII, n. 4, p. 696: "Igitur amentia perfecta semper secumfert invaliditatem matrimonii; dementia vero perfecta matrimonium invalidet tantummodo si extendatur ad ipsum objectum contractus matrimonialis." Cf. *op. cit.*, dec. XXXII, p. 282: "patet igitur consensum praestitum ab amente esse semper invalidum, consensum vero praestitum a demente esse invalidum, si dementia vertatur circa objectum contractus." Cf. also S. R. R., *Decisiones*, XXV (1933), dec. XXXXVII, nn. 2,4, p. 406; S. R. R., *Decisiones*, XXIV (1932), dec. XXXXVIII, n. 16, p. 455; S. R. R., *Decisiones*, XXVI (1934), dec. LXXXIII, n. 3, p. 709.

[45] Cf. J. D'Annibale, *Summula Theologiae Moralis* (ed. 5., 3 vols., Romae, 1908), Vol. I, n. 30, note 18.

[46] P. Gasparri, *Tractatus Canonicus de Matrimonio* (3. ed., 2 vols., Parisiis, 1904), II, n. 884.

[47] F. X. Wernz-P. Vidal, *Ius Canonicum ad Codicis Normam Exactum*, 7 vols., Vol. VII, *Ius Poenale* (Romae: Apud Aedes Universitatis Gregorianae, 1937), n. 64: "In dies crescit opinio vix admittens dementiam partialem, si sit perfecta in determinata materia." D'Avack, *Cause di Nullità*, p. 169 ff; M. Coronata, *Institutiones Iuris Canonici ad Usum Utriusque Cleri et Scholarum*: *De Sacramentis Tractatus Canonicus* (3 vols. 2. ed., Taurini: Marietti, 1948-1949), III, n. 439 (hereafter cited *De Matrimonio*).

[48] *Op. cit.*, p. 33.

of New York does not establish a presumption in favor of the insane of any type against criminal liability. Section 1120 of that law reads: "A person is not excused from criminal liability as an idiot, imbecile, lunatic, or insane person, except upon proof that, at the time of commiting the alleged criminal act, he was laboring under such a defect of reason as: 1. not to know the nature and quality of the act he was doing; or, 2. not to know that the act was wrong."[49] In essence, definitions of other courts and legislations in the United States are the same.[50]

The Code, canonical jurisprudence, and doctrine admit the possibility of lucid intervals during which an insane person may enjoy the light of reason. When, however, there is any doubt in the matter, the presumption is against the lucid interval. Moreover, the Code establishes a presumption of delictual incapacity in the habitually insane.[51]

Gasparri accepted the doctrine of lucid intervals with hesitation. For, as he noted, many medical experts denied that there was any such thing as a truly lucid interval, feeling that these were merely quiescent states under which lurked a latent insanity. Thus, Gasparri noted, in criminal legislation the insane were not punished for crimes committed during such lucid intervals, nor was a contract considered valid when made in such a state of mind.[52] Modern psychiatry shows itself generally contrary to admitting the possibility of lucid intervals as transitory returns to sanity, but concedes the possibility of a lessening in the intensity of insanity.[53]

---

[49] Penal Law of the State of New York, Article 104—Incompetent Persons, Sec. 1120.

[50] Cf. C. H. Tuttle, "Insanity in Law (United States)," *Encyclopedia Britannica*, Vol. XII, p. 392.

[51] Cf., e.g., canon 2201 § 2; S.R.R., *Decisiones*, XV (1923) dec. XIV, p. 132, n. 11: "Nam cum furoris morbus suapte natura perpetuus, insanabilis et desesperatus sit, praesumitur durare omni tempore, et illa dilucida intervalla sunt per accidens, ideoque minime praesumuntur." See also: Michiels, *De Personis*, p. 49; E. F. Regatillo, *Institutiones Iuris Canonici* (3. ed., Santander: Sal Terrae, 1949), I, n. 182; V. M. Palmieri, *Medicina Legale Canonistica*, p. 19; D'Avack, *op. cit.*, p. 159.

[52] Gasparri, *Tractatus Canonicus de Matrimonio*, II, n. 884. Cf. also, F. Wanenmacher, *Canonical Evidence in Marriage Cases* (Philadelphia, Dolphin Press, 1935), p. 296, n. 465.

The *minus firmae mentis*[54] are the feeble-minded, i.e., persons in whose case there exists mental defectiveness not amounting to imbecility, yet so pronounced that they require care, supervision, and control for their protection as well as for the protection of others.[55] Accordingly, *mentis debilitas*[56] is an intermediary mental state between sanity and insanity.[57] The term comprises all those forms of mental illness which, though permanent, are of themselves incomplete and imperfect; these forms denote a weakness (*debilitas*) rather than a true lack (*destitutio*) of the powers of mind and will.[58] It has been defined as a *mentis infirmitas semiplena* or as an *imperfectus usus rationis aut voluntatis,* more or less permanent: "ob defectum sive congenitum sive acquisitum, vel perpetuum vel temporaneum, sed aliqualiter stabilem, in organis perceptionis vel appetitus sensibilis, qui tamen non impedit omnino usum rationis et libertatem."[59]

The term includes in general all those pathological conditions that bring about some sort of mental infirmity or disturbance, whether *ex se stabilis et perpetua* (*habitualis*) or *ex se transitoria et momentanea* (*actualis*), provided it is incomplete. Feeble-

---

[53] Cf. D'Avack, *op. cit.,* pp. 162, 181, 182: ". . . gli *amentes* durante questi periodi intervallari non riacquistino la sanità mentale, ma siano semplicemente 'constituti in conspectu umbratae quietis, nec tamen sunt mentis sanae, licet videantur'" (cf. Congregatio Concilii, *Argentinen.,* cited in *Fontes,* VI, n. 4343, p. 878). Cf. also Pickett, *op. cit.,* p. 150 ff.

[54] Canon 1650.

[55] Cf. "Insanity," *Encyclopaedia Britannica,* XII, 287.

[56] Canons 2201, § 4; 2229, § 3, n. 2.

[57] Cf. Michiels, *De Personis,* p. 52: "Debiles mentis non sunt, sicut amentes et dementes, mentaliter aegri seu morbo mentali gravi affecti, sed mentaliter infirmi, idest substantialiter sani, sed ordinaria evolutione cerebrali vel perfecta inter organa facultatum sensibilium harmonia sive stabiliter sive temporanee orbati." F. Roberti, *De Delictis et Poenis* (Impressio altera emendata, Romae: Apud Custodiam Librariam Pontificii Instituti Utriusque Iuris, 1938), I, n. 83; Olivero, *Le Parti nel Giudizio Canonico,* n. 36: "La distinzione dei destituti dell'uso di ragione (fra i quali si classificano gli amentes, i furiosi, ecc.), dai deboli di mente è distinzione di grado nello stesso ordine di infermità."

[58] Cf. D'Avack, *op. cit.,* pp. 140-141.

[59] J. Noval, "De semi-amentibus et semi-imputabilitati obnoxiis," *Jus Pontificium,* IV (1924), 82.

mindedness is distinct from *amentia* and forms of *mentis exturbatio*[60] in that it changes, lessens, or weakens permanently or temporarily a person's intellectual or volitive capacity without eliminating that capacity completely.[61] Among the pathological conditions that cause feeble-mindedness may be listed the various forms of progressive insanity in their initial stages, chronic alcoholism,[62] simple drunkenness,[63] incomplete hypnotism.[64]

In a word, feeble-mindedness denotes those mental conditions in which a person does not possess powers of mind and will sufficient to act for his own good, though he has not suffered a complete loss, be it but temporary, of his mental powers, and which justifies his being deprived of juridical capacity to perform acts that reach beyond simple administration.[65] There are no peculiarities or typical features, except such as result naturally from the low degree of mentality.

Terms found in canonical literature to designate this general state of mental illness are, for example: *minus firmae mentis,*[66] *infirmitas mentis,*[67] and *mentis vitium.*[68]

In America, the term covers the entire group of mental defectives. The American Association for the Study of Feeble-Mindedness adopted the following definition of feeble-mindedness: Resolved: "1. That the term, feeble-minded, be used generically to include all degrees of mental development as result of which the person so affected is incapable of competing on equal terms with his normal fellows or managing himself or his affairs with ordinary

---

[60] The term *mentis exturbatio* applies to forms of mental disturbances which are of themselves transitory or momentary, even though they involve full or complete loss of mental powers, e.g., severe cases of drunkenness, morphinism, hypnotism. Cf. D'Avack, *op. cit.,* p. 140.

[61] Cf. D'Avack, *op. cit.,* p. 217.

[62] Cf. D'Avack, *op. cit.,* pp. 231-232.

[63] Cf. D'Avack, *op. cit.,* pp. 232-234.

[64] Cf. D'Avack, *op. cit.,* p. 242, ff.

[65] Cf. Ch. Lefebvre, "Debilitè Mentale," *Dictionnaire de Droit Canonique* (Paris: Librairie Letouzey et Ané, 1924—, Vol. IV, col. 1047 (hereafter cited "Debilité Mentale").

[66] Cf. canon 1650; PCI, Jan. 25, 1943—*AAS,* XXXV (1943) 58.

[67] Cf. canon 2147, § 2, n. 1; PCI, *loc. cit.*

[68] Cf. canon 475, § 1.

prudence. 2. That the feeble-minded be divided into three classes, viz.: *Idiots.*—Those so deeply defective that their mental development never exceeds that of a normal child of about two years. *Imbeciles.*—Those whose mental development is above that of an idiot but does not exceed that of a normal child of about seven years. *Morons.*—Those whose mental development is above that of an imbecile but does not exceed that of a normal child of about twelve years. This grouping admits of the use of the older pathological terms, such as hydrocephalic, microcephalic, paralytic, etc., as adjectives indicating the respective implications."[69]

In connection with unsoundness of mind jurists have always considered the so-called *defectus sensuum,* i.e., the imperfection or total lack of external senses, especially those of hearing and sight, and of the power of speech. The reason for accepting such a relationship is that such defects, particularly in more serious cases, may accompany a lack of normal judgment (*defectus discretionis iudicii*) in general or a sort of so-called *amentia habitualis* styled *amentia naturalis* or idiocy.[70]

In Roman Law, persons so afflicted were placed under guardianship, the *cura debilium.*[71]

Article II. The Processual Disability of the Mentally Ill

The study of procedural law, as well as the mere assistance at a trial, reveals that no less a degree of maturity and mental stability are required properly to exercise court action than is necessary to administer one's property. To prevent the violation of justice by fraud and deceit, the law ordains that unless a person is capable of sufficient knowledge and deliberation, he may be deprived of the right personally to exercise court action.

Lega expresses a fundamental principle of processual law, extant in every legislation: *"Prior conditio ad legitimam iurium defensionem est, eos qui agunt aut respondent in iudicio seu actores seu reos plena frui rerum cognitione et suae deliberationis libertate*

[69] Cf. Goddard, X., "Feeble-mindedness," pp. 140-141.

[70] Cf. D'Avack, *op. cit.,* p. 200.

[71] Cf. Inst. (1, 23) 3; D. (27, 10) 2; (3, 1) 2; C. (5, 4) 25.

quo tutius valeant iuribus consulere. Secus non per se isti audiantur in iudicio sed per alios qui eos repraesentant legitime seu ipsis a iure constitutos quales sunt parentes, tutores, curatores."[72]

The intrinsic natural capacity to be juridically responsible and liable for an act constitutes what theologians and canonists term *sufficiens discretio judicii,* or *maturitas judicii ad actum intelligendum et eligendum,* or *maturitas judicii actui proportionata.* This ability consists of two distinct but interdependent elements, one of which refers to the intellect, i.e., the *maturitas cognitionis,* and the other to the will, i.e., the *maturitas voluntatis.* Accordingly, those who lack altogether or enjoy only partially the capacity to understand and will automatically lack or have reduced their natural capacity to act in trials. Recognizing this defect of natural capacity, the law places under disability such persons as are considered incapable of properly exercising their procedural rights.[73] Therefore, in order validly to stand in judgment, they must either supply their deficiency or integrate their limitation through the representation or the intervention of other persons who act in their stead in judgment.

This principle is applied in the Code when the lawmaker states:

---

[72] Lega-Bartoccetti, *Commentarius,* I, 303. Cf. also A. Toso, "De constitutione curatoris in foro ecclesiastico," *Jus Pontificium,* XIX (1939), 155 ff. (hereafter cited "De Constitutione Curatoris"); Roberti, *De Processibus,* I, n. 202; F. Della Rocca, *Istituzioni di Diritto Processuale Canonico* (Torino: Tip. Torinese, 1946), n. 79.

[73] "A physical disability is a disability or incapacity caused by physical defect or infirmity, or bodily imperfection, or mental weakness or alienation; as distinguished from civil disability, which relates to the civil *status* or condition of the person, and is imposed by the law." H. C. Black, *A Law Dictionary,* sub v. *Disability,* p. 371. "In New York, the word 'incompetency' is used to designate the condition or legal status of a person who is unable or unfitted to manage his own affairs by reason of insanity, imbecility, or feeble-mindedness, and for whom, therefore, a committee may be appointed; and such a person is designated an 'incompetent' "—*op. cit.,* sub v. *Incompetency,* p. 613. Conversely, "legal capacity is the attribute of a person who can acquire new rights, or transfer rights, or assume duties, according to the mere dictates of his own will, as manifested in juristic acts, without any restraint arising from his *status* or legal condition."—*op. cit.,* sub v. *Capacity,* p. 166.

Canon 1648, § 1. *Pro minoribus et iis qui rationis usu destituti sunt, agere et respondere tenentur eorum parentes aut tutores vel curatores.* Canon 1650: *Bonis interdicti, et ii qui minus firmae mentis sunt, stare in iudicio per se ipsi possunt tantummodo ut de propriis delictis respondeant, aut ad praescriptum iudicis: in ceteris agere et respondere debent per suos curatores.* These two canons regulate the processual incapacity of the two general classes of the mentally ill considered above, namely, the *usu rationis habitu destituti* and the *mente debiles,* the insane and the feeble-minded. These mentally ill persons are in what may be designated as a permanent state of juridic incapacity (*status permanens incapacitatis*) ; there is, it may be said, a presumption against their capacity. Quite different from their condition is that of the merely *mente exturbati.*[74] The latter persons are, indeed, naturally incapable of human acts in general and, consequently, of processual acts, as long as they are in the grip of their mental disturbance. Their condition, however, is not marked by the note of stability (*status aliqualiter stabilis*) ; rather, it may be styled a passing condition of incapacity (*conditio transiens incapacitatis*). Their processual incapacity during any given period of a trial must be proved, as it is not presumed.[75]

According to canons 1648, § 1, and 1650, the *usu rationis destituti* and the *minus firmae mentis* must sue (*agere*) and defend (*respondere*) their cases through their legitimate representatives. Because of their mental conditions, they are debarred from acting

---

[74] Cf. above, page 42, note 60.

[75] Cf. D'Avack, *Cause di Nullità,* p. 191; Pugliese, "La Necessità del Curatore," p. 185, writes: "Tra le cause che producono lo stato momentaneo, non duraturo, di *amentia,* i suddetti Autori, sequendo criteri psichiatrici, enumerano l'epilessia e altri morbi funzionali del sistema nervoso. Gli ammalati di questa categoria che solo *incidenter usu rationis destituuntur,* nel momento dell'accesso o negli stati pre- e postaccessuali sono considerati equiparati agli amenti; ma essendo essi abitualmente 'plene sui compotes, subiiciuntur regulis ordinariis' (Cf. Michiels, *De Personis,* p. 55). Conseguentemente, se sono maggiorenni, possono stare in giudizio, agire e rispondere, senza l'assistenza di tutori o curatori, a meno che il giudice nel caso particolare e a suo giudizio non creda conveniente assegnarne loro qualcuno."

in court either as plaintiff or as defendant.[76] It must, however, be borne in mind that, when lawfully represented, the insane or feeble-minded person is and remains the subject of the processual relation that exists in the trial between the judge, the plaintiff, and the defendant; for it is he, and not his representative, who is affected by the outcome of the trial.[77] The guardian is considered as forming one person with his ward, but the interests at stake and debated in the trial are and remain vested in the ward, and the legislator exercises special care to prevent opposing interests of the representatives from inducing them to neglect or disregard entirely the best interests of their wards.[78]

An important difference must be noted in the respective incapacity to act of the *usu rationis destituti* and of the *minus firmae mentis*. The first are absolutely incapable of performing any juridical act; the second are only relatively incapable.[79] Whereas the law declares that the feeble-minded may personally stand in court in given instances,[80] no exception is made regarding the incapacity of the insane; nor could any be made. The insane are, as Lega puts it, *"iure naturali inhabiles."*[81] All positive legislations contain this principle of natural law at least implicitly. Moreover, this processual disqualification perseveres until the insane person regains sanity.[82]

---

[76] This denial of both active and passive capacity to exercise personally court action reveals the nature of the disqualification; it is a protective measure in favor or for the advantage of the disqualified person. On the other hand, the excommunicated are never freed from their obligation to appear in court when summoned as defendants, though they may be deprived of their active capacity (cf. canons 1646, 1654, 2263); their disqualification is of the nature of a penalty. Cf. Olivero, *Le Parti nel Giudizio Canonico*, n. 19.

[77] Cf. Olivero, *op. cit.*, nn. 9-35; Roberti, *De Processibus*, I, n. 199; Della Rocca, *op. cit.*, p. 164.

[78] Cf. canon 1648, § 2.

[79] Cf. Roberti, *De Processibus*, I, n. 199; Pugliese, "art. cit.," p. 184.

[80] Cf. canon 1650.

[81] Lega-Bartoccetti, *Commentarius*, I, 305. Ivo of Chartres stated: "Furiosus quoque nullum negotium gerere potest, quia non intelligit quod agit."—*Decretum*, part. 13, cap. 89. Cf. *MPL*, Vol. CLXI, col. 820.

[82] Cf. D'Avack, *op. cit.*, p. 191: ". . . il presunto amens . . . non può

Since a judicial process requires a period of time of greater or less duration, the possibility that an insane person enjoy lucid intervals is of very slight importance as regards his capacity to stand in judgment. At most he could be questioned during the lucid interval, and his testimony must be received with great caution.

Feeble-minded persons, on the other hand, cannot be said to be *"iure naturali inhabiles"*; for they possess to some degree at least the spiritual faculties necessary to perform a naturally valid act. Only by a prescription of positive legislation are they under disability. Their disqualification, however, is not absolute but relative.[83] Indeed, there are cases in which they may personally stand in judgment, as is stated in canon 1650: "ut de propriis delictis respondeant, aut ad praescriptum iudicis."

That the feeble-minded may be summoned to answer personally for their delicts is a logical consequence of the penal law of the Church. In Canon Law, mental weakness diminishes but does not destroy imputability.[84] Mental weakness, *per se,* does not excuse from penalties *latae sententiae;* in fact, if an action is gravely sinful, notwithstanding the diminution of the liability, the feeble-minded person who perpetrates it incurs the penalty attached to it.[85] Consequently, the feeble-minded may be summoned as defendants in criminal processes, in which they answer personally for their delicts.[86]

With regard to contentious trials, should the judge consider a

---

essere ammesso . . . *ad standum in judicio* personalmente, fino a che non abbia offerto una prova positiva della sua attuale *restitutio ad sanam mentem,* sotto pena, in caso contrario, di dar luogo ad una nullità insanabile dell'intiero processo e della sentenza stessa."

[83] Cf. Roberti, *op. cit.,* n. 190; Pugliese, "art. cit.," p. 184.

[84] Canon 2201, § 4: Debilitas mentis delicti imputabilitatem minuit, sed non tollit omnino.

[85] Cf. canon 2229, § 3, n. 2. Ebrietas, omissio debitae diligentiae, mentis debilitas, impetus passionis, si, non obstante imputabilitatis deminutione, actio sit adhuc graviter culpabilis, a poenis latae sententiae non excusant."

[86] Cf. canon 1650. Cf. Olivero, *Le Parti nel Giudizio Canonico,* n. 40; Lega-Bartoccetti, *Commentarius,* I, 310, n. 6; Roberti, *De Processibus,* I, n. 202, II, 5.

feeble-minded person capable of standing personally in court, he may command him to do so. Otherwise, the lawful guardian must pursue the case.[87] Canon 1650 does not limit in any way the discretionary power of the judge in this matter. He may, however, follow the prescription of canon 1648, § 3, to guide him when considering whether or not to admit or summon the feeble-minded person or his guardian to act in a contentious trial. That norm applies specifically to minors but may be followed in cases of the mentally deficient, who for all practical purposes may be considered in a class with minors.[88] Accordingly, a mentally deficient person possessing the mental capacity of a normal person of fourteen years of age may be admitted personally to act and respond in contentious trials involving spiritual matters or issues connected with spiritual matters.[89] If, however, the feeble-minded person does not enjoy the use of reason to the degree of a normal person of fourteen years, a guardian or a proxy should represent him in court, analogically with the prescription of canon 1648, § 3.

The Code contains no special disposition concerning the disqualification of the deaf, blind, and dumb, as such. Modern methods of instruction have helped these unfortunate persons considerably. Consequently, a general norm regarding their incapacity can hardly

---

[87] Canon 1650. Cf. Olivero, *loc. cit.;* Roberti, *loc. cit.*

[88] Cf. D'Avack, *op. cit.,* p .226: ". . . è . . . presunzione generale del diritto in genere e di quello canonico in specie che il *debilis mente* nella determinazione e nell'esercizio dei suoi diritti e doveri sia equiparabile al minore." Cf. Stitt, *De Promotore Justitiae Ejusque Munere in Curia Dioecesana,* n. 102; Staffa, "De Constitutione Curatoris," p. 69.

[89] Spiritual cases are, for example: Cases regarding faith and morals, the Sacraments and sacramentals, divine worship and the sacred liturgy, dispensation from vows and oaths, rights and obligations of the clergy, beneficiaries, and religious. . . . Cf. Augustine, *Ecclesiastical Trials,* p. 5; Regatillo, *Institutiones Iuris Canonici,* II, 176-177; M. Coronata, *Institutiones Iuris Canonici,* Vol. III, *De Processibus* (3. ed., Taurini-Romae: Marietti, 1948), n. 1090 (hereafter cited *De Processibus*). Among cases connected with spiritual matters may be numbered: those relating to church revenues, *ius patronatus,* legitimacy of birth, administration of church property. . . . Cf. Augustine, *op. cit.,* pp. 5-6; Coronata, *loc. cit.;* Regatillo, *op. cit.,* II, 177.

be given, but each case must be evaluated separately.[90] With the help of experts, if necessary, the ecclesiastical authority can determine whether the afflicted person is capable of personally exercising his processual rights, or whether the prescriptions of canon 1648, § 1, or of canon 1650 must be applied.

To the extent of their disability, the insane and the feebleminded lack what the Code terms *persona standi in iudicio*,[91] in the sense that they are debarred from personally exercising court action. Court action executed by a person disqualified because of mental derangement is null and void, because an essential condition of valid acts is lacking when a person does not possess necessary qualities of intellect and will.[92] Moreover, when issued to parties

---

[90] Cf. Bouix, *Tractatus de Judiciis Ecclesiasticis*, I, 168-169: ". . . jam in multis regionibus ita locupleti instructione donantur surdi et muti, ut generaliter sua jura satis intelligant, eaque persequi et defendere possint. Hinc attento solo jure naturali, non videntur posse impediri, quin tanquam Actores et Rei judicio interveniant, nisi de eorum personali incapacitate constiterit. Et licet canonistae supponant legislationem Justiniani quoad hoc fuisse in foro ecclesiastico receptam, dubium saltem esse potest utrum hodie jus illud perseveret; cum ipsius fundamentum, ob novam surdos et mutos instruendi methodum, videatur cessasse. Hinc quidquid sit de legum saecularium in variis regionibus circa hoc dispositione, cum nulla recens ecclesiastica lex contrarium decernat, non mihi videtur judicium ecclesiasticum nullitate laborare, ex eo solo quod Actor vel Reus surdus mutus fuerit." More recently Chelodi-Ciprotti wrote: ". . . . Reliqui vero, in quibus plus minusve (intellectus) evolutus cernitur, . . . surdi et muti et coeci simul, surdi et muti tantum, singuli in quolibet casu iudicandi sunt, pro gradu usus rationis quo pollent et educationis quam assecuti sunt. Regulas generales statuere nec convenit nec iuvat; in dubio decernere pertinent ad artis peritos."—J. Chelodi-P. Ciprotti, *Ius Canonicum de Personis* (ed. 3., Trento: Libreria Moderna Editrice, 1942), p. 153, n. 91. b. Cf. also Della Rocca, *op. cit.*, p. 168, n. 79.

[91] Cf. canons 1892, n. 2; 1648, § 1; 1650. The phrase is discussed more at length below, pp. 1021 ff.

[92] Cf. above, pp. 43-45 and canon 1680, § 1: Nullitas actus tunc tantum habetur, cum in eo deficiunt quae actum ipsum essentialiter constituunt, aut sollemnia seu conditiones desiderantur a sacris canonibus requisitae sub poena nullitatis. One may note here the following statement which may find application in a rare case: "Quamvis capacitas processualis requiratur pro omnibus et singulis actibus processus, nihilominus si incapax durante processu fit capax, videtur ratihabitione sanare actus praecedentes . . ." Roberti, *De Processibus*, I, n. 199.

of whom at least one had not the *persona standi in iudicio,* a judicial sentence itself is vitiated with irremediable nullity.[93]

Thus, for the validity of court action and of the judicial sentence it is necessary that a mentally ill party be represented in the trial by his lawful guardian, unless it is shown that he regained that degree of mental maturity (*maturitas animi*), which is regarded as the necessary condition for *capacitas standi in iudicio.*[94]

In conclusion, it must be noted that the nullity of the sentence issued to a mentally ill party who personally exercised court action contrary to the ruling of Canons 1648, § 1, and 1650, may be proposed in one of two ways: (1) after the manner of an exception; or (2) after the manner of an action. When introduced after the manner of an exception, the complaint of nullity may be raised at any future time, as the Code calls this particular exception *perpetual.* He who avails himself of the complaint of nullity after the manner of an action must bring suit before the judge who issued the sentence within thirty years from the date of publication of the sentence.[95]

---

[93] Canon 1892, n. 2. Cf. A. Hanssen, *De Sanctione Nullitatis in Processu Canonico* (Romae: Apollinaris, 1939), n. 127: "Ratione litigantium nullitas sententiae est insanabilis, quando nempe alteruter caret capacitate iuridica vel processuali. . . ." (hereafter cited *De Sanctione Nullitatis*); Olivero, *Le Parti nel Giudizio Canonico,* n. 37.

[94] Cf. D'Avack, *op. cit.,* pp. 190-191; Toso, "De Constitutione Curatoris," p. 118. What this author states concerning the feeble-minded applies, *a fortiori,* to the insane: ". . . in foro ecclesiastico homo mentis minus firmae stare in iudicio non potest (Can. 1650), ac proinde *semper irrita* sunt *omnia,* quae ipse non gesserit per personam curatoris (Can. 1892, n. 2)." One may also note this additional effect of disqualification in the civil forum: " . . . in some jurisdictions, after an inquisition ascertains that a person is of unsound mind, and his person and estate are committed to guardian or committee, a suit at law is not maintainable, and it is regarded as a contempt of the court having by statute the custody of persons and estates of such persons to commence and prosecute an action at law against them without permission."—25 Am. Jur., *Guardian and Ward,* § 153.

[95] Canon 1893. "The difference between the two ways of availing oneself of the complaint of nullity appears, for example, in a case where a party sued a priest in the bishop's court over a piece of land, the private property of the priest. Supposing the diocesan court gave sentence in

favor of the plaintiff, and that many years afterwards the heir of the priest goes over the case and finds in the acts one of those so-called incurable nullities of the sentence. If the thirty years have elapsed, he cannot bring the action, but if, in connection with the same property, the former plaintiff or his heir has a lawsuit with the priest or his heir, the priest or the heir may raise the nullity by way of an exception, no matter how many years have elapsed since the pronouncement of the sentence." —Woywod-Smith, *A Practical Commentary,* II, n. 1813.

CHAPTER III

The Qualifications of Guardians

Article I. In the Roman Law

Under the older Roman law, the only qualifications for the office of guardian were citizenship and male sex. Slaves and other non-citizens could not exercise the office of guardianship.[1] Should a slave be appointed guardian by testament, in the absence of the express gift of liberty, he was held to receive his freedom by implication.[2] The exclusion of women from this office was justified thus by Alexander Severus: *Ultra sexum femineae infirmitatis tale officium est.*[3] As a matter of fact, the weakness attributed to sex was of no account. The true motive for their debarrment was that women could be *in potestate,* but could not have persons *in potestate* except *dominica*[4] or *quasi dominica.*[5] Under Justinian, how-

---

[1] D. (26, 5) 17; C. (5, 34) 7. Cf. Brugi, *Istituzioni di Diritto Romano,* n. 125. b; Robinson, *Selections,* p. 132; Leage, *Roman Private Law,* p. 113; Perozzi, *Istituzioni di Diritto Romano,* I, p. 466, note 5.

[2] Inst. (1, 14).

[3] C. (5, 35) 1. Cf. also D. (26, 1) 18.

[4] I.e., *potestas* over slaves.

[5] Perozzi, *op. cit.,* p. 509: "La donna è esclusa da tutti gli uffici civili o pubblici." This author illustrates in note 4: "Essa non partecipa ai comizi, non può essere magistrato, giudice, testimonio solenne, non può presentare azioni populari, nè *postulare* per altri, nè rappresentare alcuno in giudizio, nè essere investita della tutela, salvo eccezioni vedute. . . ." The cited author continues: "Le fonte giustificano la norma, invocando la *pudicitia,* la *fragilitas* e la *forensium rerum ignorantia* propria del sesso. In realtà essa dipende dal fatto che, una volta posta la famiglia sulla base del patriarcato, non poteva partecipare alla vita della città costituita da un insieme di famiglie, chi, come la donna, non poteva essere mai padre di famiglia, ma soltanto invece chi o rappresentava attualmente una famiglia o poteva rappresentarla in avvenire, cioè dunque i *patres* e i *filii familias.*" Perozzi, *op. cit.,* p. 510: "Questa stessa situazione della donna in ordine alla famiglia creava il pericolo che, fatta *sui iuris,* si giovasse della sua

ever, exceptions were admitted, so that a widow, for example, could demand appointment as *tutrix* to her children or grandchildren.[6]

Not only the *paterfamilias* but even the *filiusfamilias,* though *in potestate* himself, could be appointed to exercise the public office of guardian.[7] Justinian declared a son eligible for the guardianship of his insane parents and asserted that he was preferable for that responsibility provided he possessed the necessary ability and integrity.[8] The law, however, denied to the husband the right to be the guardian of his insane wife.[9]

Justinian's collections indicate the categories of persons freed or disqualified from exercising the function of guardian. A man did not qualify for this office until he attained his twenty-fifth year.[10] Deaf-mutes, spendthrifts, the insane, and the blind were to be relieved of the function.[11] Soldiers in active service were not to be admitted to the office of guardianship.[12] Neither were bishops and monks.[13] Priests, deacons and subdeacons could not be guardians of persons who were not related to them.[14] A person's creditors could not be his guardians as long as they remained such.[15]

Orphanages were recognized as *quasi-tutores* or *quasi-curatores*

---

indipendenza a danno degli interessi della gente e della parentela agnatizia in cui era, per non provvedere che agli interessi suoi. La donna sui iuris sostiene infatti una vita individuale in mezzo ad una società che originariamente non conosce e non ammette se non la vita collettiva. Ad impedire ciò rimase stabilito che la donna, uscita col raggiungimento della pubertà dalla tutela *impuberum,* cadesse sotto una nuova tutela, destinata a durare per tutta la sua vita, che porta il nome di *tutela mulierum.*

[6] D. (26, 1) 16; (26, 1) 18; (26, 5) 21; C. (5, 35) 1, 2, 3.

[7] Inst. (1, 14); D. (27, 10) 1, 4.

[8] D. (27, 10) 4: "Furiosae matris curatio ad filium pertinent: pietas enim parentibus, etsi inaequalis est eorum potestas, aequa debebitur." Cf., too, D. (26, 5) 12.

[9] D. (27, 10) 14; C. (5, 34) 2.

[10] C. (5, 30) 5; Inst. (1, 25) 13; D. (26, 1) 32. 2.

[11] C. (5, 68) 1; D. (26, 1) 17; C. (5, 34) 3; (5, 30) 5. 1.

[12] Inst. (1, 25) 14; C. (5, 34) 4.

[13] Nov. 123, c. 5.

[14] Nov. 123, c. 5.

[15] Nov. 72, c. 1; Nov. 94, c. 1.

and functioned as guardians in the administration of the ward's patrimony as well as in the judicial defence of his rights.[16] When a guardian had been found open to suspicion, incompetent in the discharge of his duties, or neglectful, another was to be appointed in his stead.[17]

Subsequent legislation adhered closely to the requirements as outlined in the law of Rome.[18]

Article II. In the Law of the Code

The Code makes no mention of special qualifications required of guardians in the ecclesiastical forum.[19] We may state, then, that,

---

[16] C. (1, 3) 31: "Orphanotrophos huius inclitae urbis nulla subtilitate iuris obsistente eorum quidem qui pupilli sunt quasi tutores, adulescentium vero quasi curatores sine ullo fideiussionis gravamine in emergentibus causis tam in iudicio quam extra iudicium, ut opus exegerit, ad similitudinem tutoris et curatoris personas et negotia eorum, si qua possint habere, defendere ac vindicare iubemus. . . ."

[17] C. (5, 70) 7. To insure the faithful discharge of their duties, Justinian made obligatory the following solemnities: "Et si quidem parens curatorem furioso vel furiosae in ultimo elogio heredibus institutis vel exheredatis dederit . . . ipse qui datus est ad curationem perveniat, ita tamen, ut in hac florentissima civitate apud urbicariam praefecturam deducatur, in provincia autem apud praesidem eius, praesente ei tam viro religiosissimo locorum antistite quam tribus primatibus, et actis intervenientibus tactis sacrosanctis scripturis edicat omnia se recte et cum utilitate furiosi gerere neque praetermittere ea, quae utilia furioso esse putaverit, neque admittere, quae inutilia existimaverit. Et inventario cum omni subtilitate publice conscripto res suscipiat et eas secundum opinionem disponat sub hypotheca rerum ad eum pertinentium ad similitudinem tutorum et adulti curatorum. Sin autem testamentum quidem parens non confecerit, lex autem curatorem utpote agnatum vocaverit, vel eo cessante aut non idoneo forsitan existente ex iudiciali electione curatorem ei dare necesse fuerit, tunc secundum praefatam divisionem in hac quiden florentissima civitate apud gloriosissimam urbicariam praefecturam creatio procedat."

[18] Cf. Durandus, *Speculum Iuris,* Lib. I, Partic. III, n. 5. J. Gutierrez, *Tractatus Novus de Tutelis et Curis* (Francofurti: Impensis Wolfgangi Endteri, 1650), I, VIII, nn. 1-2 (hereafter cited *Tractatus Novus*).

[19] Cf. J. M. Costello, *Domicile and Quasi-Domicile,* The Catholic University of America Canon Law Studies, n. 60 (Washington, D.C.: The Catholic University of America, 1930), p. 166.

just as in the civil forum, so in the ecclesiastical, the decision as to whether a particular person is fit or competent to act as guardian is left to the authority charged to appoint him and to the trial court.[20]

From considerations on the nature and on the function of guardianship in an ecclesiastical process may be inferred the necessity of certain qualifications with which a guardian should be endowed. Generally speaking, a person is qualified to act as guardian in a lawsuit, if he is competent personally to exercise court action and is not otherwise unsuitable or disqualified. Thus, minors, the habitually insane, feeble-minded persons, and spendthrifts—all of whom are obliged to sue and defend their own cases through guardians,[21] are automatically disqualified from acting as guardians for another needy person.[22] During the process an exception may be raised to remove from guardianship a person who himself stands in need of representation.[23] Nor can any measure taken by the judge or by the parties in the trial eliminate such native incompetency,[24] for, the responsiblities entailed in the fulfillment of the duties of guardianship require the presence of a mature, experienced mind, which those persons presumably do not possess.

---

[20] Cf. 25 Am. Jur., *Guardian and Ward,* § 30; canons 1648, 1651.

[21] Cf. canons 1648, § 1, and 1650, and pp. 43. ff, above.

[22] Writing of procurators, Hanssen states: "Ratione constituti est invalidum mandatum, si procurator caret capacitate processuali, uti minores, qui minus firmae mentis sunt et bonis interdicti"—*De Sanctione Nullitatis,* n. 73. Cf. also Noone, *Nullity in Judicial Acts,* The Catholic University of America Canon Law Studies, n. 297 (Washington, D.C.: The Catholic University of America Press, 1950), p. 71. The reason that Hanssen presents to disqualify such persons from being procurators holds for their disqualification from guardianship: "Nam qui pro seipso in iudicio stare nequit, nec pro aliis valide potest."—*loc. cit.*

[23] Among the "exceptiones fiendae contra quemlibet tutorem et curatorem," Durandus lists minority and equivalent disqualifications: "Generaliter etiam contra quemlibet tutorem et curatorem opponitur de aetate: ut quia est minor 25. an. vel alias eget alterius cura."—Durandus, *Speculum Iuris,* Lib. I, Part. III, n. 5.

[24] "Habilitatio iudicis vel partis consensus nihil operetur" was stated of procurators in similar conditions. Cf. Blasius, Altimarus, *Tractatus de Nullitatibus* (Neapoli: Typis Haeredum Lucae Antonii de Fusco, 1672), rub. XI, q. 31, nn. 1, 2.

If a person should be so handicapped by physical disability as to be prevented from properly discharging the duties of guardianship in a trial, he would be unsuitable for this office. When such a person has already been appointed guardian by the competent authority, the presiding judge—the writer believes—could proceed, *ex officio* or at the request of the *promotor justitiae* or of the *defensor vinculi,* to appoint a guardian *ad litem,* as he is empowered to do when distance makes it difficult for a guardian to attend to his duties in a process.[25]

Conviction of crime and moral delinquency render a person incompetent or unsuitable to act as guardian in some civil jurisdictions.[26] These civil law disqualifications might very well be considered by the ecclesiastical authority, especially since the church trial is conducted in a religious manner[27] and frequently bears upon important religious issues.

Canon Law requires that judicial procurators be Catholics and enjoy good moral reputation. Non-Catholics, i.e., pagans, heretics, schismatics, and apostates, are permitted to assume the role of judicial procurator in exceptional cases, dictated by necessity.[28] Since guardians are for all practical purposes very much like procurators,[29] the injunction of canon 1657, § 1, could well be

---

[25] Cf. canon 1648, § 2. See also Roberti, *De Processibus,* I, p. 554.

[26] Cf. 25. Am. Jur., *Guardian and Ward,* § 30.

[27] Cf. canons 1636 and 1874, § 1.

[28] Canon 1657, § 1. Cf. J. J. Hogan, *Judicial Advocates and Procurators,* The Catholic University of America Canon Law Studies, n. 133 (Washington, D.C.: The Catholic University of America Press, 1941), pp. 82, 84. Writing of judicial advocates and procurators, Hogan offers the following reason for the Church's requirement of Catholicity: ". . . the Church in re-emphasizing this qualification has in mind not only the lack of understanding of Church practice and procedure on the part of the average non-Catholic, but also the incongruity of finding such key positions possessed by men entertaining dogmatic prejudices with regard to the very matters under discussion."—*op. cit.,* p. 83. The very same remarks may be made of guardians whose function of representation in court is very similar to that of judicial procurators.

[29] Cf. Hogan, *op. cit.,* p. 107, note 26. Lega stated: "tutores aut curatores . . . in genere procuratorum venire censendi sunt, sed sunt quasi species propriae."—*Commentarius,* I, 302.

followed by the ecclesiastical authorities as a guiding norm when considering the admission into the ecclesiastical forum either of a Catholic not in good standing[30] or of a non-Catholic, appointed guardian by the civil authority. It should be adhered to more strictly when the ecclesiastical authority itself appoints the guardian.

Giustiniani holds that a non-Catholic guardian who is to act as plaintiff in the ecclesiastical forum must have a substitute appointed, because non-Catholics are forbidden to appear as plaintiffs in ecclesiastical trials.[31] In view of canon 1657, § 1, the writer believes that Giustiniani's position is too strict and agrees, rather, with Doheny, who, after considering the texts of canon 1651 and of Article 78 of the *Instructio,* concludes: "The meaning and connotation are somewhat different and seem to indicate a more lenient attitude toward the admission of civil-law guardians. Hence, it appears that a non-Catholic might also be permitted to act in this capacity."[32]

Against excommunicated guardians who seek to act in ecclesiastical trials may be lodged a judicial exception, since excommunicated persons are expressly prohibited from acting as plaintiffs in Church trials.[33] The appointment by the ordinary or by the ecclesiastical tribunal of an excommunicated person to act as guardian, moreover, may prove a cause of amazement or scandal to the faithful, especially in localities where religious sentiment is strong.

In the law of the Code, women are not disqualified from acting as guardians in ecclesiastical trials, since they, too, are admitted to

---

[30] Gratian considered the *infames* in relation to processual restrictions. After enumerating persons who were not to be permitted to plead or defend the causes of others, he made a general exception in favor of persons under guardianship: "Pro his enim, quorum curam gerunt, eis postulare conceditur." Moreover, he stated expressly that the *infames* could plead and defend for *pupillus, furiosus, fatuus,* "item pro his quibus propter infirmitatem curatores dari solent. . . ."—C. 2, C. III, q. 7.

[31] ". . . essendo proibito agli acattolici di essere attori nelle cause ecclesiastiche, un tutore acattolico non potrà essere attore per il pupillo e dovrà essere sostituito." R. Giustiniani, "De Curatore Dementis," *Il Diritto Ecclesiastico,* LIV (1943), 106. (Hereafter cited "De Curatore Dementis").

[32] Doheny, *Canonical Procedure in Matrimonial Cases,* I, 252.

[33] Cf. canons 2263; 1628, § 3.

act personally on their own behalf and to offer testimony on behalf of others.[34]

Are parents to be considered *ipso facto*, by reason of their parenthood, the guardians of their mentally deficient children, when the latter are *sui iuris* because of majority or emancipation? Need they be expressly designated guardians by the competent authorities in order to be able to plead or defend their children's cases validly? The authors who take up these questions do not agree in their answers. Ferraris considered the father the *legitimus curator* of his son, even though the latter were emancipated from parental authority: *"Si filius familias inciderit in amentiam et furorem, licet fuerit emancipatus pater erit legitimus curator."*[35] Noone seems to imply that parenthood gives rise automatically to the right to act as guardian, when he writes: "The parents have a natural right to represent their children in the trial. Any other curators have to be approved by the ordinary, for even a curator who is appointed by the civil authority cannot be admitted by the ecclesiastical judge without the consent of the ordinary of the ward (Canon 1651, § 1)."[36] D'Avack expresses a similar view.[37]

---

[34] Before the Code, women were rarely called upon to be questioned in the court itself; nor could they be forced to appear in court against their will. These dispositions were prompted by reasons of decency and modesty. Cf. C. 1, *de iudiciis*, II, I, in VI°: Mulieres, quas vagari non convenit, nec virorum coetibus immisceri, auctoritate literarum sedis apostolicae, vel legatorum ipsius, aut alia quacumque ad iudicium personaliter evocari vel trahi invitas causa ferendi testimonium, aut alia qualibet, quae in iure non exprimitur, prohibemus. Under the earlier English common law, married women were not ineligible to become guardians, but it was not the practice to appoint them without first obtaining their husbands' consent. This discrimination has become obsolete in modern times. Cf. 25 Am. Jur., *Guardian and Ward*, § 30.

[35] L. Ferraris, *Prompta Bibliotheca Canonica, Juridica, Moralis, Theologica, necnon Ascetica, Polemica, Rubricistica, Historica* (9 vols., Romae, 1885-1889), VII, sub v. *Tutela, Tutor, Cura, Curator*, pp. 520-532, n. 91 (hereafter cited *Prompta Bibliotheca*). This author cites Justinian's C. (5, 70) 7, who offers as a reason for his position: "Quis enim talis affectus extraneus inveniatur, ut vincat paternum? Vel cui alii credendum est res liberorum gubernandas, parentibus derelictis?"

[36] Noone, *Nullity in Judicial Acts*, p. 55.

[37] ". . . . merita di essere ricordato e tenuto presente che, a termini

On the other hand, Lega clearly implies that only after being admitted by the ecclesiastical authority do parents acquire the right to represent their children in the Church forum.[38] To support his view that parents do not become automatically the guardians of their incompetent children in ecclesiastical trials, Roberti refers to a sentence declared null by the Signatura Apostolica, because the parent was not expressly appointed guardian for his child.[39] After considering canon 1648, § 1, which states that parents, like tutors and guardians, are bound to plead or defend the cases of minors and persons devoid of the use of reason, Doheny remarks that the injunction can hardly be interpreted to mean that parents automatically become the sole guardians of the children under consideration, merely because of parenthood. He holds that like other guardians they must be designated as such by the competent authorities.[40]

From the consideration of canons 89 and 1648, § 1, and of the declaration of the Signatura Apostolica, referred to by Roberti, the writer concludes: (1) that parents become automatically, by virtue of canon 1648, § 1, the lawful guardians of mentally ill children before the age of majority; and (2) that in order to be-

del diritto canonico, i genitori ed i tutori hanno senz'altro il pieno diritto di rappresentare in giudizio gli incapaci sia come attori che come convenuti; mentre il curatore viceversa . . . o deve essere direttamente nominato dallo stesso *Ordinarius proprius* dell'incapace, o . . . deve per lo meno essere da lui formalmente approvato con suo apposito decreto. . . ." D'Avack, *Cause di Nullità,* I, 189.

[38] "Vi praescripti can. 1648, § 3, et can. 1651 statuenda est regula, iudicem ecclesiasticum pro suo foro et prouti controversiae natura ferat, admittere tutores et curatores civili auctoritate datos, multoque magis parentibus recognoscere facultatem civili iure attributam filiorum nomine agendi et respondendi in iudicio, tamen nonnullis sub limitationibus hoc canone statutis; et salva semper auctoritate iudicis ecclesiastici dandi peculiarem tutorem aut curatorem pro negotio cui agendo inhabiles sint tutor aut curator aut alteruter parentum aut uterque parens iure civili constituti." —*Commentarius,* I, 304-305.

[39] Roberti, *De Processibus,* I, n. 202, IV, note 3: "Ita SA in c. Neoboracen. null. matr. incid. de nominatione curatoris 27 ian. 1934." Cf. also Giustiniani, "De Curatore Dementis," p. 107.

[40] Doheny, *Canonical Procedure in Matrimonial Cases,* I, 25, 252.

come the lawful guardians of mentally ill children after the age of majority they must be designated as such by the competent authorities.

Pre-Code legislation, restricting bishops, regulars, and clerics as to the exercise of guardianship referred to *tutela* and *cura* in the civil forum.[41] The norms were enacted to safeguard clerical and religious dignity, to avoid interference with priestly and religious duties, and to preclude avarice and ambition.[42] The prohibition, however, was not absolute, as the texts cited reveal. Brunini studied the question of guardianship exercised by clerics in the civil forum and stated: "The only conclusion is that while the law did not forbid to clerics the guardianship of minors related through legitimate birth and of orphans and widows unable to care for themselves and the care in general of such persons as needed ecclesiastical charity, still they could not undertake such care without the permission of their superior. This is necessary in our present interpretation of canon 139, § 3. . . .

"In granting permission to clerics and to regulars to act as guardians of relatives the sacred congregation and the bishops were accustomed to include the warning that they do nothing interdicted to ecclesiastical persons or foreign to the ecclesiastical state."[43]

On the other hand, the law of the Church has never excluded clerics and religious from acting as guardians in the ecclesiastical forum. Their lawful superiors may, of course, forbid them to exercise this function.

When considering the appointment of a cleric or religious to act as guardian in the ecclesiastical forum, the competent au-

---

[41] Cf. above, pp. 17-19. See also J. Pignatelli, *Consultationes Canonicae* (II vols. in 5, Coloniae Allobrogum, 1700-1711), V, consul. 10, pp. 31-34.

[42] After citing the disqualification of bishops and monks contained in Nov. 123. 5 and adding *regularis* to the disqualified, Durandus gives a reason for their disqualification: "Non enim bene possunt tractari simul divina et humana."—*Speculum Iuris,* I, partic. III, n. 5.

[43] J. B. Brunini, *The Clerical Obligations of Canons 139 and 142,* The Catholic University of America Canon Law Studies, n. 103 (Washington, D.C.: The Catholic University of America, 1937), p. 32.

thorities might do well to consider the possibility of his becoming involved in subsequent civil suits.

In some jurisdictions in the United States, corporations, banks and trust companies, are eligible for guardianship of the estates of incompetent persons.[44] With reference to this, Doheny remarks that it is the intent of the Code that the guardian be a physical rather than a moral person.[45]

The *Promotor Iustitiae* may well be appointed guardian, especially under circumstances contemplated in canon 1648, § 1.[46] The *Defensor Vinculi,* however, cannot act as guardian.[47] His primary duty is to defend the sacred bond of marriage and the validity of ordination.[48]

From canon 1648, § 2, may be inferred a peculiar qualification, namely, that of residence proximate to the tribunal in which the guardian acts for his ward.

Analogously with the ruling of Boniface VIII regarding procurators it may be affirmed that as a rule once a person has been duly appointed guardian he is presumed capable of exercising that function so that the burden of proof to the contrary rests on the one contesting his fitness.[49]

---

[44] Cf. 25 Am. Jur., *Guardian and Ward,* § 34.

[45] Doheny, *Canonical Procedure in Matrimonial Cases,* I, 24.

[46] Cf. Stitt, *De Promotore Justitiae,* n. 130.

[47] Cf. canon 1613, § 2.

[48] Canon 1586. Cf. also Pius XII's *Allocutio ad Praelatos Auditores, ceterosque Officiales et Administratores Tribunalis S. Romanae Rotae necnon eiusdem Tribunalis Advocatos et Procuratores,* habita die 2 mensis Octobris a. 1944, *AAS,* XXXVI (1944), 281-290.

[49] C. 1, *de procuratoribus,* I, 19, in VI°: "Regulariter, qui non prohibetur expresse ad exercendum procurationis officium idoneus debeat reputari."

CHAPTER IV

THE MANNER OF APPOINTMENT OF GUARDIANS FOR THE MENTALLY ILL

Preliminary Considerations

Canon 1892 lists among processual defects that vitiate a sentence with irremediable nullity the fact that a person acted for another without a legitimate mandate.[1] Accordingly, a person is not authorized to be another's legal representative in the ecclesiastical forum unless he has been commisioned in the manner prescribed by the canons. The question of the guardian's appointment is a vulnerable point for the intrusion of judicial nullity into a trial, If the guardian lacks appointment or if his appointment is illegitimate, he has not the legal or legitimate title whereby the right to act for his principal is acquired. Consequently, his acts and the acts which the court and adverse party perform in relation to him are invalid, and the sentence is vitiated by irremediable nullity.[2]

That a person may be lawfully commisioned to act in Church trials, as guardian for a mentally deficient person, it is required: 1. That he be appointed in the manner prescribed by the law; and 2. That the competent authority designate him. These two requirements will be discussed in the following chapters.

Article I. The Manner of Appointment in Roman Law and Doctrine

In Roman Law, the guardian of the mentally deficient person could be appointed in one of two ways—i.e., by operation of law and by action of the magistrate: *"curatores aut legitimi sunt, id est*

[1] Canon 1892. Sententia vitio insanabilis nullitatis laborat, quando: 3°. Quis nomine alterius egit sine legitimo mandato.

[2] Roberti, *De Processibus,* I, n. 202, IV; Noone, *Nullity in Judicial Acts,* p. 55; Hanssen, *De Sanctione Nullitatis,* n. 65 b; Olivero, *Le Parti*

qui ex lege duodecim tabularum dantur, aut honorarii, id est qui a praetore constituuntur."[3]

According to the Twelve Tables, the *cura furiosi* fell to the *adgnati* and *gentiles*: "*Si furiosus escit, adgnatum gentiliumque in eo pecuniaque eius potestas esto.*"[4]

Thus it was the law itself that designated the insane person's guardian. *Adgnati* in the Roman sense were persons who were regarded as related to each other, either because they were in the common *potestas* of some ancestor, or because they would have been in such *potestas* were the ancestor still alive.[5] *Gentiles,* on the other hand, were the organized members of a *gens,* an aggregate of agnatic families bearing a common name. The juxtaposition of *adgnati* and *gentiles* in the text cited leads to the following interpretation: if the nearest agnate (*proximus adgnatus*) cannot be guardian, the *furiosus* falls under the *cura* of his *gentiles.*[6] Accordingly the right and duty to be guardian was attributed to a person in the order of the interest he had in the preservation of a ward's property because of a possible succession to ownership.[7] This provision of the Twelve Tables was lauded by Ulpian: "*Le-*

nel Giudizio Canonico, n. 37; Doheny, *Canonical Procedure in Matrimonial Cases,* I, 514. This doctrine is based on canon 1680.

3 The text is attributed to Ulpian, *Libri Regularum,* XII. 1. Cf. Baviera's reconstruction: *Tituli XXVIII ex corpore Ulpiani qui vulgo Domitio Ulpiano adhuc tribuuntur,* XII. *De Curatoribus,* 1, in *Fontes Iuris Romani Antejustiniani,* pars altera: *Auctores* (Florentiae: Barbera, 1940), p. 277.

4 Cf. Bruns, *Fontes Iuris Romani Antiqui,* p. 23.

5 Cf. D. (26, 4) 1; (26, 4) 7: "Sunt autem adgnati, qui per virilis sexus personas cognatione iuncti sunt, quasi a patre cognati, veluti frater eodem patre natus, fratris filius neposve ex eo, item patruus et patrui filius neposve ex eo." Cf. Also Inst. (1, 15) 1.

6 Writing of *adgnati* with reference to *tutela,* Gaius states: "Si plures sunt adgnati, proximus tutelam nanciscitur." Cf. D. (26, 4) 9; cf. also Inst. (1, 16) 7: "Cum autem, ad adgnatos tutela pertineat, non simul ad omnes pertinet, sed ad eos tantum, qui proximo gradu sunt, vel, si eiusdem gradus sint, ad omnes."

7 Cf. Inst. (1, 17) which may apply here: ". . . plerunque, ubi successionis est emolumentum, ibi et tutelae onus esse debet. Plerumque, quia, si a femina impubes manumittatur, ipsa ad hereditatem vocatur, cum alius est tutor." See also Perozzi, I, 524.

gitimae tutelae lege duodecim tabularum adgnatis delatae sunt et consanguineis, item patronis, id est his qui ad legitimam hereditatem admitti possint: hoc summa providentia, ut qui sperarent hanc successionem, idem tuerentur bona, ne dilapidarentur."[8]

Should an insane person be without a *curator legitimus*, because he had no *adgnati* or *gentiles* to qualify for guardianship, the appointment of the guardian was made by the magistrate. Within the limits of the city of Rome, the magistrate usually authorized to appoint guardians was the *praetor urbanus*. The governor usually appointed guardians in the provinces.[9]

Ulpian warned the designating authority to proceed with caution when appointing a guardian for an insane person: "*Observare praetorem oportebit, ne cui temere citra causae cognitionem plenissimam curatorem det, quoniam plerique vel furorem vel dementiam fingunt, quo magis curatore accepto onera civilia detrectent.*"[10] Thus, after verifying the existence of *furor* or *dementia* in the person to be subjected to guardianship, was the magistrate to decree the appointment. The measures, however, to be adopted in

---

[8] D. (26, 4) 1. Note, however: "Interdum alibi est hereditas, alibi tutela, ut puta si sit consanguinea pupillo: nam hereditas quidem ad adgnatam pertinet, tutela autem ad adgnatum. Item in libertinis, si sit patrona et patroni filius: nam tutelam patroni filius, hereditatem patrona optinebit." —D. (26, 4) (1, 1).

[9] Cf. D. (26, 5) 8: "Furioso et furiosae et muto et surdo tutor vel curator a praetore vel praeside dari poterit." Cf. also D. (27, 10) 5; Inst. (1, 20) 4; (1, 23) 3; C. (1, 70) 7, 5-6. Note also this declaration, made by Ulpian: "Tutoris datio neque imperii est neque iurisdictionis sed ei soli competit, cui nominatim hoc dedit vel lex vel senatus consultus vel princeps." Cf. D. (26, 1) (6, 2). Cf. Bonfante, *Corso di Diritto Romano,* I, 421. Jolowicz remarks, however: "At no time does there appear to have been any *lex* granting the power of appointment to the magistrate; it seems to have been regarded as inherent in the *imperium.*" Finally, note the requirement of jurisdiction: "Quod autem permittitur tutorem dare provinciae praesidi, eis tantum permittitur, qui sunt eiusdem provinciae vel ibidem domicilium habent."—D. (26, 5) 1, 2: "Neque a praeside alterius provincae neque a magistratibus municipalibus tutorem ortum ex alia civitate nec domicilium ubi nominatur habentem iure dari posse ab eo, cuius iurisdictioni subiectus non est, certissimi iuris est."—C. (5, 34) 5.

[10] D. (27, 10) 6.

order to examine the mental state of the subject and the manner of appointing the guardian were not regulated by law, but left to the discretion of the magistrate.[11]

In early post-classical times, the *cura legitima furiosi* was displaced entirely by the *cura furiosi decretalis* (*cura dativa, curatores honorarii*), since the *adgnatus* needed official confirmation. This seems to be the import of a statement found in Justinian's Institutes: *"Furiosi quoque et prodigi, licet maiores viginti quinque annis sint, tamen in curatione sunt adgnatorum. Sed solent Romae praefectus urbis vel praetor et in provincia praesides ex inquisitione*[12] *eis dare curatores."*[13]

The fact that the *adgnati* had to be confirmed as guardians by the legitimate authority reveals an evolution in the Roman concept of guardianship. In the earlier law, guardianship was conceived as a private right, analogous to *patria potestas* and a substitute for the latter; this right entailed a number of duties towards the ward's person and property.[14] With time, the manner of appointing guardians changed this initial concept. When the magistrate appointed a guardian, the person designated usually had no hereditary rights to his ward's property. Slowly guardianship came to be considered a public office, whose duties gave rise to rights with respect to the ward and his property. The State felt that it was its duty to protect the needy. Hence, its action to provide guardians and its supervision over the discharge of the duties of guardianship, which gradually became a *munus,* a public office, whose function it was to safeguard a private person's welfare in the general interest of

---

[11] Cf. Staffa, "De Constitutione Curatoris," p. 64.

[12] D. (26, 3) 7 outlines the *inquisitio*: "Si quaeratur, an ex inquisitione recte datus sit tutor, quattuor haec consideranda sunt: an hic dederit qui dare potuit, et ille acceperit cui fuerit dandus, et is datur cuius dandi facultas erat, et pro tribunali decretum interpositum." Cf. also C. (5, 42) 4.

[13] Inst. (I, 23) 3. Cf. Schulz, *Classical Roman Law,* p. 192; Robinson, *Selections,* p. 155-156; Perozzi, *Istituzioni di Diritto Romano,* I, 527. The last author cited challenges the opposite view held by Bonfante and De Francisci. Cf. E. Volterra, "Interdizione," *Enciclopedia Italiana,* Vol. XIX.

[14] Perozzi, *op. cit.,* I, 460.

state.[15] Indeed, in one of his letters Severus wrote: "*Omnem me rationem adhibere subveniendis pupillis, cum ad curam publicam pertineat, liquere omnibus volo.*"[16]

A *cura furiosi testamentaria* strictly so called did not exist in Roman Law.[17] If a father designated a guardian for his insane son, the designated person did not automatically become guardian at the time the testament went into effect. A magistrate had to confirm him as *curator*.[18] The father's action, however, was not useless, since it served as an application (*postulatio*), proposing a certain person (*nominatio*). *Causa cognita,* the magistrate usually appointed the person designated.[19]

---

[15] Cf. Perozzi, *op. cit.*, I, 460-461; 527; Robinson, *op. cit.*, p. 139; Jolowicz, *Historical Introduction*, p. 249. A. Pertile, *Storia del Diritto Italiano, dalla Caduta dell' Impero Romano alla Codificazione* (2. ed., 6 vols., Torino: Unione Tipografico-Editrice, 1892-1902), III, 410 (hereafter cited *Storia del Diritto Italiano*).

[16] Cf. D. (26, 6) (2, 2).

[17] Cf. Inst. (1, 23); Cf. Schulz, *op. cit.*, p. 197; Perozzi, *op. cit.*, I, pp. 526-527; Brugi, *Istituzioni di Diritto Romano*, 122. c; Jolowicz, *op. cit.*, pp. 121, 251.

[18] Cf. Inst. (1, 23) 1; Gutierrez, *op. cit.*, I. 12, 6.

[19] D. (27, 10) 16: "Si furioso puberi quamquam maiori annorum viginti quinque curatorem pater testamento dederit, eum praetor dare debet secutus patris voluntatem: manet enim ea datio curatoris apud praetorem, ut rescripto divi Marci continetur." Cf. Robinson, *op. cit.*, pp. 156-157; Perozzi, *op. cit.*, I, 526. It may be noted here that a guardian was not appointed to take charge of a mentally defective person whose father cared for him: Cf. C. (5, 70) 7: "Quis enim talis adfectus extraneus inveniatur, ut vincat paternum?" Paternal solicitude was considered sufficient to assure the proper care of the insane person.

In the law of Justinian, at least, the *curator* was appointed in much the same way as the *tutor*: cf. Bonfante, *op. cit.*, I, 422. Moreover, the principles regulating *tutela* and *cura* were very similar: cf. D. (44, 4) (4, 25): "Quae in tutore diximus, eadem in curatore quoque dicenda erunt." The terms *cura* and *tutela* were used freely in texts—cf. D. (26, 7) 1, (26, 10) 1, (13, 7) 16 and in headings (*rubrica titulorum*): cf. D. (26, 3), (26, 5), (26, 8); C (5, 33), (5, 42), (5, 43); Inst. (1, 24), (1, 26). Consult B. Windscheid, *Diritto delle Pandette,* Traduzione dei Professori C. Fadda e P. E. Bensa con note e riferimenti al Diritto Civile Italiano (Nuova ristampa stereotipa, 5 volumi, Torino: Unione Tipografico-Editrice Torinese, 1925-1926), II, 729 ff.

Article II. The Manner of Appointment in Subsequent Civil Legislation and Doctrine

During the Middle Ages, changes occurred in the distribution of civil offices and in the functions of magistrates to whom the Roman sources reserved the appointment of guardians; and the task of selecting guardians fell to the *iudex*.[20] Though the dispositions of Roman Law regarding the manner of appointing guardians remained intact in the civil forum up to the time of the Napoleonic Code,[21] sixteenth-century commentaries on the *Corpus Iuris* reveal that a trend was under way to establish the practice that the insane, even as the spendthrift, first be interdicted, or deprived of the exercise of their rights, by the judge, and subsequently be placed under guardianship.[22] The common teaching, however, adhered to the practice of Roman Law; but more than previously writers insisted that the judge conduct an investigation to ascertain mental illness before issuing a decree of guardianship.[23] Indeed, clear mention is made of a *votum* to be sought from experts.[24] Still, authors and commentators on the *Corpus Iuris Civilis* excluded the neces-

---

[20] Cf. Durandus, *Speculum Iuris*, Lib. I, Part. III, *de Curatore*, n. 1, *Scias ergo*. This was true of the appointment of both *tutor* and *curator*. Cf. also Part. III, *De Tutore*, § *Si tutor*, n. 2; § *Si vero*, n. 3. Part. III, *De Curatore*, § *Viso*, § *Cum autem*.

[21] Cf. Staffa, "De Constitutione Curatoris," p. 65. The Napoleonic Code was promulgated on March 21, 1804, and achieved universal renown. Moreover, it became the exemplar of foreign civil codes, particularly of those of Latin countries. Cf. "Code," *Larousse*, Tome 2e, *Larousse du XXe Siècle*, publié sous la direction de Paul Auge (6 vols., Paris: Librairie Larousse, 1929), Vol. II, sub v. *"Code"* (hereafter cited as: *Larousse*, Vol. II, "Code.")

[22] Cf. Staffa, "art. cit.," p. 65, note 25, where the following authors are cited: Bartolus, *in Digestum*, XLV, 1. 6. n. 1; Montanus-Gutierrez-Cavalcanus, *Tractatus de tutore, curatore et usufructu* (ed. a. 1675), p. 98, n. 18; p. 359, nn. 5-6. *Glossa in Digestum*, X. V, 1. 6. ad v. *is cui bonis interdictum est.*

[23] Cf. Baldus, *In Digestum*, (27, 10) 6; Gothofredus, *In Digestum*, (27, 10) 6; Montanus-Gutierrez-Cavalcanus, *op. cit.*, p. 98, n. 9.

[24] Cf. Bartolus, *loc. cit.;* Baldus, *In Digestum*, (27, 10) 6; Gutierrez, *op. cit.*, I. 19. 7; Cf. Staffa, "art. cit.," p. 66, and note 27.

sity of citing the insane person and of conducting a judicial process to prove his insanity, as well as the necessity of instituting a judicial process and of issuing a formal sentence to restore the exercise of his rights to a person who recovers his mental health.[25]

The trend which required formal judicial procedure to deprive a mentally ill person of the administration of his property gained momentum and supporters, so that finally the Napoleonic Code introduced the necessity of a special process to disqualify a major for reasons of mental instability.[26] Subsequently the civil codes of other nations prescribed the same procedure, so that nowadays, in the civil jurisdictions generally, mental illness must be ascertained and the afflicted persons must be placed under disability by the courts through a special judicial process.[27] Scholars, however, do not agree as to whether the process and the pronouncement that concludes it are to be considered of voluntary or of contentious jurisdiction.[28] Wach, for instance, defends the position that these acts are of voluntary jurisdiction,[29] while Chiovenda maintains that the process—as it is conceived in the Italian Civil Law statutes which enjoin the interdiction of the mentally ill—is one of contentious jurisdiction.[30]

---

[25] Cf. Gutierrez, *op. cit.*, I. 19. 7: ". . . potest dari talis curator cum inquisitione, vel absque ea." See also Staffa, *loc. cit.* and notes 28, 29, where he cites several authors.

[26] Cf. *Art. 489.* Le majeur qui est dans un état habituel d'imbecillité, de demence ou de fureur, doit être interdit même, lorsque cet état présente des intervalles lucides. *Art. 492.* Toute demande en interdiction sera portée devant le tribunal de première instance. *Art. 493.* Les faits d'imbecillité, de demence ou de fureur, seront articulés par écrit. Ceux qui poursuivront l'interdiction presenteront les témoins et les pièces.

[27] Cf. 25 Am. Jur., *Guardian and Ward,* §§ 22, 40, 45.

[28] Cf. Staffa, "art. cit.," p. 67.

[29] Staffa, *loc. cit.,* summarizes Wach's thought thus: ". . . iudicium circa statum mentis infirmi necessario requiritur, sed unice praemittitur ad eius capacitatem iuridicam integrandam. Species tantum iudicii habetur, et scopus ad quem dirigitur est infirmi tutela, id est provisio in ipsius favorem, non contra eum."

[30] Staffa, *loc. cit.,* presents Chiovenda's viewpoint: "Notat e contra Chiovenda statum mentis infirmi obiective pugnare cum iure, quod oeconomicas relationes inter cives tuetur: huius ergo anormalitatis remotio

Article III. The Manner of Appointment in the Law of the Code and Canonical Doctrine

The canonists engaged in drafting the fourth book of the Code were confronted with suggestions regarding the manner of appointing guardians. From the Archbishop of Esztergom (Strigonia), Hungary, came the proposal that the new law contain more precise norms regarding guardianship.[31] The motion was made to include special processual norms under the new title *"de interdictione personarum"*; and it was suggested that the seeking of an expert's opinion be made obligatory.[32] The final draft of the Code, however, presented but very general norms regarding the entire institute of guardianship, and the Codifiers left the details to the prudent judgment of the Ordinaries.[33] Indeed, the Code does not establish that the Ordinary follow the procedure to which civil magistrates are bound, even in those instances when the ecclesiastical authority

---

tamquam voluntatis legislatoris applicatio est consideranda in infirmum, ideoque tamquam actus iudisdictionis contentiosae." Staffa himself then concludes: "Haec tamen, quae a lege civili italica eruuntur, non impediunt, prout ipse Chiovenda explicite admittit, quominus in systemate ab italico diverso, praevalenter consideretur interdicendi tutela, et processus interdictionis inter actus iurisdictionis voluntariae recenseatur."

[31] Cf. F. Roberti, *Codex Iuris Canonici Schemata,* Lib. IV, *De Processibus;* (Romae: Typis Polyglottis Vaticanis, 1940), F, Can. 112, note 6, p. 137: "Praeterea id etiam lege constituendum erit, quomodo possit iure ecclesiastico quis sub curatela poni, quaenam sint curatoris obligationes, cui debeat rationes gesti muneris reddere, quomodo et a quo et coram quo possit ad respondendum trahi." (hereafter cited *Schemata*).

[32] Cf. *Schemata,* D, can. 127, note 2: "Quaeritur an requiratur sententia interdictionis: O censet difficile statui posse specialem processum interdictionis, ideo proponit *ii quos iudex prodigos aut interdicendos iudicaverit;* Ma adhibendas censet physicas inspectiones peritorum; Ma specialem processum statuendum autumat sub tit. *De interdictione personarum."*

[33] Cf. canons 1648, § 3, 1651; *Schemata,* D, can. 127, note 2: "Dl praefert canonem generalem; quam opinionem omnes denique probant." Roberti later declared that it was not the mind of the codifiers that a real trial be instituted to declare a mentally ill person under disability and then place him under the control of a guardian. Cf. Staffa, "De Constitutione Curatoris," p. 70, note 55.

the substitutes for a civil law guardian one of his own choice, nor does it suggest that the judge follow that procedure.[34]

It is interesting to note the various norms suggested and considered before the codifiers agreed on the general prescription of canon 1651, § 2. In the order of their succession, they are:

a. Ordinarius tamen ad curatoris dationem devenire non debet nisi postquam, audita persona cui dandus est curator, auditisque pariter qui de eadem pleniorem notitiam habent et peritis physicis, ac visis documentis ad rem facientibus, decreto suo statuerit praefatam personam ad tuenda sua iura non satis aptam esse.[35]

b. Quod si Ordinarius admittendum non censeat curatorem ab auctoritate civili alicui datum, et alium in foro ecclesiastico assignandum esse iudicet, ad novi curatoris dationem devenire non debet, nisi postquam audita persona cui dandus est curator, auditisque pariter qui de eadem pleniorem notitiam habent et peritis physicis, ac visis documentis ad rem facientibus, decreto suo statuerit ad tuenda sua iura non satis aptam esse.[36]

c. Ordinarius potest quoque aliam curatoris personam constituere pro foro ecclesiastico, si, omnibus mature perpensis, ac praesertim audita, si fieri possit, persona, accitis quoque quatenus opus fuerit, peritis, visisque documentis ad rem facientibus, id statuendum esse prudenter censuerit.[37]

d. Ordinarius potest quoque alium curatorem constituere pro foro ecclesiastico, si, omnibus mature perpensis, ac praesertim audito, si fieri possit, curatore ab auctoritate civili dato, id statuendum esse prudenter censuerit.[38]

Now though these proposed norms do present more details than canon 1651, § 2, they do not establish the necessity of a trial to place a person under disability because of his mental condition before appointing a guardian to exercise his processual rights.

Civil legislations at large require judicial proceedings to declare a person's disability before placing him in the control of a guard-

[34] Cf. J. Torre, *Processus Matrimonialis* (Neapoli: M. D'Auria, 1947), p. 81.

[35] *Schemata,* D, can. 127, § 2, p. 138.

[36] *Schemata,* E, Can. 127, § 2, p. 139.

[37] *Schemata,* F, can. 113, § 2, p. 139.

ian.[39] Maroto made the following general statement: *"In designandis tutoribus vel curatoribus Superior Ecclesiasticus, servatis generalibus canonum praescriptionibus et deficientibus in nostro jure normis particularibus, ad regulas juris civilis prudenter, juxta casus confugiet."*[40] This rather general statement must not be pressed to require the ecclesiastical authority to proceed as must the civil courts, but ought to be regarded in the light of the discussion that follows on the law of the Church. Indeed, as Torre remarks: *"In codice juris canonici non statuitur ut Ordinarius regulas pro magistratu in iure civili statutas sequi debeat, si censeat alium curatorem sufficiendum esse."*[41] Nor is there any expression in the Code which might suggest that the extra-judicial appointment of a guardian is invalid or even as much as contrary to law.[42]

It can hardly be argued from canon 1651 that the Ordinary must proceed judicially in appointing a guardian.[43] Certainly the consent he gives to the civil law guardian to act in the ecclesiastical court[44] is an act of voluntary jurisdiction. It would seem, too, that the alternative he enjoys of appointing a guardian of his own choice when he deems such action fit, would likewise be exercised through an act of voluntary jurisdiction.[45] Again there is no ex-

---

[38] *Schemata,* G, can. 111, § 2, p. 139. The following suggestion was made: "Delentur verba: *ac praesertim audito si fieri possit curatore ab auctoritate civili dato.*" The resulting norm passed into the Code.

[39] Cf. above, pp. 68 ff; A. Toso, "De Constitutione Curatoris in Foro Ecclesiastico," *Ius Pontificium,* XIX (1939), 118. (Hereafter cited "De Constitutione Curatoris.")

[40] P. Maroto, *Institutiones Iuris Canonici ad Norman Novi Codicis,* (2 vols. Romae: Vol. I, 3. ed., 1921; Vol. II, 1919, Apud Commentarium pro Religiosis) I, n. 441, A, 4°.

[41] Torre, *Processus Matrimonialis,* p. 81.

[42] Cf. Toso, "art. cit.," p. 119: ". . . nullum occurrit in Codice I.C. verbum, ex quo argui possit aut irritam aut illicitam esse extra-judicialem curatoris constitutionem." Staffa, "art. cit.," p. 76: "Nec adest . . . lex quae nullitatem curatelae secumferat via simpliciter administrativa constitutae."

[43] Cf. G. Cocchi, *Commentarium in Codicem Iuris Canonici,* 8 vols. Vol. VII, *De Processibus* (3. ed., Taurinorum Augustae: Marietti, 1940), n. 63.

[44] Cf. can. 1651, § 1.

[45] Cf. Giustiniani, "De Curatore Dementis," p. 108. Cf. S.R.R.,

pression in § 2 that can be construed to indicate the necessity of a judicial process.

Recourse might possibly be made to canon 1552, § 2, n. 1, to urge the necessity of a judicial process to declare a person incompetent before placing him under guardianship; for a person is manifestly deprived of a right when he is placed under disability to exercise personally his own rights. Closer consideration, however, of the entire canon leads to the conclusion that a judicial process is not strictly required to decide any rights or facts that may be the matter of a contentious trial.

The first paragraph defines what is meant by the term *Ecclesiastical trial*—the legal discussion and settlement before an ecclesiastical court of a disputed matter upon which the Church has the right to judge. In the second paragraph is outlined the subject matter of the two types of trials: *contentious trials* have for their object the prosecution and execution of the rights of physical or moral persons, or the declaration of the juridical facts concerning such persons, while *criminal trials* examine offenses with a view to inflicting or declaring a penalty.

It is important to note that the *judicium contentiosum* is a trial in which rights or juridical facts are *contested.* Unless a controversy, or dispute, exists, a contentious trial cannot be had. Thus, for example, unless a particular juridical fact is contested, the steps which the competent authority takes to verify it and the declaration which he makes concerning it cannot be called respectively a contentious trial and a judicial sentence. Where there is no controversy, the competent authority proceeds non-judicially to ascertain the fact and then issues a document stating his ruling.

Consequently, to argue from canon 1552, § 2, n. 1, the strict necessity of instituting a formal trial in the ecclesiastical forum to appoint a guardian, it must be shown first that the appointment

---

Decisiones, XXIV (1932), dec. XLV, n. 2. 2°, p. 430: ". . . res tota committatur prudentiae pastorali, cui nulla forma procedendi in iure praescribitur, ne quidem in can. 1651, qui specificum casum spectat, quo iam curator ab auctoritate civili datus sit, non excludendo scilicet, ut curator primo ab Ordinario constituatur (can. 1648, § 1 et § 3)."

is necessarily a matter of controversy.[46] Therefore, at least when the appointment is not disputed, the Ordinary proceeds non-judicially, exercising his so-called voluntary jurisdiction.[47] If, however, a person's incompetency and his guardian's appointment are contested, it may be advisable to resort to a formal judicial process.[48] Nevertheless, in view of a response of the Commission for the Authentic Interpretation of the Code,[49] the strict necessity of such a process in any case at all cannot be proved. The writer holds, with Staffa, that the Ordinary is free to act extra-judicially even when the appointment of the guardian is contested.[50] Since the appointment of a guardian usually falls to the Ordinary, whose task it is to seek the good of the community and to provide for the assistance of its needy members,[51] with him lies the decision

---

[46] Cf. Staffa, "De Constitutione Curatoris," p. 71: "In canone 1552, § 2, n. 1, non enumerantur . . . quaestiones semper ac necessario iudicio contentioso dirimendae, sed controversiae indicantur, quae, si in iudicium veniunt, obiectum sunt iudicii contentiosi; ideoque illis contraponuntur quae sunt obiectum iudicii criminalis, quaeque in numero veniunt subsequenti eiusdem paragraphi." The author cited concludes: "Canon igitur 1552, § 2, n. 1, tunc tantum merito invocari posset, si probatum fuisset curatoris nominationem obiectum esse iudicii contentiosi. Quod e contra quaeritur et probandum est."

[47] Cf. canon 201, §§ 2-3. Woywod-Smith, *A Practical Commentary,* I, 92: "The term 'voluntary jurisdiction' is used in contrast to 'jurisdictio contentiosa or judicialis.' The voluntary jurisdiction embraces the legislative and administrative power; the judicial, as the name suggests, has to do with the power exercised in the ecclesiastical court of deciding litigated questions or rights by judicial procedure and punishing transgressions of the law after trial and conviction."

[48] The following authors state categorically that, if contested, disqualification must be proved through a formal judicial process: Roberti, *De Processibus,* I, n. 202; Noone, *Nullity in Judicial Acts,* p. 54; Toso, "art. cit.," p. 119; A. C. Jemolo, *Il Matrimonio del Diritto Canonico* (Milano: Vallardi, 1940), n. 194, who cites an unedited decision of the Apostolic Signatura, *Pratensis,* April 29, 1939.

[49] Cf. below, p. 78.

[50] Cf. Staffa, "art. cit.," p. 78: "Censemus ergo in hoc casu quaestionem sive via administrativa sive via iudiciali dirimi posse."

[51] Staffa, *loc. cit.;* Jemolo, *op. cit.,* p. 379.

as to whether the appointment is to be made *via administrativa* or *via iudiciali.*[52]

Article 78, § 3, of the *Instructio* of 1936 has been cited to support the opinion that requires a judicial process to declare incompetency and upholds the judicial nature of the Ordinary's decree appointing a guardian.[53] The texts reads: "In curatore constituendo ab Ordinario procedendum est iuris ordine servato, audita altera parte, necnon vinculi defensore."[54]

Now, the phrase *procedendum est iuris ordine servato* must be rightly understood. The obvious meaning of the phrase is that the procedure established by law must be observed.[55] Since the power of jurisdiction is either judicial or voluntary,[56] the Ordinary may proceed either judicially or non-judicially in exercising that power. Which of these manners of procedure is imposed by the Article under consideration? Authors differ in their answers.

Jemolo, for instance, maintains that the article imposes judicial proceedings to ascertain a person's incapacity because of mental illness and then place him under the control of a guardian.[57] Differing with Lega, who, commenting on canon 1648, § 3, stated that the Ordinary proceeded non-judicially in appointing a guardian,[58] Toso cites Articles 78, § 3, 77, and 74 of the *Instructio,* and argues that the *Instructio* plainly refers to the appointment of a guardian after the ecclesiastical tribunal has taken up the case, and concludes

[52] Cf. Staffa, *loc. cit.*

[53] Cf., e.g., Jemolo, *op. cit.*, n. 194.

[54] Cf. *AAS* (1936), 330. In appointing a guardian, the Ordinary must proceed according to law, after hearing from the other party and from the defender of the bond.

[55] Cf. Staffa, "art. cit.," p. 72.

[56] Cf. canon 201, §§ 2-3. See above, p. 73, note 47.

[57] Cf. Jemolo, *op. cit.*, n. 194. This author corroborates his position by citing a case presented to the Apostolic Signatura in 1933. The Supreme Tribunal ruled that, before declaring the plaintiff mentally ill, the bishop must have him examined by two experts and held invalid the appointment of the guardian made by the Vicar General.

[58] Cf. *Commentarius,* I, p. 307, n. 6: "Ordinarius distinguitur *a iudice,* quia hic censetur agere uti iudex seu iudicialiter in constitutione curatoris ...pendente iudicio; dum Ordinarius aestimatur interponere potestatem administrativam, seu extra-iudicialem."

that the Ordinary must proceed judicially whenever the guardian is to be appointed after the case has been initiated, and that he may proceed non-judicially whenever a guardian is to be appointed before the initiation of proceedings, provided the appointment is not contested.[59] After stating that the Code contains neither an absolute prescription requiring a sentence to declare a person's disability nor special procedural norms to follow in arriving at such a declaration, Roberti goes on to say that if a dispute arises concerning a person's disqualification, a sentence declaring disability must be issued after proceeding according to law with the participation in the process of both parties, the *Promotor Justitiae* and, in special cases, of the *Defensor Vinculi.*[60] Pugliese and Noone follow Roberti

[59] Cf. Toso, "De Constitutione Curatoris," pp. 118-119: "At dum cl. Lega sententiam suam ex hoc derivare videtur. quod agatur de curatoris constitutione *ante susceptam causam,* vicissim S.C. de Sacramentis apertissime loquitur de constitutione curatoris '*parti conventae,* quae rationis usu sit destituta vel minus firmae mentis,' quare 'citatio tutori vel *curatori* (quo pars de facto caret) *denuncianda* est' (Art. 77): Scilicet loquitur de constitutione curatoris parti conventae, postquam actoris 'libellum vel oralis petitio admissa fuerit' (Art. 74) ac proinde *post causam susceptam.* Est igitur tenendum, Ordinarium *iudicialiter* procedere debere quoties curator constituendus est post causae susceptionem, *extraiudicialiter* quoties agitur de constituendo curatore, causa nondum suscepta et nemine contradicente."

[60] *De Processibus,* I, n. 202, II. 3. Roberti bases his opinion on Article 78, § 3, of the *Instructio* and on a declaration of the Signatura Apostolica (in c. Praten., April 29, 1939), which ruled: "Si ergo non citato infirmo, eidemque non concessa facultate excipiendi sive contra accusationem sive contra decisionem in ipsum latas, datus sit curator, hic est illegitime constitutus, et si stet in iudicio pro suo pupillo, stat sine legitimo mandato, cum consequenti nullitate sententiae." Cf. Roberti, *loc. cit.* Against Roberti it may be stated that this ruling speaks of a *decisio,* not of a *sententia,* and that the procedure indicated is not necessarily judicial. Granted, however, that the Signatura did impose a judicial procedure in this particular case, this order should not be interpreted as an injuction to proceed always in that manner. As a matter of fact, as Staffa puts it: ". . . notandum censemus neque ante Codicem neque postea Supremum Trib. Signaturae Apostolicae aut Sacram Romanam Rotam iudicialem processum ad curatorem constituendum necessarium unquam dixisse. . . . Unica decisio quae contra adduci potest, in causa quam innuimus, contrarium stylum et praxim inducere non valet, quia unica est, et statim adversitatibus et controversiis obnoxia." Cf. Staffa, "art. cit.," p. 76.

in requiring a formal judicial process to prove a person's disqualification, when contested.[61]

Staffa, on the other hand, examines the norms contained in the *Instructio* and concludes that they do not exact a judicial process for the valid appointment of a guardian.[62] First of all, he explains why, in appointing a guardian, the Ordinary must hear from the other party and from the Defender of the Bond.[63] It is a measure suggested by caution and prudence, to prevent the appointment of a person who might contend in favor of or against the sacred bond of matrimony for reasons opposed to truth and justice.[64] Then he proceeds to demonstrate that the words *iuris ordine servato* do not oblige the Ordinary to proceed judicially even in appointing a guardian to act in matrimonial cases.[65]

The *Instructio,* it must be noted, in no wise changed the provisions of the Code related to the matters upon which it touched. Its purpose was rather to arrange the norms of the Code in a manner calculated to facilitate the task of diocesan tribunals engaged in the study of marriage cases and to illumine the provisions of the Code by proposing jurisprudence and norms of the Rota.

---

[61] Cf. Pugliese, "La Necessità del Curatore," p. 185. Noone, *Nullity in Judicial Acts,* p. 54.

[62] Cf. Staffa, "art. cit.," pp. 72-73.

[63] Cf. *Instructio,* Art. 78, § 3: "audita altera parte, necnon vinculi defensore."

[64] Cf. Staffa, "art. cit.," p. 72: "Ante omnia notandum est hunc articulum casum respicere, in quo alteruter coniux matrimonium iam accusavit. Absque difficultate ergo intelligitur, quomodo, etiamsi ad curatorem constituendum iudicialis processus non requiratur, actor et Defensor Vinculi ab Ordinario convocandi sint, ut dicant si quid habeant contra personam, cui cura est committenda. Caute enim et sapienter id voluit legislator, ne in curatoris officium eligatur persona, quae pro vinculo aut contra decertet, ob rationes veritati et iustitiae adversas. Hoc tamen necessitatem non implicat iudicialis processus, et a processu etiam administrativo postulatur prudentiae conformi." Aguirre suggests another reason: "Haec norma pro hoc casu particulari ideo fortasse est data, quia praesumendum videatur in genere declarationem circa infirmitatem mentis interesse alterius partis et vinculi defensoris ob influxum, quem potest habere in ipsam sententiam de nullitate matrimonii."—"De Curatore Dementis," p. 296.

[65] Staffa, "art. cit.," pp. 72-73.

"In hisce regulis iudices ipsi et tribunalium administri praecipuos canones de processibus agentes accurate apteque dispositos reperient, necnon brevem facilemque eorundem explanationem, ex iurisprudentia praesertim erutam atque ex Normis S. R. Rotae, quo plenius ipsis iidem Codicis canones, quibus derogatum non est, sint perspecti, eosque expeditius singulis aptare possint matrimonialibus causis."[66] This citation reechoes expressions found in the *Motu Proprio "Cum Iuris Canonici,"* of September 15, 1917, with which the Supreme Pontiff assigned to the Sacred Congregations as their ordinary duty the task of safeguarding the observance of the prescripts of the Code and of issuing *Instructiones* concerning the application of the law of the Code.[67] The *Instructio* is not a new law nor does it contain authentic interpretations of any kind.[68] Therefore, though the *Instructio* does suggest practical steps to be taken by the Ordinary in appointing guardians for matrimonial cases,[69] it could not oblige him to proceed judicially, as such an injunction would restrict the discretionary power the Ordinary enjoys by virtue of canon 1651 and would thus introduce a change in the law of the Code.

Nor does the ruling of Article 78, § 3, necessarily conflict with the general norm of canon 1651. As a matter of fact, the phrase *iuris ordine servato* is an expression used to indicate both judicial and non-judicial, or administrative, procedure.[70] Consequently the phrase offers no grounds to confine the Ordinary to judicial procedure.[71]

---

[66] *Instructio, Decretum,* § 5, *AAS,* XXVIII (1936), 313.

[67] The *Motu Proprio* mentioned is found in *AAS,* IX (1917), 483-484, as well as in reprints of the Code of Canon Law.

[68] Cf. J. R. Schmidt, "The Juridic Value of the *Instructio* Provided by the Motu Proprio *'Cum Iuris Canonici'* September 15, 1917"—*The Jurist,* I (1941), 289-316. Writing of *Instructiones* in general, Schmidt affirms: ". . . if . . . the Congregations could issue restrictive-extensive authentic interpretations, the *Instructiones* would be considered new laws for all practical purposes, and the stability of the Code . . . would be hopeless." Cf. p. 316 of this article.

[69] Cf. Art. 78, § 3.

[70] Cf. Staffa, "art. cit.," p. 72.

[71] Cf. Staffa, "art. cit.," pp. 72-73: ". . . si articulus 78, § 3, necessi-

The strongest argument against the necessity of a regular trial to appoint a guardian is the declaration made to that effect by the Pontifical Commission for the Authentic Interpretation of the Code on January 5, 1943. The *dubium* proposed and the *responsum* offered read: D. Utrum vi canonis 1651 § 1 et § 2 ad curatorem dandum iis, qui rationis usu destituti vel minus firmae mentis sunt, requiratur regulare iudicium, an sufficiat decretum Ordinarii, praevia eiusdem prudenti inquisitione. R. Negative ad primam partem; affirmative ad secundam.[72] Therefore, in order to assign a guardian to those who are destitute of reason or weak-minded, a regular trial is not required; rather, a decree alone of the Ordinary after prudent inquiry suffices.

An important consequence of the fact that a judicial process is not required in order to disqualify the mentally ill and place them under guardianship in the ecclesiastical forum is that the Vicar General is competent in this matter unless the Ordinary has reserved it to himself or to an ecclesiastic of his own choosing.[73]

While ruling out the necessity of a regular trial, the Pontifical Commission indicates that the Ordinary is to exercise his voluntary

---

tatem induceret iudicialis processus ad curatorem constituendum, respectu systematis praecedentis, iuxta Codicis normas etiam post ipsum applicandas, gravis haberetur mutatio, cui sufficiens fundamentum non praebet clausula, quae modo Codici perfecte congruo interpretari valet." In a note the same author adds: "Hanc interpretationem confirmavit ille qui articulum redegit." —p. 73, note 63. Ciprotti, too, in his commentary on the *Instructio* maintains that the appointment of a guardian is not a judicial act and consequently may be made by the Vicar General.—cf. *Le Nuove Norme per i Processi di Nullità di Matrimonio Presso i Tribunali Diocesani* (Roma, 1937), p. 46.

[72] PCI, Jan. 25, 1943—*AAS* XXXV (1943), 58, II, 1; 439. On page 439 are found "quaedam corrigenda in Vol. XXXV (1943) Commentarii Acta Apostolicae Sedis." Among the *Corrigenda* is found: "Pag. 58. Ad verba 'Utrum vi canonis 1651 § 1' addatur 'et § 2.'" Giustiniani did not note this correction in his comment on the *responsum*: Cf. "De Curatore Dementis," p. 108.

[73] Canon 368, § 1. Vicario Generali, vi officii, ea competit in universa dioecesi iurisdictio in spiritualibus ac temporalibus, quae ad Episcopum iure ordinario pertinent, exceptis iis quae Episcopus sibi reservaverit, vel quae ex iure requirant speciale Episcopi mandatum.

jurisdiction[74] *after prudent inquiry*. The competent authority must, therefore, precede the decree of appointment with some sort of investigation. The principal aims of the inquiry may be summed up under two headings:

a. The person to be placed under guardianship should be examined to ascertain the *fact* of his mental illness,[75] as well as to determine the degree of the illness,[76] since insanity and feeble-mindedness involve different degrees of incapacity.[77]

b. A person fit to act as guardian must be sought out.[78]

To ascertain the fact and the degree of a person's mental illness, the Ordinary may question people who have associated with that person so that he may gather information regarding his discourse and conduct that may reveal his mental condition; or, again, he may resort to the services of experts, doctors or psychiatrists. Though he is not obliged by law to seek the opinion of such experts when appointing a guardian,[79] the Ordinary may deem it

---

[74] Cf. Giustiniani, "art. cit.," p. 108: "Parlando di decreto è manifesto che ammette come il provvedimento sia un atto amministrativo lasciato al prudente giudizio dell'Ordinario, quindi non si richiedono perizie, intervento dell'altro coniuge ecc." See also Aguirre, "De Curatore Dementis," p. 295.

[75] Ulpian's warning to the praetor has lost none of its timeliness. Cf. above, p. 64. See Toso, "De Constitutione Curatoris," p. 119.

[76] Indirect proofs are sufficient. As a matter of fact, direct proofs of mental illness are impossible. Cf. S. R. R. *Decisiones*, XIII (1921), dec. IX, n. 5: "Probatio directa non est possibilis; est enim amentia morbus in mente latens, qui sensibus non percipitur; sed admittitur probatio indirecta, quae conficitur recurrendo ad coniecturas et praesumptiones verbis et factis innixas, quae sanae menti repugnant; ab effectibus enim causa rite deducitur."

[77] Cf. Canons 1648, § 1, and 1650; see above, pp. 46 ff. See also Staffa, "art. cit.," p. 77, note 78; Aguirre, "art cit.," p. 295.

[78] Cf. Staffa, *loc. cit.*: ". . . arguere non possumus curatorem absque debita cautela et praeviis investigationibus constitui posse, et infirmi iura aliorum cupiditati absque protectione derelinqui. Antequam enim curatorem constituat, omnibus mediis quae eum a dolo praemunire valent, Ordinarius certior fieri debet sive de infirmitate sive de curatelae necessitate et opportunitate, sive de idoneitate personae cui curatoris officium deferendum est." Aguirre, *loc. cit.* See above, pp. 52-61.

[79] Cf. Torre, *Processus Matrimonialis*, p. 81: "Consideratur constitutio

advisable to do so, especially when confronted by a person whose abnormal mental state is not immediately discernible. A monomaniac, for instance, may appear quite normal to an official who is not versed in psychiatric science, whereas an expert will demonstrate that his mental state does not permit him the normal exercise of his rights.[80]

The prior adjudication of insanity or feeble-mindedness by civil courts may be followed by the ecclesiastical authorities.[81] Indeed, public documents are accepted as means of proof even in formal trials.[82] It should, however, be noted that the ecclesiastical authority is not bound to observe the decision of the civil court as to the mental condition of the person under consideration. Moreover, the person under civil disability, as well as the opposing party, the Promotor of Justice, and, in marriage cases, the Defender of the Bond, may request a pronouncement by the ecclesiastical authority.[83] Finally, as Doheny remarks, the mere fact that a person

---

curatoris quasi actus administrativus . . . prudentiae pastorali relictus, nec requiritur . . . peritale infirmi examen nisi ipse Ordinarius hoc censeat opportunum, ad suum judicium efformandum." The opinion of experts, however, is required by law in marriage cases of lack of consent: S.R.R., *Decisiones,* XVIII (1926), dec. XXIII, nn. 1-3, p. 183-184; S.R.R., *Decisiones,* XX (1928), dec. XXVIII, n. 9, p. 267; S.R.R., *Decisiones,* XXIV (1932), dec. XLV, n. 2, 2°, p. 430; S.R.R., *Decisiones,* XXVIII (1936), dec. XXXIII, n. 2, pp. 304-305. Cf. canon 1982.

[80] Cf. Palmieri, *Medicina Legale Canonistica,* p. 28. This author offers a clear treatment of the subject of judicial experts in cases of defect of matrimonial consent on account of insanity. Cf. Pickett, *Mental Affliction and Church Law,* pp. 157-161. The reader is directed to these and other writers for detailed information on the nature, end, method, and authority of the services of judicial experts. The canonical norms concerning experts are found mainly in canons 1792-1805, 1976-1982.

[81] Noone writes: "The ecclesiastical judge may, but he is not obliged to, follow the opinion of civil authorities concerning the prodigality or mental weakness of the litigants."—*Nullity in Judicial Acts,* p. 53. Cf. also Coronata, *De Processibus,* n. 1176; Roberti, *De Processibus,* I, n. 202; The same may be said of the *Ordinarius.*

[82] Cf. canons 1812 and 1813, § 2.

[83] D'Avack has this to say: ". . . riterrei che al fatto dell' eventuale esistenza di una precedente sentenza d'interdizione del soggetto per infermità mentale emanata dall'autorità civile non possa riconoscersi altro valore

has been confined in an asylum for the insane does not, of itself, constitute full proof of insanity, as confinement in institutions may at times be accomplished by fraud or intrigue.[84]

Where regional tribunals have been constituted by the Holy See to judge matrimonial cases,[85] the archbishop of the see in which the tribunal is situated is to appoint the guardian "ad norman art. 78 *Instructionis,* collatis consiliis cum Ordinario partis conventae cui tutor vel curator constituendus est."[86] Accordingly, the archbishop, or his delegate, is to consult the mentally ill person's Ordinary, and to hear from the other party as well as from the Defender of the Bond.[87]

---

che quello di una semplice *praesumptio iuris tantum* d'incapacità processuale, nel senso che, fino a prova in contrario egli debba effettivamente presumersi incapace, ma facendo salvo il suo diritto di dimostrare in modo positivo la sua riacquistata sanità mentale e quindi la sua piena capacità processuale attuale; nel qual caso egli dovrà essere autorizzato ad *agere et respondere in judicio* personalmente, senza bisogno della constituzione di alcun rappresentante processuale."—*Cause di Nullità,* p. 190.

[84] Cf. Doheny, *Canonical Procedure in Matrimonial Cases,* I, 827-828. In one of its decisions, the Sacred Rota summarized the chief proofs of mental illness: "in primis per testes, qui actus cum sana ratione nullo modo convenientes ab infirmo habitualiter gestos, idest clarae manifestationes amentiae, viderunt et eiusdem sermones audierunt; deinde per peritos, qui de infirmo ab ipsis, si casus ferat, visitato eiusque actis aliunde probatis iudicium scientificum ferre debent; postremo per documenta praesertim publica, quae v.g. testantur infirmum in asylo amentium rite fuisse inclusum."—Cf. S.R.R., *Decisiones,* XXII (1930), dec. XII, n. 15, pp. 134-135.

[85] Cf. below, p. 86.

[86] Cf. *Normae pro Exsequendis Litteris Apostolicis "Qua Cura,"* Art. 14—*AAS,* XXXII (1940), p. 306.

[87] See above, p. 74.

CHAPTER V

The Ecclesiastical Authorities Competent to Appoint Guardians

Article I. Approval of the Civil Law Guardian

Canon 1648, § 1, obliges guardians of persons without the use of reason to plead and defend their wards' cases. By canon 1650, weak-minded persons are obliged to plead and defend their cases through their guardians, except when they must answer for their offenses and when ordered by the judge to appear personally in court. In canon 1651, § 1, the general obligations and consequent rights involved in canons 1648, § 1, and 1650 are made dependent on the consent of the ward's proper Ordinary when the guardian has been appointed by the civil authority, so that an ecclesiastical judge may not admit such a guardian into court unless the proper Ordinary's consent has been previously obtained.

Thus, then alone has a guardian designated by the civil authority the right to exercise action in ecclesiastical courts, when (1) he has been lawfully appointed by the civil authority, and (2) the proper Ordinary has consented to his representing his ward in court. These two conditions must be verified before the judge may lawfully admit him into court.

a. *First condition*: he must be lawfully appointed by the civil authority.

Statutes of civil jurisdiction which determine those empowered to appoint guardians for insane and feeble-minded persons present differences with which the ecclesiastical authority in each particular jurisdiction should be familiar.[1]

[1] D. (26, 3) 7: Si quaeratur, an ex inquisitione recte datus sit tutor, quattuor haec consideranda sunt: an hic dederit qui dare potuit, et ille acceperit cui fuerat dandus; et is datur cuius dandi facultas erat, et pro tribunali decretum interpositum. The Ordinary may follow like procedure when considering lawful appointment of civil law guardians.

In a certain sense, the government itself is the supreme guardian of incompetent persons; the individual guardian represents the government in its solicitude for the welfare of the wards.[2]

In the United States, the different jurisdictions act through the courts of equity or of probate to appoint guardians for the mentally incompetent.

Unless authorized by statutes, parents are without power to appoint testamentary guardians for adult imbecile children. When an insane person is an infant, a guardian charged to care for him is considered as commissioned because of the person's infancy; such a guardian may be appointed by will or by deed and continues in his charge until the ward reaches majority. When the ward becomes of age, a committee or guardian may be appointed by the courts to take charge of his person and estate because of his insanity.[3]

b. *Second condition*: The ward's proper Ordinary must give his consent.[4]

The required consent may be sought by the guardian himself or by the tribunal that is to handle the cause. The Code does not specify.

As a rule, the ecclesiastical authority relies on the decision of the civil authority as to the necessity of a guardian in a particular case and as to the choice it makes of the person to act as guardian.[5] Generally that guardian is admitted to act for his ward in the ecclesiastical forum.[6] It is, however, possible that a guardian appointed by the civil authority may be unsuited to defend his ward's best interests in a Church trial, because, for instance, he is gen-

---

[2] Cf. 25 Am. Jur., *Guardian and Ward*, § 205.

[3] Cf. 25 Am. Jur., *Guardian and Ward*, § 17.

[4] A similar ruling exists in the civil forum in the United States: "inasmuch as the authority of a guardian is limited to the state of his appointment, he cannot sue in a court, even of the United States, held within another state, except so far as authorized to do so by the laws of the latter jurisdiction." 25 Am. Jur., *Guardian and Ward*, § 147.

[5] Roberti, *De Processibus*, I, n. 202, II; Aguirre, "De Curatore Dementis," pp. 294-295.

[6] Cf. *Instructio*, art. 78. See also Toso, "De Constitutione Curatoris," p. 117.

erally opposed to the Church's judicial powers and hostile to the Church[7] or because he seeks his own advantage and temporal good rather than to safeguard the ward's interests and liberty in spiritual matters.

Consequently, canon 1651, § 1, most wisely ordains that a guardian commissioned by the civil authorities is to be admitted before the ecclesiastical tribunal only after the proper Ordinary's consent has been obtained. For this Ordinary is in a position to appraise rightly the persons and peculiar circumstances of the case.[8] Moreover, he is free to grant or to withold his consent.[9]

The consent required is that of the ward's proper Ordinary: *consensus Ordinarii proprii illius cui datus est* (*curator*).[10] Who is the ward's proper Ordinary when he is already under guardianship?

One's proper Ordinary is he in whose territory one has a domicile or quasi-domicile.[11] Since an insane person necessarily retains the domicile of him to whose power he is subject, in our case the guardian, it follows that an insane person's proper Ordinary is his guardian's proper Ordinary.[12]

The Code does not contain special norms to determine the domicile of a feeble-minded person. Since his status, when under guardianship, is analogous to that of a minor and of a wife not lawfully separated from her husband—they are all *sub potestate alterius*—we may apply canon 20 and conclude that the ward *minus firmae mentis* retains his guardian's domicile, just as a wife retains her

---

[7] Cf. Lega-Bartoccetti, *Commentarius,* I, p. 311, n. 7.

[8] Cf. Lega-Bartoccetti, *loc. cit.*

[9] Cf. Torre, *Processus Matrimonialis,* p. 81: "in ista confirmatione vel electione, Ordinarius maxima gaudet libertate et nullo modo tenetur eamdem eligere personam, quam auctoritas civilis elegit, vel familiares praesentant."

[10] Canon 1651, § 1. Lega adds: "nec sufficit quod sit Ordinarius loci iudicii." *Commentarius,* I, 311; Naz, "Curateur," *DDC,* IV, 887.

[11] Canon 94, § 1.

[12] Canon 93, § 1, and 94 § 1. If the notion of a necessary quasi-domicile is accepted, the Ordinary of the guardian's quasi-domicile also would be the insane person's proper Ordinary. The possibility of a necessary quasi-domicile is discussed below. Cf. below, pp. 92-93.

husband's domicile and a minor retains the domicile of him to whom he is subject.[13] A feeble-minded person's proper Ordinary, then, would be his guardian's proper Ordinary. It must be noted here, however, that since a feeble-minded person is capable of acquiring a quasi-domicile,[14] the Ordinary of the territory in which this quasi-domicile is located may also be considered a proper Ordinary.

When a mentally ill person has two proper Ordinaries, the one of his guardian's domicile and the one of his own quasi-domicile, it seems that the consent of either would suffice for the civil law guardian's admittance into court by the ecclesiastical judge. Prescriptions of civil law and peculiar circumstances may counsel that one Ordinary be preferred to another in a given case.

Canon 198 lists those whom the law generally includes under the term *Ordinary*: the Roman Pontiff; the residential bishop, abbot *nullius,* prelate *nullius,* administrator apostolic, vicar apostolic, prefect apostolic; those who, in case of vacancy of the above offices, succeed to the office during vacancy by provision of the law or of approved constitutions; and major superiors in exempt clerical religious organizations.[15]

Is a vicar-general's consent sufficient? Since the vicar-general is included under the term *Ordinarius*[16] and canon 1651, § 1, does not contain a restrictive phrase requiring a special mandate from the Bishop, the vicar-general's consent would suffice for the legiti-

[13] Canon 93, § 1.

[14] See below, p. 96.

[15] Canon 488, n. 8, indicates explicitly which religious superiors are included under the designation *major superiors*: The abbot primate and the abbot general of a monastic Congregation, the abbot of an exempt monastery, the supreme moderator of a religious community and the provincial superior, the vicars of the same (i.e., of the foregoing four categories), and all others who have authority like to that of provincials. If they belong to a clerical exempt religion, these superiors must be considered juridically as ordinaries. Cf. M. J. Keene, *Religious Ordinaries and Canon 198,* The Catholic University of America Canon Law Studies, n. 135 (Washington, D.C.: The Catholic University of America Press, 1942), p. 3.

[16] Canon 198, § 1.

mate admission of a guardian appointed by the civil authority, unless the Ordinary has reserved this affair to himself.[17]

At this point we may cite the special prescription obtaining in countries where regional tribunals have been established by the Holy See to judge matrimonial cases. Such tribunals were established in Italy by Pope Pius XI in his Motu Proprio *"Qua Cura"* of December 8, 1938.[18] Similar tribunals were constituted in the Philippine Islands in 1940[19] and in Canada in 1946.[20] Article 14 of the *Normae pro exsequendis Litteris Apostolicis "Qua Cura,"* issued by the S.C. de Disciplina Sacramentorum,[21] reads :"Archiepiscopi Sedis tribunalis regionalis erit tutorem aut curatorem admittere vel designare ad norman art. 78 Instructionis,[22] collatis consiliis cum Ordinario partis conventae cui tutor vel curator constituendus est."[23] This same injunction is found *ad litteram* in the corresponding *Normae* sent to the regional tribunals of the Philippines and of Canada. The Archbishop of the See in which the special tribunal is located is to admit a guardian after consulting the defendant's Ordinary.

When considering the granting or the withholding of his consent, the Ordinary should bear in mind both canon 1651, § 2: *Ordinarius potest quoque alium curatorem constituere pro foro ecclesiastico, si, omnibus mature perpensis, id statuendum esse prudenter censuerit,* and article 78, § 1, of the *Instructio*: *Ubi tutor vel curator a civili auctoritate constitutus adest, hic ordinarie*

---

[17] Canon 368, § 1. It has been demonstrated above (pp. 71 ff.) that the appointment of guardians in the ecclesiastical forum is not a judicial act. Consequently, the Vicar General is *per se* competent to appoint guardians. If he is competent to appoint a guardian, *a fortiori* he is competent to grant consent to a civil law guardian to represent his ward before an ecclesiastical tribunal.

[18] Cf. *AAS,* XXX (1938), 410-413.

[19] Cf. *AAS,* XXXIII (1941), 363 ff.

[20] Cf. *AAS,* XXXVIII (1946), 281 ff.

[21] Cf. *AAS,* XXXII (1940), 304-308.

[22] The *Instructio* referred to is the *Provida Mater Ecclesia,* issued by the same Sacred Congregation on August 15, 1936. Cf. *AAS,* XXVIII (1936), 313-361.

[23] Cf. *AAS,* XXXII, (1940), 306.

admittatur, nisi peculiares rationes Ordinario aliud suadeant (cf. can. 1651). These norms reveal the mind of the legislator regarding the granting of consent to the guardian appointed by the civil authority. Ordinarily he should be admitted to act in Church trials.[24] Only after seriously considering the pros and cons in a particular case and finding special reasons to deny his consent, should the proper Ordinary withhold his permission and proceed to appoint a different guardian for the ecclesiastical forum.

Among the reasonable causes sufficient to justify the appointment by the Ordinary of a guardian in place of the one appointed by the civil authority may be mentioned the following: a conflict of interests and difficulties arising from distance, as mentioned in canon 1648, § 2;[25] the fact that the guardian in civil law is a *vagus* or has only a quasi-domicile;[26] hostility of the guardian to the Church or ecclesiastical judges.[27] When such causes are found to exist, Lega suggests that, if the intervention of the *promotor iustitiae* can supply for the defective activity of the guardian, the latter be granted consent to act in the ecclesiastical forum rather than that a substitute guardian be appointed by the Ordinary.[28] This alternative he advises especially when the sentence will touch on civil matters, to insure its being upheld in the civil forum.[29]

By way of conclusion one may ask whether the proper Ordinary's consent is required for the validity of the civil law guardian's admission into the ecclesiastical court.

From the wording of canon 1651, § 1: *Ut curator ab auctoritate civili alicui datus a iudice ecclesiastico admittatur, debet accedere*

---

[24] Cf. Aguirre, "De Curatore Dementis," p. 295: "Expedit profecto ut ubi tutor vel curator a civili auctoritate constitutus adsit, hic admittatur etiam in foro ecclesiastico, nisi graves rationes aliud suadere videantur, quae norma expresse statuitur pro causis de nullitate matrimonii in art. 78 Instructionis S.C. de disc. Sacram. d. 15 augusti 1936."

[25] Cf. Giustiniani, "De Curatore Dementis," p. 106; Roberti, *De Processibus,* I, n. 202, III.

[26] Cf. Doheny, *Canonical Procedure in Matrimonial Cases,* I, 24.

[27] Cf. Lega-Bartoccetti, *Commentarius,* I, 311.

[28] Cf. Lega-Bartoccetti, *Commentarius,* I, 311-312; Aguirre, "art. cit.," p. 295; Naz, "Curateur," *DDC,* IV, 887.

[29] Lega-Bartoccetti, *ibid.,* p. 312.

consensus Ordinarii proprii . . . can be gathered the obligation (*debet*) to secure the Ordinary's consent; but the invalidity of that guardian's admission into court without that consent cannot be strictly argued from the text.

Canon 166, § 1, of the procedural law of the Oriental Rites reads: *Ut curator ab auctoritate civili alicui datus a iudice ecclesiastico valide admittatur, debet accedere consensus Hierarchae proprii illius cui datus est.*[30] In this canon which corresponds to canon 1651, § 1, of the Code, it is expressly stated that the consent is required for the validity of the admission.

Commentators on the Code generally do not explain whether the *consensus Ordinarii proprii* is required for validity by our law. D'Avack states that the Ordinary's formal approval by means of a decree is required; otherwise, the civil law guardian *invalide agit.* But he offers no reason in support of his assertion other than to cite canon 1651;[31] nor does he say *invalide admittitur.*

Even were we, however, to grant that the admission without proper consent were valid, we would have to concede that such admission is illicit, since it is contrary to law. Consequently, the guardian would still lack—precisely because he has been unlawfully admitted into court—the *legitimum mandatum* required by canon 1892, n. 3; and this defect in his appointment would vitiate the process and the final sentence.[32]

---

[30] Cf. Motu Proprio de Iudiciis pro Ecclesia Orientali: *Sollicitudinem Nostram—AAS,* XXXXII (1950), 5-120.

[31] "Il curatore . . . qualora sia stato . . . deputato dall'autorità civile, deve per lo meno essere da lui (the proper Ordinary) formalmente approvato con suo apposito decreto, altrimenti *invalide agit* (1651)"—D'Avack, *Cause di Nullità,* p. 189. See also Torre, *op. cit.,* p. 81: "Attamen necesse est, priusquam denuncietur citatio curatori vel tutori a civili auctoritate dato, examinare utrum ista persona confirmata fuerit necne, ab Ordinario, quia, absque confirmatione, nullo modo repraesentatio infirmi mente valida est ad effectus canonicos."

[32] Cf. Hanssen, *De Sanctione Nullitatis,* n. 65; Roberti, *De Processibus,* I, n. 202, IV. Speaking of a guardian *illegitime constitutus,* a decision of the Apostolic Signatura concluded: ". . . et si stet in iudicio pro suo pupillo, stat sine legitimo mandato cum consequenti nullitate sententiae." Cf. Roberti, *op. cit.,* n. 202, II, 3, note 2. Cappello observes: "Consensus Ordinarii seu legitima constitutio curatoris requiritur ad valorem iudicii,

Article II. Appointment of Guardians by the Ordinary

I. Identity of the Competent Ordinary

If a guardian has not been appointed by the civil authority, or if the one so appointed is not admitted by the Ordinary to serve as guardian in the ecclesiastical court, the Ordinary himself shall appoint one;[33] for, when the guardian appointed by the civil authority fails to receive the proper Ordinary's consent to act in the ecclesiastical forum, his ward is left without a guardian for this forum. Should the ward still require representation by a guardian because of his mental condition, another guardian must be appointed by the ecclesiastical authority.

The ecclesiastical authority competent to appoint this new guardian is the authority who rejected the civil law guardian,[34] i.e., the ward's proper Ordinary, as explained above.[35]

The *Ordinarius* of canon 1651, § 2, is the same as that of § 1, since § 2 is obviously the alternative which the Ordinary enjoys in cases where he denies consent to the civil law guardian. The *eiusdem Ordinarii erit eum designare* of article 78, § 2, of the *Instructio* clearly indicates the identity of the Ordinary in the demonstrative adjective *eiusdem* (the same). This Ordinary's delegation would be required for the validity of the appointment before the trial by the *Ordinarius loci iudicii* or by the *officialis* as such, since the placing of a person under guardianship is an act of jurisdiction and the power of jurisdiction can be exercised directly over subjects only.[36] Canon 1648, § 2, however, authorizes

---

ut manifesto liquet ex ipso conceptu repraesentationis."—*Summa Iuris Canonici,* III, n. 92, 2.

[33] Canon 1651, § 2. Ordinarius potest quoque alium curatorem constituere pro foro ecclesiastico, si omnibus mature perpensis, id statuendum esse prudenter censuerit. *Instructio,* Art. 78, § 2: Si tutor vel curator non est a civili auctoritate constitutus, vel, etsi constitutus, ab Ordinario non fuit admissus, eiusdem Ordinarii erit eum designare.—*AAS,* XXVIII (1936), 330.

[34] Cf. Toso, "De Constitutione Curatoris," p. 117.

[35] Cf. pp. 83 ff.

[36] Cf. canon 201, § 1.

them to appoint a guardian *ad litem* under certain circumstances during the course of a trial.[37]

II. Determination of the Proper Ordinary

To determine the *Ordinarius proprius* of insane and of feeble-minded persons not already under guardianship, resort must be had to the principles of the Code concerning domicile and quasi-domicile; for one's proper Ordinary is he in whose territory one has a domicile or quasi-domicile.[38]

a) Principles of the Code governing domicile and quasi-domicile. Canonical doctrine recognizes two forms of domicile and quasi-domicile, viz., voluntary domicile or quasi-domicile[39] and legal or necessary domicile or quasi-domicile.[40]

To acquire a voluntary domicile, it is required: (1) that a person be present in a parish, quasi-parish, diocese, etc., and (2) that this presence either be associated with the intention of remaining permanently in that place unless something calls one away, or actually extend over a period of ten complete years.[41] To acquire a voluntary quasi-domicile a person must either (1) be actually present in the specific territory with the intention of remaining at least for the greater part of the year unless something calls him away, or (2) actually reside in the territory for a greater part of the year regardless of intention.[42] Voluntary domicile and quasi-domicile, then, are characterized by two requisites: actual presence

---

[37] Cf. below, pp. 97 ff.

[38] Canon 94, § 1.

[39] Cf. canon 92.

[40] Cf. canon 93. The term *necessary* domicile is not found in the Code, but it is used universally by authors who discuss canon 93, § 1. "The necessary domicile is a juridical institution as old as Roman Law, but the attribution, in law, of such a domicile to the insane is new with the Code," writes Pickett, citing D. (50, 1) and (Vindex), "Domicilium et Quasi-domicilium," *Jus Pontificium,* VI (1926), 34-44. Cf. Pickett, *Mental Affliction and Church Law,* p. 112.

[41] Canon 92, § 1.

[42] Canon 92, § 2.

and intention of remaining, which intention the law supplies if simple residence is protracted over a given period of time.[43]

Necessary domicile is acquired by disposition of the law. It does not depend, as to its acquisition, on actual personal presence and the intention of remaining, as does voluntary domicile. As Costello states it: "It matters not whether the person actually resides in the place, or whether he has the positive intention of not residing there; he has a domicile nevertheless, a domicile conferred by operation of the law, a *domicilium legale, necessarium*."[44]

According to canon 93, § 1,[45] a wife necessarily acquires and retains the domicile of her husband, unless she is legitimately separated from him; an insane person acquires and retains the domicile of his guardian; and a minor acquires and retains that of his parents or guardian. This is a form of necessary domicile borrowed from others: *Species necessarii domicilii mutuati*.[46]

Authors speak of another form of necessary domicile, proper of persons who are required to reside in a given place independently of their own will but who acquire their own domicile and not someone else's. This form of domicile they term *domicilium necessarium personale seu proprium*. In this category they enumerate the following: beneficed clerics, in the place of their benefice;

---

[43] Costello explains the difference between domicile and quasi-domicile: "(Quasi-domicile) has ever been regarded as an extention of the domicile, an attenuated domicile, a *domicilium improprium*. In fact, the only difference in notion between the domicile and the quasi-domicile consists in the intention. To constitute a domicile, an intention of permanent residence is necessary; to constitute a quasi-domicile, it is sufficient that one have the intention of remaining for the greater part of the year."—*Domicile and Quasi-Domicile*, p. 111.

[44] Costello, *op. cit.*, p. 161 Cf. also, Pickett, *op. cit.* p. 112.

[45] This canon does not state anything explicitly about the acquisition of legal domicile, but simply enumerates those persons upon whom it is conferred; its acquisition, then, is effected through one's entrance among the classes of persons enumerated.

[46] Cf. U. Beste, *Introductio in Codicem*, (ed. 3., Collegeville, Minn.: St. John's Abbey Press, 1946), p. 141; J. J. McBride, *Incardination and Excardination of Seculars*, The Catholic University of America Canon Law Studies, n. 145 (Washington, D.C.: The Catholic University of America Press, 1941), p. 319.

religious, in the religious house to which they are affiliated;[47] Cardinals (except those who are Bishops of non-suburbicarian dioceses) in the city of Rome; life prisoners, in the place of their confinement; and soldiers, in their stationary garrisons. "One author places in this list also secular clerics in the diocese in which they are incardinated, on the strength of canon 111, where clerical *vagi* are outlawed, and of canons 143 and 144, where the secular cleric is shown to have no free will in selecting any residence outside the diocese."[48]

Can a person have a necessary quasi-domicile? The Code makes no mention of such a quasi-domicile. An array of distinguished authors, however, stand for the possibility of a necessary quasi-domicile, since the law of the Code does not exclude such a possibility and the idea of a necessary quasi-domicile does not appear otherwise untenable.[49] The silence of canon 93, § 1, as to quasi-domicile—thus argues Michiels—can be explained by the fact that

[47] Novices, however, follow the general rules of domicile and quasi-domicile. Cf. Beste, *op. cit.*, p. 141: "Novitii vero reguntur iure laicorum; quocirca, si minorennes, sequuntur domicilium necessarium parentum vel tutorum et simul sibi comparant quasi-domicilium in domo novitiatus; adepta maioritate, valent principia proxime praecedentis canonis"—i.e., of canon 92.

[48] McBride, *op. cit.*, pp. 319-320; Cf. also Beste, *op. cit.*, p. 141; Regatillo, *Institutiones Iuris Canonici,* I, n. 192. McBride points out the differences between these necessary domiciles: "In addition to all these types of domiciles (the second group) being proper instead of borrowed, another point of differentiation between them and those mentioned in canon 93, § 1, is that only one element, the formal, is supplied by law. There is no evidence to show that any one of these categories would have a legal residence in a place where they never yet have been. It is their will alone which has been constrained by law to consent actually to go to a certain place and remain there, and since they are not free to leave on their own authority, they are considered as still belonging there even if they later leave without permission. Hence, it is not justifiable to put them in the same category with wives, the insane, and minors, for whom even the basic element of residence itself is supplied by law, nor may the same juridical effects be invoked."—*op. cit.*, p. 320; cf. Costello, *op. cit.*, pp. 169-174.

[49] Cf. Michiels, *De Personis,* p. 151; Chelodi, *Ius Canonicum de Personis,* n. 92; Cappello, *Summa Iuris Canonici,* I, n. 194; Coronata, *Institutiones Iuris Canonici,* I, n. 127.

it would have been superfluous to include quasi-domicile in the provisions made by that norm; for, there is no difference in the modes of acquisition of necessary domicile and quasi-domicile, as there is in the case of voluntary domicile and quasi-domicile.[50] Moreover, the necessary domicile, or imposed participation in the domicile of another, is a protective right countenanced by the law. Wernz-Vidal go on to add that this protective right admits of a wide and favorable interpretation, so that it may be extended to include necessary quasi-domicile.[51] Again, if the possibility of a necessary quasi-domicile is excluded, the whole purpose of canon 93, § 1, would frequently be defeated, since the dependents mentioned therein would of necessity be reduced to the status of *vagi,* as often as the persons on whom they depend possessed but a quasi-domicile.[52] Consequently, it seems at least highly advisable that the idea of necessary quasi-domicile be accepted.

Canon 95 regulates the loss of domicile and quasi-domicile: *Domicilium et quasi-domicilium amittitur discessione a loco cum animo non revertendi, salvo praescripto can. 93.* A voluntary domicile or quasi-domicile, then, is lost by leaving the place of domicile or quasi-domicile with the intention of not returning. A person necessarily retains (*necessario retinet*) his legal, necessary domicile, as long as he continues in the state or the condition to which that domicile has been annexed; upon the cessation of the fact upon which it was founded, this necessary domicile ceases. It is presumed, however, to have passed into a voluntary domicile unless it is apparent that the place has been definitely abandoned.[53]

"The law regards the loss of domicile as a *res odiosa,* and does not countenance a presumption of its loss, even though in the case of voluntary domicile the person is at liberty to abandon it."[54]

---

[50] Canon 92, §§ 1-2, outlines the differences. Cf. above, pp. 90-91; Michiels, *loc. cit.*

[51] Cf. Wernz-Vidal, *Ius Canonicum,* II, n. 12.

[52] Cf. Pickett, *op. cit.,* p. 115.

[53] Cf. Costello, *op. cit.,* pp. 161, 166; M. L. Gibbons, *Domicile of Wife unlawfully Separated from Her Husband,* The Catholic University of America Canon Law Studies, n. 249 (Washington, D.C.: The Catholic University of America Press, 1947), pp. 94, 98 ff.

[54] Gibbons, *op. cit.,* p. 98; Costello, *op. cit.,* pp. 145-146. In support of

b) The domicile and quasi-domicile of the mentally ill who are not already subject to a guardian.

The foregoing applies differently to the mentally incompetent, depending on whether they are insane or feeble-minded.

Since an insane person is not capable of eliciting the intention either of leaving a place or of choosing a place, it appears that of himself he is incapable of losing a domicile, once properly acquired, and of electing a new domicile or quasi-domicile.[55]

---

his affirmation, the latter cites: S.R.R., *in Causa Gratianopolitana,* 17 iul 1912, Dec. XXXI, nn. 4, 9—S.R.R., *Decisiones,* IV (1912), 365-366; 368-369.

[55] Cf. Doheny, *Canonical Procedure in Matrimonial Cases,* I, p. 23, note 32. "In view of the second section of canon 93 it is clear that the insane person, unlike the married woman and the minor cannot acquire a proper quasi-domicile. Some canonists, indeed, are of the opinion that an insane person can acquire a quasi-domicile by actual residence in a place for the greater part of a year. (Cf. De Meester, *Compendium,* I, n. 317). This opinion cannot be admitted. Not a single argument can be urged in its favor, and it is clearly opposed to a cardinal rule of interpretation as enunciated in canon 18. This canon declares that laws are to be understood according to the proper signification of the words, considered in their text and context. A careful reading of section two of canon 93 with a backward glance at section one reveals the unmistakable intention of the legislator to exclude insane persons from acquiring a quasi-domicile. In canon 93, § 1, wives, minors and insane persons are declared to have necessary domiciles. In the next breath, as it were, canon 93, § 2, permits wives and minors to acquire a quasi-domicile of their own. The logical conclusion is that insane persons cannot acquire a proper quasi-domicile.

"This conclusion is strengthened by the fact that a quasi-domicile (even that constituted by actual residence) must be acquired by a personal action performed *humano modo.* The act by which a quasi-domicile is acquired must be a human act, for from involuntary and unconscious actions no juridical effect can follow, since those things which in law depend on one's own personal action and are not induced by a fiction of law, presuppose in the agent a reflection of the mind and the *voluntas agendi.* But insane persons are incapable of a human act, since they are deprived of the use of reason. It must be concluded, therefore, that they cannot acquire a proper quasi-domicile." So writes Costello, *op. cit.,* pp. 168-169; "Non videtur ratio declarandi infantes quoque et amentes acquierere quasi-domicilium, si de facto per sex menses in quodam loco commorentur." Claeys Bouuaert, F.—Simenon, G., *Manuale Juris Canonici ad Usum Seminariorum* (Vols. I, and III, 3. ed., Vol. II, 1. ed., Gandae et Leodii,

In other words, the domicile of one who, after becoming *sui iuris,* becomes insane remains the domicile which he had before he became mentally incompetent,[56] because he is personally incapable of effecting a change of domicile.[57]

Indeed, as Costello writes: "It must be remembered, however, that although this necessary domicile *as such* ceases upon the cessation of the fact upon which it was founded, it is presumed to have passed into a voluntary domicile unless it is clear that it has been definitely abandoned."[58]

On becoming insane, a wife does not *per se* lose the domicile or quasi-domicile of her husband. For, the fact of her becoming insane does not subtract her from her dependence on him, and it is precisely from this dependence that her necessary domicile issues.[59] If, at the request of her husband, she is placed under guardianship, then her domicile or quasi-domicile becomes that of her guardian.[60]

1930-1931), I, n. 245; see also Doheny, *Canonical Procedure in Matrimonial Cases,* I, 25.

[56] Cf. 17 Am. Jur., *Domicil,* § 70: ". . . the domicil of one who, after attaining majority, becomes mentally incompetent remains the domicil which he had when he became insane."

[57] Since an insane person is incapable of losing a properly acquired domicile, the writer disagrees with Costello who writes: "If the insane person has no guardian . . . it would seem that he must be placed in the category of *vagi."—Op. cit.,* p. 169. A reason for this opinion is not advanced either by Costello or by the author he cites, N. Farren, *Domicile and Quasi-Domicile* (Dublin: M. H. Gill and Son, 1920), p. 94. See also Pickett, *op. cit.,* pp. 113, 117, 120.

[58] *Op. cit.,* p. 161.

[59] Cf. Pickett, *op. cit.,* p. 116.

[60] Canon 93, § 1. Cf. Pickett, *op. cit.,* p. 116-117. Pickett goes on to say: "Lacking a guardian, either ecclesiastically or civilly appointed, the insane wife who is legitimately separated from her husband has no domicile *voluntary* or *necessary* and is, therefore, a *vaga."* The present writer, however, cannot conceive how a wife legitimately separated from her husband becomes a *vaga* after becoming insane. If she had neither a domicile nor a quasi-domicile before becoming insane, she was already a *vaga* and one may not speak of her as becoming a *vaga.* If she possessed a domicile or quasi-domicile before losing her mind, she can hardly lose either, as explained above (cf. pp. 93 ff). Pickett himself maintains that "the very

Residence alone will not effect the change of an insane person's domicile. It follows, then, that the mere placing of an adult lunatic in an asylum, situated in territory other than that of his properly acquired domicile, does not work a change of domicile, no matter how long the confinement continues. Should the institution, however, become his legal guardian, the lunatic's domicile would change in accordance with canon 93, § 1.

Feeble-minded persons, on the other hand, are generally capable of exercising choice and intention, elements regarded as essential to effecting a change in domicile.[61]

Since they are capable of performing human acts, they are also capable of acquiring and retaining a voluntary domicile.[62] Moreover, when they already have a necessary, legal domicile,[63] they can acquire a proper and voluntary quasi-domicile, according to the norms stated in canons 93, § 2, and 92, § 2. Besides, on becoming *sui iuris,* after attaining majority or, in case of a wife, after being lawfully separated from her husband, a feeble-minded person can acquire a proper, voluntary domicile. It must be remembered, however, that a necessary domicile is presumed to pass into a voluntary domicile unless it is clear that it has been abandoned.[64]

The proper Ordinary, determined according to the foregoing, has the power to appoint a guardian for a mentally ill person who stands in need of assistance or representation in the ecclesiastical forum. The proper Ordinary of non-exempt religious is the local Ordinary of the place in which the religious' residence is situated, whereas exempt religious have as their proper Ordinaries their particular major superiors.[65]

This power may be delegated as there is no prescription in the Code that forbids delegation.[66]

---

concept (of domicile) is inseparably conjoined with a note of permanency." Cf. *op. cit.*, p. 113.

[61] Cf. 17 Am. Jur., *Domicil,* § 70.

[62] Cf. Pickett, *op. cit.*, p. 113.

[63] Cf. above, p. 91 ff.

[64] Cf. above, p. 93.

[65] Cf. canons 500; 615; 618 § 1; 198 § 1; 488, n. 8.

[66] Cf. Canon 1651. See J. Tobin, *De Officiali Curiae Diocesanae* (Romae: Apud Aedes Pontificae Universitatis Gregorianae, 1936), p. 221,

C. Appointment by the Ecclesiastical Judge.

The law of the Code empowers the presiding judge to appoint a guardian to exercise court action when he thinks that the ward's rights are in jeopardy because they conflict with the rights of his lawfully appointed guardian or because, on account of distance, the guardian cannot at all, or can only with difficulty, represent his ward in court.[67]

The appointing of a guardian to act for a person already under the control of another guardian is not peculiar to the law of the Code. This possibility was admitted even in the Roman Law.[68]

In the civil forum, guardians are barred from acting for their wards when a conflict of interests arises. "But if the action is one brought by the guardian, in his personal or in a different official capacity, in which his interest is opposed to that of the ward, he cannot defend for the ward either as general guardian or as guardian ad litem."[69] Civil codes, however, do not contemplate the necessity of appointing a guardian *ad litem* to offset difficulties arising from distance. Such difficulties are not likely to arise in the secular forum. Since the ecclesiastical forum is worldwide, distance may render very difficult the offering of assistance to a ward by his already appointed guardian.[70]

On perceiving the existence of the above-mentioned causes, the

---

who speaks of such delegation in reference to the *officialis* and *vice-officialis*. Cf. Doheny, *Canonical Procedure in Matrimonial Cases,* I, 252.

[67] Canon 1648, § 2. Si iudex existimet ipsorum iura esse in conflictu cum iuribus parentum vel tutorum vel curatorum, aut ipsos tam longe distare a parentibus aut tutoribus vel curatoribus, ut hisce uti aut minime aut difficulter liceat, tunc stent in iudicio per curatorem a iudice datum.

[68] Cf., e.g., D. (26, 1) 13: "Solet etiam curator dari aliquando tutorem habenti propter adversam tutoris valetudinem vel senium aetatis." See also D. (26, 10) 9; C. (5, 36) 4: "Licet tutorem habenti tutor dari non potest, tamen certis ex causis alius idoneus substitui sententia competentis iudicis solet, id est in locum suspecti, qui convictus ac remotus est, et in locum excusati vel defuncti vel relegati tutoris."

[69] 25 Am. Jur., *Guardian and Ward,* § 154. Cf. also *op. cit.,* § 157, as well as the Italian Civil Code, articles 224, 266.

[70] Cf. Lega-Bartoccetti, *Commentarius,* I, 306.

judge may proceed *ex officio* to appoint a guardian *ad litem.*[71] This follows necessarily from the wording of canon 1648, § 2: *si iudex existimet, tunc stent in iudicio per curatorem a iudice datum.* These expressions imply that the judge himself takes the initiative in appointing the guardian. It can hardly be objected that the danger to the ward's rights is an affair which pertains to a private person and that, consequently, the judge can interfere only at the request of the party.[72] Just as the law provides for the protection of the incompetent by means of the institute of guardianship, so does it safeguard and promote the purpose of this institute by giving the presiding judge power to substitute a guardian, under given conditions, with a guardian of his own choice.

Needless to say, the judge should bear in mind the best interests of the ward when appointing a guardian *ad litem.*

The appointment of a guardian is an act of jurisdiction. Since jurisdiction can be exercised only over subjects,[73] one must determine just when a person becomes a subject of a judge, or of a tribunal. In Ferraris' work is found: *"Quantum ad fundandam iurisdictionem iudicis, initium iudicium capit a citatione, ac propterea inducit citatio praeventionem et litis pendentiam."*[74] Thus with the summons rises the tribunal's exclusive jurisdiction in a particular case and over the parties engaged in the controversy.[75] The prescription of canon 1725 contains a similar teaching: Cum citatio legitime peracta fuerit aut partes sponte in iudicium venerint:

---

[71] Cf. Lega-Bartoccetti, *loc. cit.*

[72] Cf. canon 1618.

[73] Cf. Can. 201, § 1. See M. J. Reinhardt, *The Rogatory Commission*, The Catholic University of American Canon Law Studies, n. 288 (Washington, D.C.: The Catholic University of America Press, 1949), pp. 1-4; 53-59.

[74] *Prompta Bibliotheca,* ad v. *Iudicium,* n. 44 (additiones ex aliena manu).

[75] The summons itself must be considered an act of jurisdiction; for it proceeds from the command of the judge, ordering the defendant to appear in court. Cf. Reinhardt, *op. cit.,* p. 105. Cappello, *Summa Iuris Canonici,* III, n. 146.

1° Res desinit esse integra;[76]

2° Causa fit propria illius iudicis aut tribunalis, coram qua actio instituta est;[77]

3° In iudice delegato firma redditur iurisdictio ita ut non exspiret resoluto iure delegantis;[78]

4° Interrumpitur praescriptio, nisi aliud cautum sit, ad norman can. 1508.[79]

5° Lis pendere incipit; et ideo statim locum habet principium: "Lite pendente, nihil innovetur."[80] Hence, one may conclude: (1) that a judge has *per se* no authority to appoint a guardian before the citation has been delivered;[81] and (2) that he alone may appoint a guardian *ad litem* during this trial.[82]

Toso maintains that the Ordinary may appoint a guardian even after the case is already before the court.[83]

---

76 The case is before the tribunal, and the matter involved in the controversy is no longer a private affair, but one in which the public authority is interested.

77 Consequently, if the plaintiff had the choice between the courts of the dioceses A and B, once the court of diocese A issued the summons to the defendant, diocese B is precluded by law from judging the case in the first instance.

78 The litigants become his subjects and remain so throughout the trial. This effect of the summons is of particular concern to the present discussion.

79 The reason for this is that from the moment that property or rights are made a subject of litigation, the good faith essential to prescription cannot persevere. Cf. Woywod, *A Practical Commentary*, II, n. 1683.

80 Thenceforth no change may be made (1) in the complaint of the plaintiff; (2) in the allegations of his reasons for asking redress; or (3) in the property or in the rights under litigation.

81 Vaughan suggests: "He (the *officialis*) could be authorized to choose, constitute and substitute guardians (tutores vel curatores) for minors and those lacking use of reason and to either approve or substitute for guardians named by civil authorities."—W. E. Vaughan, *Constitutions for Diocesan Courts*, The Catholic University of America Canon Law Studies, n. 210 (Washington, D.C.: The Catholic University of America Press, 1944), n. 44. Cf. also Tobin, *De Officiali Curiae Dioecesanae*, p. 221, n. 404; Doheny, *Canonical Procedure in Matrimonial Cases*, I, 252. Staffa, "De Constitutione Curatoris," p. 78.

82 Cf. Staffa, "art. cit.," p. 79.

83 ". . . decretum . . . manare potest . . . ex Ordinario . . . ante vel post inceptum iudicium"—"De Constitutione Curatoris," p. 118.

Since, however, the summons renders the case proper to the judge or the court,[84] and the controversy is withdrawn from the limits of voluntary jurisdiction,[85] the writer holds with Staffa[86] that the tribunal alone may appoint or substitute a guardian *lite pendente.* Canon 1648, § 2, confirms this opinion, inasmuch as it supposes the process already instituted[87] and mentions only the *iudex* as the authority entrusted with the substitution of a guardian under the circumstances indicated.[88] That the tribunal is competent to appoint a guardian whenever the need of one first emerges during the course of the process because, for instance, one of the contending parties becomes mentally ill follows from the general principle of law thus expressed by Javolenus: *"Cui iurisdictio data est, ea quoque concessa esse videntur sine quibus iuridictio explicari non potuit."*[89] Canon Law accepted this principle[90] and retained it in the Code.[91] In the case under consideration the appointment of a guardian is an act required for the valid pursuance of the process. Therefore, the court must have the authority to appoint the guardian.[92]

---

[84] Canon 1725, n. 2; *Instructio,* art. 85.

[85] Canon 1725, n. 1: Res desinit esse integra; *Instructio,* art. 85. Cf. also PCI, July 8, 1940—*AAS*, XXXII (1940), 317.

[86] Cf. "art. cit.," pp. 79, 80.

[87] Cf. Lega-Bartoccetti, *Commentarius,* I, 310.

[88] Staffa, "art. cit.," p. 79: "Curatoris nominationem lite pendente unice iudici competere, demum confirmatur can. 1648, § 2, qui, iudicium inceptum praesupponendo, nominationem curatoris pro iis qui usu rationis sunt destituti iudici tribuit, si ipsorum iura existimet: 'esse in conflictu. . . .", etc.

[89] D. (2, 1) 2.

[90] Cf. Cc. 1, 5, 11, 29, X, *de officio et potestate iudicis delegati,* I, 29; Reg. 42, 53, 80, R. J., in VI°.

[91] Canon 200, § 1: Potestas iurisdictionis ordinaria et ad universitatem negotiorum delegata, late interpretanda est; alia quaelibet stricte; cui tamen delegata potestas est, ea quoque intelliguntur concessa, sine quibus eadem exerceri non potest.

[92] "Facultas dandi curatorem est de omnino necessariis (iudici) quia sine tali facultate iurisdictio in causa minoris esset omnino inanis."—P. Passerini, *Commentaria in Sextum Librum Decretalium* (2 vols., Romae: 1667-1670), II, tit, 1, nn. 55-56. (This citation is taken from Staffa, "art. cit." p. 79, note 86). Pinna makes a like statement: "Sin autem amentia

On the other hand, unless it was properly delegated at some earlier time, the tribunal may not substitute a guardian until the trial has begun. For only at this point does it obtain jurisdiction over the parties involved. Before the case is in progress, the Ordinary, or his delegate, alone is authorized to appoint or substitute guardians.[93]

---

supervenerit durante processu, curator, non modo quoties agatur de actore mente infirmo, sed ipsi quoque convento amenti, dandus erit a iudice; nam constitutio curatoris est actus necessario connexus cum exercitio potestatis iudicialis"—J. M. Pinna, *Praxis Iudicialis Canonica* (Romae: Catholic Book Agency, 1952), pp. 32-33.

[93] "Il can. 1648, § 2, prevede il caso che il giudice (quindi a giudizio iniziato) riconosca l'esistenza di un contrasto d'interessi tra pupillo, genitori, curatore o che sia inefficace la loro rappresentanza e autorizza il giudice a dare al pupillo un altro rappresentante speciale. Ma nel silenzio del *Codex* si deve pensare che, quando questi casi si verifichino prima dell'inizio del giudizio, spetti all' Ordinario di provvedere alla nomina del curatore speciale."—Giustiniani, "De Curatore Dementis," p. 106; Toso, "De Constitutione Curatoris," p. 118.

CHAPTER VI

THE GUARDIAN'S RIGHT TO STAND IN ECCLESIASTICAL TRIALS

Preliminary Considerations

When a judge receives a bill of complaint (*libellus litis*) and ascertains that he is competent to take cognizance of and decide a case, he must investigate the parties' rights to stand in judgment;[1] for, if the outcome of the judicial process is to be valid, both the plaintiff and the defendant must have the right to stand in judgment. Indeed, the sentence is vitiated by incurable nullity if it has been issued to parties of whom at least one had no right to stand in court.[2]

The expression *persona standi in iudicio*[3] is used in the Code to designate the right to stand in judgment and applies to both the plaintiff and the defendant. Augustine seems to restrict the expression to include only the rights of the plaintiff. He writes: "This term (viz. *habere personam standi in iudicio*) might be rendered by *right to prosecute.*" Moreover, he entitles the commentary on canon 1652, which regulates the rights of religious to stand in court, "Religious as Plaintiffs."[4] This application of the expression only to the plaintiff is contrary: (1) to canon 1892, n. 2: Sententia vitio insanabilis nullitatis laborat, quando: 2°. *Lata est inter partes, quarum altera saltem non habet personam standi in iudicio,* which clearly implies that the expression is not restricted to denote merely the plaintiff; (2) to the discussion attendant upon the text of the present law: "Quidam . . . loca verborum *stare in iudicio* ponerent *actor esse potest.* Verum affirmatur verba stare in iudicio ampliorem habere extensionem et

[1] Cf. canons 1609, § 2; 1646; 1709, § 1; 1892, n. 2.

[2] Canons 1892, n. 2; 1646-1654.

[3] Cf., e.g., canons 1652; 1892, n. 2.

[4] Augustine, *Ecclesiastical Trials,* p. 96, note 2; p. 101.

facultatem interveniendi tribuere etiam ei qui actor non sit,"[5] and (3) to the common doctrine.[6]

Similarly, the phrase *stare in iudicio* means the same as *agere* and *respondere*.[7]

The norms that regulate a person's right to stand in judgment are contained in the chapter of the Code entitled *De Actore et de Reo Convento*.[8] Canon 1646 lays down the general rule that every person not prohibited by the Sacred Canons may institute a suit as plaintiff and that the person who is legitimately sued must answer. The succeeding canons provide for instances which regard: (1) persons not fully developed and persons of abnormal mental condition;[9] (2) religious;[10] (3) moral persons and corporations;[11] and (4) excommunicated persons.[12]

Authors spell out the qualifications that a person must possess in order to enjoy full procedural capacity. These qualifications are: (1) *Capacitas partis;* (2) *legitimatio ad causam;* and (3) *legitimatio ad processum*.[13] They go on to explain that the Code's

---

[5] Roberti, *Schemata*, E, c. 122, note 1.

[6] Cf. A. Couly, *"Les Parties en Cause,"* Le Canoniste, XLVIII (1926), 347: ". . . le droit d'ester en justice—stare in judicio—qui est comme le couronnement et la sanction pratique de la capacité juridique d'une personne physique ou morale. On peut donc le définir, 'le droit de se présenter en justice soit comme défendeur soit comme demandeur';" J. Noval, *Commentarium Codicis Iuris Canonici*, Lib. IV, *De Processibus*, Pars 1, *De Iudiciis* (Augustae Taurinorum: Marietti, 1920), n. 257 (hereafter referred to as *De Iudiciis*); Coronata, *De Processibus*, n. 1171, note 8; J. J. Krol, *The Defendant in Contentious Trials*, The Catholic University of America Canon Law Studies, n. 146 (Washington, D.C.: The Catholic University of America Press, 1942), pp. 67-68.

[7] Cf. e.g., canons 1648, §§ 1-3; 1650; 1653, §§ 1-6; 1654, §§ 1-2.

[8] Tit. IV, Caput I, Canons 1646-1654. The capacity of persons to exercise court actions in ecclesiastical tribunals is founded on principles of natural law and regulated by the positive law and decrees of the competent ecclesiastical authorities. Cf. Cappello, *Summa Iuris Canonici*, III, n. 88; Lega-Bartoccetti, *Commentarius*, I, p. 309, n. 3.

[9] Canons 1648, 1650, 1651.

[10] Canon 1652.

[11] Canons 1649, 1653.

[12] Canon 1654.

[13] Cf. Roberti, *De Processibus*, I, n. 197; S. Goyeneche, *De Processibus*,

expression *legitima persona standi in iudicio* comprises the qualifications *legitimatio ad causam* and *legitimatio ad processum.*[14]

1. *Capacitas Partis*

The capacity to be a party in a trial (*capacitas partis*) cannot exist except in a subject possessing rights. In other words, it is in virtue of his juridic capacity that a person can be a party in a trial, as that *capacitas partis* stems from and is dependent on capacity of right (*capacitas inridica*).[15] As Chiovenda stated it, the capacity to be a subject of a processual relation is but the capacity of right applied in a trial.[16] It follows that if a person has

---

Vol. I, *De Iudiciis in Genere,* Pro manuscripto (Romae: S. Joannis Lat.); Hanssen, *De Sanctione Nullitatis,* nn. 64, 65, 68, 72. These authors make mention also of *ius postulandi,* which has greater importance in civil courts than in ecclesiastical tribunals in which a person possessing the three qualifications listed may validly plead his own cause. In fact, Wernz-Vidal do not mention *ius postulandi.*—Cf. *De Processibus,* n. 203, note 16. Noone (*Nullity in Judicial Acts,* pp. 49-51; 51-52; 64-65) follows Wernz-Vidal, as does Król (*op. cit.,* p. 66). Lega adhered to terms found in the Code and did not introduce into his treatise the terminology derived from the German civil lawyers.

[14] Cf. Roberti, *op. cit.* I, n. 197, II, and n. 231; Cappello, *Summa Iuris Canonici,* III, n. 89; Goyeneche, *op. cit.,* p. 148; Hanssen, *op. cit.,* n. 68; Król, *op. cit.,* p. 67. Król says that it includes also the notion of *capacitas iuridica.* It would be more exact to state that the Code's expression presupposes juridic capacity. Król (*op. cit.,* p. 67) and Noone (*op. cit.,* p. 49) offer English equivalents for the phrases in question: *legitimatio ad causam* is expressed as the legitimation to act in a determined cause; *legitimatio ad processum* is expressed as procedural capacity.

[15] Canon 87 is the fundamental norm regarding capacity of right in the Church.

[16] G. Chiovenda, *Istituzioni di Diritto Processuale Civile* (Napoli, 1936), n. 206: "La capacità d'esser soggetto d'un rapporto giuridico processuale non è altro che la capacità giuridica trasportata nel processo." Cf. also Olivero, *Le Parti nel Giudizio Canonico,* n. 9; Della Rocca, *Istituzioni di Diritto Processuale Canonico,* p. 165, wrote: "La capacità di essere parte altro non è che la capacità giuridica (personalità giuridica, subbiettività giuridica, capacità di diritti) applicata al processo civile, l'idoneità cioè di essere soggetto di diritti processuali." Roberti explains: "(capacitas partis) connectitur cum capacitate iuris substantivi, sed non semper cum ea coincidit. Omnes qui habent cap. iuris. habent quoque capac. partis; sed aliquando capacitate partis pollent etiam ii qui non gaudent plena capacitate

no rights in a particular jurisdiction, he may not, as a rule, obtain the protection of that jurisdiction's tribunals.[17]

2. *Legitimatio ad Causam*

This qualification is necessary before a person who enjoys juridic capacity and the subsequent capacity to be a party in a judicial case may be admitted either as a plaintiff or as a defendant in a definite cause. It may also be referred to as the legitimation to act in a determined cause.[18] Strictly it is not the *actio* itself, but rather a condition or qualification that must be realized in the plaintiff in order to exercise his *actio*.[19]

Unless a person has this juridic relationship, he is estopped from litigating in a trial either in person or through a representative, such as a guardian or proxy. A person, however, may possess passive legitimation—i.e., the ability to be a defendant, and at the same time be devoid of active legitimation—i.e., the right to be a plaintiff.[20] Again, a person may enjoy active legitimation in respect to some cases specified by law[21] and be debarred from acting in all other cases.[22]. In criminal cases, for instance, the Pro-

---

iuridica. Ex quo etiam ostenditur capacitatem partis naturam habere omnino processualem."—*De Processibus,* II, n. 198.

[17] Olivero, *op. cit.,* n. 18: "Un diritto di azione non può darsi ad alcuno che in genere non possa avere alcun diritto, o non quella forma di diritti, relativamente ai quali si fa questione, o per cagione del quale un diritto di azione sussiste. Quindi non può la protezione giuridica essere concessa di contro ad una persona inesistente o non capace di diritti."

[18] Król, *op. cit.,* pp. 66 ff; Noone, *op. cit.,* pp. 64 ff.

[19] Cf. Hanssen, *op. cit.,* n. 68, speaks of *Legitimatio ad causam* as *facultas deducendi causam determinatam in iudicium* and as *condicio ad actionem promovendam, quae si desit, repellitur actor ab agendo in quocumque stadio litis.* Wernz-Vidal note: *"in praxi (legitimatio ad causam) reducitur ad quaestionem utrum quis habeat acitonem vel ea careat."—De Processibus,* n. 203, note 16. Roberti offers the following notion of *legitimatio ad causam*: *"facultas certam actionem proponendi vel eidem respondendi; seu est qualitas certae personae agnita ut ipsa valeat determinatam actionem proponere vel ut coram ipsa actio proponatur."—Op. cit.,* I, n. 231.

[20] Cf. canon 1646. Cf. Noone, *op. cit.,* p. 65.

[21] Cf. canons 1652; 1654, § 1.

[22] Cf. canons 1650; 1652; 1654, § 1; 2263.

moter of Justice alone enjoys active legitimation,[23] while the person liable for the penalty attached to a law or precept possesses passive legitimation.[24]

3. *Legitimatio ad Processum*

By *legitimatio ad processum* is meant the qualification in virtue of which a party in a trial can personally execute procedural acts which produce their proper juridic effects.[25] It is opposed to personal subjective incapacity to exercise one's rights advantageously. Just as in substantive law a person may possess rights and yet be estopped from personally exercising those rights, so in procedural law an individual may enjoy juridic capacity and the required juridic relationship to a particular cause but still be debarred from personally positing processual acts.[26]

The study of procedural law, as well as the mere assistance at a trial, reveals that no less a degree of maturity and mental stability is required properly to exercise court action than is necessary to administer one's property. To prevent the violation of justice by fraud and deceit, the law ordains that unless a person is capable of sufficient knowledge and deliberation, he may be deprived of the right personally to exercise court action.[27]

Those who lack procedural capacity are debarred from acting in judgment as plaintiff and as defendant.[28] This denial of both active and passive *legitimatio ad processum* reveals the nature of this disqualification; it is a protective measure against personal, subjective incapacity.

---

[23] Canon 1934.

[24] Canon 2226, § 1.

[25] Cf. Roberti, *De Processibus,* I, n. 199; Król, *op. cit.,* p. 66; Noone, *op. cit.,* pp. 51-52. Wernz-Vidal, *op. cit.,* I, n. 203, note 16: (legitimatio ad processum) "pendet a capacitate ponendi actus processuales."

[26] Cf. Roberti, *De Processibus,* I, n. 199; Olivero, *Le Parti nel Giudizio Canonico,* n. 35.

[27] Lega-Bartoccetti, *Commentarius,* I, 303: "Prior conditio ad legitimam iurium defensionem est, eos qui agunt aut respondent in iudicio seu actores seu reos plena frui rerum cognitione et suae deliberationis libertate quo tutius valeant iuribus consulere. Secus non per se isti audiantur in iudicio."

[28] Cf. Olivero, *op. cit.,* n. 19.

The law affords protection proportionate to their general needs to minors,[29] to the insane,[30] to prodigals,[31] and to feeble-minded persons.[32].

Modern civil jurists make a sharp distinction between *legitimatio ad causam* and *legitimatio ad processum. Legitimatio ad causam* is conceived by them as an objective prerequisite for a lawsuit rooted in a right that can be enforced by judicial action; in other words, a right enforceable by court action begets juridic relationship to a case, i.e. a so-called action. *Legitimatio ad processum* is conceived as the subjective, personal ability of the litigants to execute personally procedural acts.[33]

The Code, on the other hand, includes both these concepts in the expression *persona standi in iudicio.*[34]

Consequently, in canonical trials, the absence of either qualification vitiates a sentence with irremediable nullity. For they are required for the validity of a sentence by canon 1892, n. 2., in the expression *persona standi in iudicio.*[35]

An exposition of the rules which govern the rights of persons to stand in judgment is important in this treatise; for, when considering the question of admitting a mentally ill person's guardian to stand in a canonical trial, the ward's juridic capacity (*capacitas iuridica*) and relationship to the cause (*legitimatio ad causam*) must be examined and his lack of procedural capacity (*legitimatio ad processum*), because of mental illness, must be ascertained.

Just as a sentence is vitiated by irremediable nullity if it has

---

[29] Canon 1648.

[30] Canon 1648.

[31] Canon 1650.

[32] Canon 1650.

[33] Cf. Roberti, *De Processibus,* I, n. 231; Hanssen, *op. cit.,* n. 68; Noone, *op. cit.,* pp. 49, 64 ff.

[34] Cf. canons, 1650; 1652; 1653; 1654; 1892, n. 2. Roberti, *op. cit.,* I, n. 231; Hanssen, *op. cit.,* n. 68.

[35] Cf. Roberti, *op. cit.,* I, n. 231; Hanssen, *op. cit.* n. 68; Roberti indicates briefly the essential difference in these qualifications: "Legitimatio ad processum est praesuppositum processus, quod requiritur ad validitatem singulorum actuum processualium. Legitimatio ad causam est praesuppositum litis, quod sufficit ut exsistat tempore decisionis."—*Op. cit.,* I, n. 231.

been issued to parties of whom at least one had not the right to stand in court, so is it null if someone acted in the same of another without a legitimate mandate.[36] These two causes of irremediable nullity, contemplated in canon 1892, may appear in trials in which a guardian pleads or defends the case of a mentally ill person. It these cases, the ward is strictly the party in the trial:[37] he is the subject in whom the right under discussion is claimed to inhere; his substantial rights will be affected by the outcome of the trial. His guardian is considered as forming one person with him, as long as he acts for his ward and in the name of his ward.[38] In the mentally ill person, consequently, must be found the qualifications required by a law of parties in trials, except, of course, those qualifications which the law supposes he lacks and which are supplied through the agency of the guardian. On the other hand, the guardian is the legal representative of his ward and he must demonstrate his legal right to represent his protégé before the ecclesiastical tribunal.

Consequently, the following pages will discuss briefly disqualifications that arise from the status of infidels, excommunicated Catholics, baptized non-Catholics, and religious, and conclude with consideration on the guardian's decree of appointment.

---

[36] Canon 1892, nn. 2, 3.

[37] "Partes in iudicio sunt '*illi qui petunt executionem alicuius juris, et illi relate ad quos petunt*'. Non sunt partes illi qui petunt nomine aliorum, e.g., tutor, curator, etc."—F. Roberti, *Iuris Processualis Compendium* (Romae: Apud Custodiam Librariam Pontificii Instituti Utriusque Iuris), I, n. 113. That the guardian is not strictly the party when acting for his ward is apparent in the opposition contained in canon 1757, § 3, n. 1: Qui partes sunt in causa, aut partium vice funguntur veluti tutor in causa pupilli. Guardians, however, are included in the term *pars litigans* of canon 1733 (Si pars litigans moriatur aut statum mutet aut cesset ab officio cuius ratione agit), so that Olivero rightly observes that the Code is not consistently exact in the use of the term *pars*.

[38] Cf. Roberti, *op. cit.*, n. 191, 199; Lega-Bartoceetti, *Commentarius*, I, 302; Olivero, *op. cit.*, nn. 9, 35; Della Rocca, *op. cit.*, pp. 164 ff.; Stitt, *De Promotore Iustitiae*, n. 56; Aguirre, "De Curatore Dementis," p. 296; 25 Am. Jur., *Guardian and Ward*, § 149.

Article I. The Ward's Freedom from Canonical Disqualification

A. Disqualifications of Infidels

In order to become a subject of rights and obligations in the Church, a person must be validly baptized. This principle is stated in canon 87: *"Baptismate homo constituitur in Ecclesia Christi persona cum omnibus christianorum iuribus et officiis. . . ."* Valid baptism, therefore, begets juridic capacity in the Church. By becoming a member of the Church, one receives both the privileges and the obligations of its law, just as entrance into civil society and obtaining membership therein of themselves give a person the legal capacity to enjoy the privileges of the law of that society and to be bound by its mandates.[39]

An infidel, though he be a catechumen,[40] does not generally enjoy juridic personality in the Church; he is not a subject of ecclesiastical rights, either substantive or processual, nor has he any direct, subjective obligations towards the Church as an external, juridically constituted society.[41] Since they enjoy no ecclesiastical

---

[39] In civil law today, all persons whether they be subjects or externs are persons in law, though citizenship is required as far as certain political rights,—e.g., the right to vote—are concerned. In order, however, that one may be designated as a *persona Christiana* in the Catholic Church, valid baptism is required. Cf. Cocchi, *Commentarium,* II, *De Personis,* 3. ed., 1948, 14; Claeys Bouuaert-Simenon, *Manuale Juris Canonici,* I, 137.

[40] Because they are unbaptized, catechumens are still infidels. They may have received the gift of Faith but they do not possess that bond of union with the Church which is acquired only through a valid Baptism of water. Since they are still classed as infidels, whatever is noted in this section on infidels applies to them. Cf. J. A. McCloskey, *The Subject of Ecclesiastical Law According to Canon 12,* The Catholic University of America Canon Law Studies, n. 165 (Washington, D.C.: The Catholic University of America Press, 1943), p. 49.

[41] Cf. A. Ottaviani, *Institutiones Iuris Publici Ecclesiastici* (2 vols., Vol. I, 3. ed., Romae: Typis Polyglottis Vaticanis, 1947), I, n. 160: "... quemadmodum nonnisi ii qui de Christi ovili sunt, pastoralibus curis Petri sunt commissi ('pasce oves meas') ac proinde legibus Ecclesiae reguntur ac diriguntur, ita etiam ii tantum qui eiusdem gregis participes sunt facti, virgae et baculo pastoris seu iudicis et poenis ecclesiasticis subiiciuntur." Cf. also Olivero, *op. cit.,* n. 20.

rights and do not recognize the authority of the Church,[42] infidels are ordinarily denied the opportunity of standing in judgment in Church tribunals.[43]

In a preliminary draft of the Code, the possibility of infidels, heretics, and other non-Catholics to enjoy an *actio* was explicitly regulated: *"Infideles, haeretici et acatholici actione fruantur quoties animae salus, aut Ecclesiae vel fidelium utilitas videantur iudici eam postulare."*[44] Other *schemata* and the final draft of the Code did not include this norm. A footnote, however, to *Schema C,* can. 106, § 5, which regarded the *excommunicati tolerati,* read: *"Quid de acatholicis? R recolit haereticos esse ipso facto excommunicatos; My et Ma infidelibus actionem concederent, quia agendo videntur semper aliquam observantiam Ecclesiae profiteri; Dl actionem infidelium censet non admittendam; N sequentem formulam proponeret: Infideles, haeretici, etc.* as above.[45] The commission later decided on canon 1654, omitting any mention of infidels, heretics, etc.

Special reasons, however, especially in connection with matrimonial cases, may occasion an unbaptized person's being allowed to act as plaintiff in an ecclesiastical court.[46] This is an exceptional case and in such contrast to fundamental principles of law, that some authors hold that the ensuing trial may not properly be styled an ecclesiastical process.[47] In these cases, the natural or civil

---

[42] Cf. Olivero, *op. cit.,* n. 20; Roberti, *De Processibus,* I, n. 231, IV, 1.

[43] Cf. Roberti, *op. cit.,* I, n. 231, IV: "Carent legitimatione activa [ad causam] . . . infideles generaliter, qui cum iura in Ecclesia non habeant, nec eius auctoritatem agnoscant, ne ab eius iurisdictione quidem protectionem iuridicam exigere valent; qua prohibitione . . . non negantur iura naturalia et civilia infidelium immo et eorum actiones, sed generaliter tantum prohibetur ne eas coram Ecclesia proponant. . . ."

[44] *Schemata,* A, can. 140, § 3.

[45] *Schemata,* C, can. 106, § 5.

[46] Roberti writes: "rationes autem variae esse possunt, e.g. utilitas partis catholicae quae matrimonium inire cupiat cum acatholico de cuius matrimonii valore dubitatur, privilegium fori, ut puta si infidelis clericum conveniat, et generaliter ratio litis consortii necessarii vel etiam simplicis." —*De Processibus,* I, n. 231, IV, 1.

[47] Cf. Cappello, "De Acatholicorum Incapacitate Agendi in Foro Eccle-

juridic capacity of the plaintiff is taken into consideration by the ecclesiastical authority.[48]

It must be added here that when an infidel seeks to act as plaintiff in a matrimonial case recourse must be made to the Holy Office, to which is reserved the right to admit non-Catholics to act as plaintiffs in ecclesiastical courts. The Holy Office issued this declaration on January 27, 1928:[49] "Utrum in causis matrimonialibus acatholicus, sive baptizatus sive non baptizatus, actoris partes agere possit?" The answer given was: "Negative, seu standum C.I.C., praesertim can. 87. Si quidem autem speciales occurrant rationes ad admittendos acatholicos ut actores in huiusmodi causis, recurrendum ad Supremam S.C.S.O. in singulis casibus."[50]

This disposition of the Holy Office was incorporated into the *Instructio "Provida Mater Ecclesia"* issued by the *S.C. de Disci-*

---

siastico," IV—*Miscellanea Vermeerseh,* I, 396-399; Hanssen, *De Sanctione Nullitatis,* n. 64.

[48] Cf. Cappello, *loc. cit.;* Hanssen, *loc. cit.* Olivero (*Le Parti nel Giudizio Canonico,* n. 20) advances a new view: He holds that in admitting this exception the Holy Office has created a new type of person in the Church, procedural in character and in substance, existing apart from a subject of substantial rights.

[49] The decision was approved by the Supreme Pontiff on January 26, and was dated from the Holy Office January 27, 1928. A subsequent question (cf. *AAS,* XXXI [1939], 131) refers to this decision as given by the Holy Office on January 18, 1928. Cf. T. L. Bouscaren, *The Canon Law Digest* (3 vols., Milwaukee: Bruce Publishing Company, 1934, 1943, 1954), I, 762-763; II, 530-531.

[50] *AAS,* XX (1928), 75. Cf. Bouscaren, *op. cit.* I, pp. 762-763. Roberti observes, commenting on the cited declaration of the Holy Office and the reference made to Canon 87 which he cites in full: "Iamvero non est dubium quin 'actio' inter iura est accensenda: quae in ipsis fontibus romanis (Ita Celsus in 61. D. XLIV. 3) dicitur: "ius persequendi iudicio quod sibi debetur! Merito autem ab Ecclesia tutela iuridica destituuntur ii qui eius auctoritatem agnoscere recusant, sc.: a) Infideles, qui, cum sint extra Ecclesiam, nullum ius in eadem sibi vindicare possunt. Iidem iura servant in ordine naturali et civili, sed eorumdem nequeunt ab Ecclesia protectionem invocare . . . Nec praetereundum est acatholicos facile posse ecclesiasticam sententiam spernere, quae forte ipsis extiterit contraria . . ." Roberti, "Animadversiones," *Apollinaris,* I, (1928), 215.

plina Sacramentorum on August 15, 1936. Art. 35, § 3 of the *Instructio* reads: Actoris partes agere nequeunt in causis matrimonialibus acatholici sive baptizati sive non baptizati; si quidem autem speciales occurrant rationes ad eosdem admittendos, recurrendum est in singulis casibus ad S.C.S.O.[51]

On April 20, 1931, in a private reply to the Bishop of Harrisburg, the Holy Office stated that diocesan curias are competent to adjudicate summary cases[52] even when an infidel acts as petitioner.[53] Therefore, the debarment of non-baptized persons from acting as plaintiffs in matrimonial cases is restricted to formal trials; they are not estopped from acting as plaintiffs in summary cases under canon 1990.

In view of the foregoing: (a) In the event that both parties involved in a marriage case are infidels or that one party is an infidel and the other a non-Catholic, the case may not be brought up for decision in a formal ecclesiastical trial, unless the Sacred Congregation of the Holy Office authorizes it. A sentence issued by an unauthorized court would be vitiated by irremediable nullity.[54] (b) In formal trials involving an infidel and a Catholic: if the infidel seeks the role of plaintiff, the above-mentioned Congregation must give its authorization before the cause can be properly instituted; when the Catholic sues against the infidel, that authorization is not required.[55]

Authors extend the disposition given by the Holy Office on January 27, 1928, to deny infidels capacity to stand in judgment in any contentious trial in which they seek the role of plaintiff.[56]

---

[51] *AAS*, XXVIII (1936), p. 313ff.

[52] Cf. Canon 1990.

[53] Cf. Bouscaren, *op. cit.*, II, p. 552.

[54] Canon 1892, n. 2. Cf. Doheny, *Canonical Procedure in Matrimonial Cases*, I, pp. 115, 129; Noone, *Nullity in Judicial Acts*, p. 50; Roberti, *De Processibus*, I, nn. 198, 221; Wernz-Vidal, *De Processibus*, n. 210.

[55] Cf. Beste, *Introductio in Codicem*, pp. 851-854.

[56] Roberti, in his comment on that declaration of the Holy Office, writes: "Ultimo quaerimus utrum exposita declaratio afficiat tantum causas matrimoniales an omnes causas quae ab acatholicis proponantur. Non est dubium quin declaratio spectet tantum causas matrimoniales; sed cum eaedem rationes valeant et pro reliquis causis, censemus a pari et pro his

The general disqualification, however, which bars infidels from bringing action in an ecclesiastical court cannot violate their natural rights. A sufficient reason may exist to justify the admittance of an unbaptized person before church tribunals. For example, he may be permitted to sue a cleric before an ecclesiastical judge.[57] It is suggested here that the infidel seek the permission of the local ordinary when desirous of appearing in a church trial as plaintiff. So doing, he will anticipate any exceptions against his person for lack of the right to stand in ecclesiastical judgments,[58] and will make inoperative the sanction of canon 1892, n. 2,, regarding the sentence; for, authors who consider this peculiar situation of an infidel appearing in judgment before an ecclesiastical tribunal state that the permission of the ordinary of the place where the tribunal is located will give the unbaptized person the right to stand in judgment in such an instance. They deduce the power of the ordinary to grant this permission from the fact that the Code permits him in exceptional cases to allow non-Catholic advocates and procurators to exercise procedural activity in church courts.[59]

As regards criminal trials, it is obvious that infidels cannot be cited to them as defendants. The principle enunciated in canon 12—"legibus mere ecclesiasticis non tenentur qui baptismum non receperunt"—applies to criminal law. Canon 2241, § 1, reads: "censura est poena qua *homo baptizatus* delinquens et contumax, quibusdam bonis spiritualibus vel spiritualibus adnexis privatur"; and canon 2291 states: "poenae vindicativae quae omnes *fideles* pro delictorum gravitate afficere possunt. . . ." Consequently, there would be no point to an infidel's appearing as a defendant in a criminal trial *in foro ecclesiastico;* for the Church could not punish him in the event of his being convicted.[60]

---

vigere interpretationem."—*Apollinaris,* I (1928), 217. Cf. also Hanssen, *De Sanctione Nullitatis,* n. 70; Olivero, *Le Parti nel Giudizio Canonico,* n. 24.

[57] Cf. Roberti, *De Processibus,* I, n. 231, IV, 1.

[58] Cf. canon 1628, § 1.

[59] Roberti, *op. cit.,* I, n. 213, IV, 1; Noone, *op. cit.,* p. 50; canon 1657, § 1.

[60] Ottaviani, (*Institutiones Iuris Publici Ecclesiastici,* I, n. 160) writes: ". . . infideles omnes penitus exempti sunt a potestate ecclesiastici magistra-

B. Disqualifications of Excommunicated Catholics

a. *Excommunicati vitandi* and *excommunicati tolerati* after declaratory or condemnatory sentence.

The *persona standi in iudicio* of the *excommunicati vitandi*[61] and of the *tolerati* after sentence is delineated in canon 1654, § 1: *Excommunicatis vitandis aut toleratis post sententiam declaratoriam vel condemnatoriam permittitur ut per se ipsi agant tantummodo ad impugnandam iustitiam aut legitimitatem ipsius excommunicationis; per procuratorem, ad aliud quodvis animae suae praeiudicium avertendum; in reliquis ab agendo repelluntur.*

This is a clear statement concerning the personal right to stand in judgment possessed by these categories of excommunicated persons. Though these persons retain the juridical personality conferred upon them by baptism, the censure of excommunication places on them a bond restricting seriously their rights in the Church.[62] Very severe and rigorous is the restriction regarding

---

tus, videlicet, tamquam rei conveniri nequeunt, qualibet de causa, coram tribunalibus Ecclesiae. 'Quid enim mihi—inquit Apostolus—de iis qui foris sunt iudicare?' (I Cor. 5. 12)." Cf. also canon 201, § 1: Potestas iurisdictionis potest in solos subditos directe exerceri.

[61] According to canon 2258, § 2, an excommunicated person is not *vitandus* unless: (1) he has been excommunicated *nominatim* by the Apostolic See; (2) the excommunication has been publicly proclaimed; and (3) it has been expressly stated in the decree or sentence that he is *vitandus.* This canon also safeguards the ruling of canon 2343, § 1, n. 1, which declares that anyone who lays violent hands on the Supreme Pontiff is *ipso facto vitandus.*

[62] McCloskey distinguishes between members and subjects of the Church: "A *member* of the Church possesses complete (*plena*) juridic personality (capacity), because he not only is bound by the obligations imposed by the Church, but he may also enjoy the corresponding rights which are granted to the members of the various states of life that exist in the Church, e.g., the clerical state, the religious state, the lay state. One who is only a *subject* of the Church, on the other hand, possesses incomplete (*minus plena*) juridic personality (capacity), because he is generally held to all the obligations, but is deprived of the rights. either entirely or partially."—*The Subject of Ecclesiastical Law According to Canon 12,* pp. 129-130; cf. also Coronata, *De Processibus,* n. 1173, note 4.

their legitimation to act in ecclesiastical processes. In fact, personally they may institute only the *actio* to impugn the justice or legality of their excommunication.[63] For the sake of averting spiritual harm, they may promote court action by proxy. Excepting these two cases, the judge is bound to reject their application for judicial protection.[64] In all other cases they are excluded from instituting a suit in ecclesiastical courts. Thus their active legitimation is severely curtailed.[65]

The lack of active legitimation has for a serious consequence that the sentence issued at the end of a judicial process in which the *excommunicati vitandi* or *tolerati post sententiam* act as plaintiffs is invalid.[66] This is the logical conclusion to be drawn from the consideration of canons 1654, § 1, and 1892, n. 2. No positive sanction of nullity need be attached to the law prohibiting them from initiating a lawsuit. The prohibition itself deprives them of

---

[63] This is a legitimate act of self-defense. Cf. Cappello, *Summa Iuris Canonici,* III, n. 95.

[64] Torquebiau writes: "S'ils sont *demandeurs,* le juge est tenu de les exclure, c'est-à-dire de rejeter leur demande, soit d'office, soit à la requête du defendeur (Can. 1654, § 1; 1628, § 3)";—cf. *Traité de Droit Canonique,* sous la direction de R. Naz (4 vols., Paris: Letouzey et Ané, 1948-1949), IV, n. 232 a. (The following authors collaborated in the production of the *Traité di Droit Canonique*: P. Claeys Bouuaert, C. de Clercq, H. Durand, E. Jombart, Ch. Lefebvre, P. Torquebiau).

[65] Writing of a certain class of communists, Del Corpo has this to say: ". . . nemo est qui illum de haeresi non arguat et inter excommunicatos non recenseat (c. 2314, § 1, n. 1); et, qua talis, valent pro ipso, quoad usum iurium ecclesiasticorum, quorum unum est ius actionis, cann. 87 et 1628, § 3."—"De Jure Agendi in Iudiciis Ecclesiasticis Communistarum aliorumque Acatholicorum," *Monitor Ecclesiasticus,* LXXV (1950), p. 98, n. 4.

[66] Cf. Roberti, *De Processibus,* I, n. 208, III: "Defectus legitimationis activae ad causam cum agitur de excommunicatis vitandis aut toleratis quorum excommunicatio inflicta vel declarata est per sententiam vel per modum praecepti, est absolutus; ideoque processus et sententia nullitate laborant ob defectum personae standi in iudicio." Cf. also Hanssen, *De Sanctione Nullitatis,* n. 70; Coronata, *De Processibus,* n. 1156, b: "Ratio cur exceptio de incompetentia absoluta aut excommunicatione vitandi vel post sententiam semper proponi possit, est quia talia iudicia nulla sunt" (Coronata bases his statement on canons 1892 and 1893).

a necessary qualification to obtain a valid sentence—namely, the *persona standi in iudicio,* required for validity by canon 1892, n. 2.[67]

The reasons for this disqualification are summed up in the words of Pope Innocent IV, as recorded by the Council of Lyons (1245): "ut ex hoc magis censura Ecclesiastica timeatur, communionis periculum evitetur, contumaciae vitium reprimatur, et excommunicati (dum a communibus actibus excluduntur) rubore suffusi ad humilitatis gratiam, et reconciliationis effectum facilius inclinentur."[68]

The *excommunicati vitandi* and *tolerati post sententiam* possess passive legitimation to act—i.e., they have *persona standi in iudicio* as defendants. Therefore, when lawfully summoned, they have the right to appear in court in order to defend themselves against a suit brought against them; and they have also the obligation to answer the summons, lest they derive profit from their own malice.[69]

---

[67] Lega is of the opinion that the legislator did not intend to state that the judicial acts of such excommunicated persons are invalid; but this opinion, found on page 331 of the *Commentarius,* contradicts what had been previously stated on page 259.—Cf. Lega-Bartoccetti, *Commentarius,* I, 259, 331. After stating that these excommunicates do not enjoy active legitimation, Wernz-Vidal rightly observe: "Excommunicati etiam vitandi non absolute et intrinsece sunt inhabiles ad agendum, sed sola prohibitione Ecclesiae impediuntur." The conclusion, however, which they draw from this statement is against the obvious meaning of canon 1654, § 1 and 1892, n. 2.: "quare si a iudice ex officio non repelluntur nec a reo exceptio proponatur, sententia robur debitum obtinet." They do, however, offer a remedy to the defendant: "adhuc tamen exceptio proponi potest ad impediendam executionem."—Cf. Wernz-Vidal, *Ius Canonicum,* VI, n. 206, note 30.

Roberti stands for the nullity of the judicial sentence: "Si agatur de excommunicatis vitandis vel tolerandis post sententiam declaratoriam vel condemnatoriam, ii ex officio semper excludendi sunt, salvo tamen praescripto canonis 1654, § 1 (c. 1628, § 3). Sententia in his casibus illegitime prolata, laboraret insanabili nullitate (c. 1892, 2°.)—"*De Processibus,* I, n. 158, I, 1, a; see also, *op. cit.,* I, n. 208. Cf. also *Traité de Droit Canonique,* IV, n. 600; Hanssen, *op. cit.,* pp. 83, 84.

[68] Cf. C. 1, *de exceptionibus,* II, 12, in VI°.

[69] Canon 1646. Cf. Roberti, *op. cit.,* I, n. 208; Cappello, *Summa Iuris Canonici,* III, n. 95. 2; Lega-Bartoccetti, *Commentarius,* I, 329; *Traité de Droit Canonique,* IV, n. 232 b.

Among the instances wherein an *excommunicatus vitandus* or *sententiatus* may act to avert spiritual harm are included matrimonial cases.[70] In the interest of their salvation, therefore, these persons may be admitted to impugn the validity of their marriage *per procuratorem*.[71] It follows that the *exceptio excommunicationis* which would generally exclude any action initiated by them[72] does not bar these excommunicated persons from acting through a proxy to impugn the validity of their marriage. The defender of the bond, however, should mention the fact of excommunication in his objections to the character and credibility of the plantiff.[73]

b. *Alii excommunicati.*

This category of excommunicated persons consists of all who are not *vitandi* or *sententiati*. The members of this group may generally stand in judgment both as plaintiffs and defendants;[74] but they may be repelled from acting as plaintiffs by reason of a judicial exception, invoked in view of their excommunication.[75] When such an exception is raised, the excommunicated person loses active legitimation to the case, and the trial must normally be suspended until he clears himself of the censure.[76] This con-

---

[70] Cf. Roberti, *De Processibus,* I, n. 205; Regatillo, *Institutiones Iuris Canonici,* II, n. 435; P. R. Coyle, *Judicial Exceptions,* The Catholic University of America Canon Law Studies, n. 193 (Washington, D.C.: The Catholic University of America Press, 1944), pp. 106ff.; cf. also Cappello, *Summa Iuris Canonici,* III, n. 95, 1.

[71] Cf. canon 1654, § 1.

[72] Cf. canons 1654, § 1, 2263.

[73] Cf. Coyle, *Judicial Exceptions,* p. 107.

[74] Cf. canon 1654, § 2.

[75] Cf. Król, *The Defendant in Contentious Trials,* p. 74; Beste, *Introductio in Codicem,* p. 801; Cappello, *Summa Iuris Canonici,* III, n. 95, 3; Coyle, *Judicial Exceptions,* p. 106; Noone, *Nullity in Judicial Acts,* p. 67. Cf. canon 169, § 2, of the procedural law of the Oriental Rites: Alii excommunicati generatim stare in iudicio queunt, nisi exceptio opponatur ad normam can. 143, § 3. Can. 143, § 3 corresponds exactly to can 1628, § 3 of the Latin Code.

[76] Cf. Roberti, *De Processibus,* I, n. 208. Hanssen, *De Sanctione Nullitatis,* n. 70; Torquebiau, *loc. cit.*

clusion seems to be the clear implication of canons 1628, § 3; 1654, § 1; 2223, § 4; and 2263.

When, however, an *excommunicatus toleratus* is acting to avert some spiritual harm, as when he impugns the validity of his marriage, the exception of excommunication would not hold against him. This follows logically, *a fortiori,* from what was stated about the *excommunicati vitandi* and *sententiati* in similar cases.[77] Nor does the Code oblige him to act through a proxy, as it does the latter in these cases.

Canon 1628, § 3, allows that the exception of excommunication be raised at any period or stage of the trial, provided that it be raised before the final sentence.

C. Disqualifications of Baptized Non-Catholics

Under the expression *baptized non-Catholics* fall schismatics, heretics, and apostates.[78] These persons are in every respect subject to the authority of the Church; for by valid baptism they were made her subjects.[79] Since they have juridic personality in the Church, their status differs radically from that of infidels. But the obstacles of heresy, schism, and apostasy impede the bond of communion with the Church and curtail their rights most seriously.[80]

The Code does not directly deny them the right to stand in judgment. It does so, however, indirectly by placing them under the censure of excommunication. Canon 2314, § 1, reads: *Omnes a christiana fide apostatae et omnes et singuli haeretici aut schismatici incurrunt ipso facto excommunicationem.* Consequently, they lack active legitimation[81] and may be denied the right to stand in judgment as plaintiffs on the grounds that they are excommunicated.[82]

Moreover, the Sacred Congregation of the Holy Office has declared that baptized non-Catholics are unable to act as plaintiffs in

---

[77] Coyle, *op. cit.,* p. 107.

[78] Cf. canon 1325, § 2, § 3.

[79] Cf. canon 87.

[80] Cf. canon 87.

[81] Canon 1654. Canon 2263 also applies here.

[82] Cf. Noval, *De Processibus,* n. 250; Olivero, *Le Parti nel Giudizio Canonico,* n. 24.

matrimonial cases, calling attention to the observance of canon 87.[83] Recourse must be had in each case to that Sacred Congregation when special reasons exist for admitting these non-Catholics as plaintiffs, to impugn the validity of their marriage.[84] The permission of the Holy Office is required for the validity of the sentence.[85]

As stated above, this response of the Holy Office refers directly and immediately to the right to act as plaintiff in formal trials impugning the validity of marriage; but in virtue of its reference to canon 87, authors extend it to cover every contentious trial,[86] recognizing in apostasy, schism, and heresy *as such* sources of disability distinct from that of excommunication.[87] Ordinarily, therefore, baptized non-Catholics do not have legitimation to act as plaintiffs in Church trials.[88] Consequently, should they appear as plaintiffs in an ecclesiastical trial without the proper authorization, the opposing party may raise an exception against their right to stand in judgment, basing his opposition on canon 87 and 1654.

For the lawful admission of baptized non-Catholics as defendants in contentious and criminal trials, no special permission is required, as the law states without qualification that a defendant who is lawfully summoned must respond and as subjects of the Church they may be summoned.[89]

D. Disqualifications of Religious

(1) *General Principle.*

Without the consent of their Superiors, religious have no personal standing in court.[90] This is the general principle regarding

[83] Cf. Resp. 27 ian. 1928, cited above, p. 111.

[84] *Ibid.*

[85] Cf. Del Corpo, *op. cit.*, 98; Cappello, *op. cit.*, III, p. 141-142.

[86] Cf. above, p. 112.

[87] Cf. Del. Corpo, "De iure agendi in iudiciis ecclesiasticis," p. 102; Olivero, *op. cit.*, n. 21, Roberti, "Animadversiones," to Response of Jan 27, 1928—*AAS*, XX (1928), 75., *Apollinaris*, I (1928). (Hereafter cited "Animadversiones".)

[88] Cf. Wernz-Vidal, *De Processibus*, n. 210.

[89] Cf. canons 1646, 87.

[90] Canon 1652: Religiosi sine Superiorum consensu non habent personam

the court rights of religious; and it applies to all religious, whether they have solemn or simple vows.[91] Novices, however, are not religious properly so-called;[92] and though they enjoy the benefits and privileges of religious,[93] they do not lose their right to stand in judgment.[94] Men or women who lead a community life under the government of superiors and according to approved constitutions or regulations but without the three vows required of religious life are not properly religious.[95] Consequently they are not *per se* included under the provisions of canon 1652;[96] by force of their constitutions, however, they may be under limitations as to their right to stand in judgment.[97]

The principle of canon 1652 is a natural consequence of the nature of the religious profession. By the vow of poverty a religious abdicates the habitual or actual right of holding or administering property, and by the vow of obedience he becomes dependent on the will of his superior. It follows that, generally speaking, they need the consent of their superiors to plead or defend their rights in court.[98]

---

standi in iudicio, nisi in casibus qui sequuntur . . . Cf. Woywod-Smith, *A Practical Commentary,* II, n. 1626.

[91] Cf. Lega-Bartoccetti, *Commentarius,* I, 313, 316; Król, *The Defendant in Contentious Trials,* p. 70.

[92] Cf. canon 488, n. 7.

[93] Cf. canon 567, § 1.

[94] An argument may be construed from canon 19. See also Hanssen, *De Sanctione Nullitatis in Processu Canonico,* n. 69; Noone, *Nullity in Judicial Acts,* p. 56.

[95] Canon 673, § 1. Cf. Woywod-Smith, *A Practical Commentary,* I, n. 578.

[96] Cf. Król, *The Defendant in Contentious Trials,* p. 71.

[97] Cf. Roberti, *De Processibus,* I, n. 207. V; Hanssen, *De Sanctione Nullitatis in Processu Canonico,* n. 69.

[98] Cf. Augustine, *Ecclesiastical Trials,* p. 101; Lega-Bartoccetti, *Commentarius,* I, 313: "Unde ex voto paupertatis, religiosus personam non habet standi in iudicio, nempe *in rem suam seu nomine suo*"; p. 316: "Etenim ob votum paupertatis et obedientiae simul iuncta, religiosus est quasi filius familias non sui iuris sed in tutela positus cum *velle* et *nolle* amplius non habeat. Cumque in religionem aut in alium bona, iura, actiones suas transtulerit *sine consensu* superioris *non habet personam standi in iudicio. . . .*" Cf. also *ibid.,* p. 317. Cf. V. Pichler, *Candidatus Jurispruden-*

This principle holds whether a religious is to act as plaintiff or as defendant in the case.[99] It applies, however, to religious as individuals when suing or defending a case in their own name,[100] and not to religious *collective sumpti* as a moral person (e.g., a convent, province, or order as such)[101] or when a religious acts *nomine religionis* by reason of his office (i.e., as rector, or administrator).[102] When a religious is appointed to a certain office, e.g., as rector of a church, administrator of a pious foundation, chaplain of an institution, permission to stand in judgment, as plantiff and defendant, *ratione ipsius officii,* is included in the appointment.[103]

(2) *Exceptional Cases.*

The Code admits of exceptions to the foregoing general principle. In these exceptional cases, a religious may stand in judgment without his superior's consent.

First exception: if the suit is concerned with vindicating against the religious organization rights which the religious has acquired

---

tiae Sacrae seu Juris Canonici, secundum Gregorii Papae IX Decretalium Titulos Explicati (3. ed., Sumptibus G. Schluter and M. Happash, 1726-1728), *De Judiciis,* lib. II, tit. 1, n. 9 (hereafter cited *Candidatus*); A. Reiffenstuel, *Jus Canonicum Universum* (5 vols. in 6, Romae, 1831-1834), lib. II. tit. 1, n. 165.

[99] Cf. Lega-Bartoccetti, *Commentarius,* I, 316: "Religiosus . . . *sine consensu* superioris *non habet personam standi in iudicio* sive ut *actor* sive uti *reus.*" Since the principle applies to all religious, whether they have solemn or simple vows, Coronata's statement regarding religious with simple vows cannot be defended: "Religiosi vero votorum simplicium, circa bona quorum dominium retinent, valide, non autem licite, convenire aut conveniri possunt, ut videtur; de licentia autem Superiorum etiam licite." Cf. *De Processibus,* n. 1177. The Code does not make the distinction, neither may we. Cf. Król, *op. cit.,* p. 71; Reiffenstuel, *loc. cit.*

[100] Cf. Roberti, *De Processibus,* I, n. 207, I; Wernz-Vidal, *De Processibus,* n. 206; Cappello, *op. cit.,* III, n. 93.

[101] Cf. Lega-Bartoccetti, *Commentarius,* I, 312; Goyeneche, *De Processibus,* I, 151; cf. Cappello, *op. cit.,* III, n. 93, 1.

[102] Cf. Wernz-Vidal, *De Processibus,* n. 206; Goyeneche, *loc. cit.*

[103] Cf. Augustine, *Ecclesiastical Trials,* p. 102; Wernz-Vidal, *De Processibus,* n. 206; Roberti, *De Processibus,* I, n. 207; Coronata, *De Processibus,* n. 1177; Goyeneche, *De Processibus,* I, 151; Król *The Defendant in Contentious Trials,* p. 71.

by his profession.[104] Such rights are, for example: the right to remain in religion;[105] the right to return to religion when unjustly expelled;[106] the right to proper sustenance;[107] the right to share in the benefits and privileges of his community.[108] Moreover, he may impugn the validity of his religious profession without seeking his superior's consent.[109] Though he may defend any and all spiritual rights accruing to him from his religious profession without that consent, he would need permission to vindicate spiritual rights not arising from his profession, e.g., the validity of marriage previous to his entrance into religion.

Finally, in order to vindicate such rights as he acquired by profession in a suit against strangers to the community, his parents, for instance, who might impugn his profession, he must obtain his superior's consent; for in such a case he would not be defending himself against the religious organization.[110]

Second exception: if he legitimately lives outside the religious house, and the defense of his rights becomes urgent.[111] A religious may be legitimately absent from his community by reason of his studies,[112] because of ill health,[113] or when his community has been dispersed or the religious are prevented from leading community life because of persecution.[114] The defense of his rights

---

[104] Canon 1652, n. 1. Cf. Woywod-Smith, *A Practical Commentary,* II, n. 1626. Cf. Pichler, *op. cit.,* lib. I, tit. I, n. 9.

[105] Cf. Roberti, *De Processibus,* I, n. 207, V; Coronata *De Processibus,* n. 1177; Cappello, *op. cit.,* IV, n. 93, 2. 1°; Reiffenstuel, *op. cit., lib.* II, tit. 1, n. 170..

[106] Cf. Augustine, *Ecclesiastical Trials,* p. 102; Roberti, *loc. cit.;* Coronata, *loc. cit.*

[107] Cf. Coronata, *ibid.,* note 3; Noone, *Nullity in Judicial Acts,* p. 56; Cappello, *loc. cit.*

[108] Cf. Roberti, *loc. cit.;* Noone, *loc. cit.*

[109] Cf. Conc. Trident., sess. XXV, *de regularibus,* C. 19; Roberti, *loc. cit.*

[110] Cf. Roberti, *loc. cit.;* Lega-Bartoccetti, *Commentarius,* I, 317.

[111] Canon 1652, n. 2. Cf. Woywod-Smith, *A Practical Commentary,* II, n.. 1626.

[112] Cf. canon 606, § 2. Roberti, *loc. cit.;* Augustine, *Ecclesiastical Trials,* p. 102. Cf. Pichler, *loc. cit.;* Reiffenstuel, *ibid.,* n. 167.

[113] Cf. Roberti, *loc. cit.;* Noone, *Nullity in Judicial Acts,* p. 56.

[114] Cf. Król, *op. cit.,* p. 71, note 35.

may become urgent because of impending prescription or to avoid being deprived of his possessions.[115]

A question arises with regard to exempt religious who are illegitimately absent from their communities. Certainly they do not fall under the exception contemplated in canon 1652, n. 2. The general principle of this canon applies to them. Consequently, they may not stand in court as plaintiffs except with their lawful superior's consent. When they are to be summoned to court as defendants, "the safest norm of action would be to secure the consent of the superior . . . If the superior's consent cannot be obtained at all, or at least not in due time, then in virtue of canons 616, § 1, and 500, § 1, the consent of the local ordinary would give the religious the right to stand in judgment, and thus preclude the possibility of an irremediably null sentence."[116] Non-exempt religious, on the other hand, are under the jurisdiction of the local ordinary (can. 500, § 1). To determine the identity of their ordinary, the principles enumerated above[117] must be applied. It is this ordinary's right to permit his subject to stand in judgment when such permission is required according to can. 1652.

Third exception: if religious wish to denounce their superior.[118] Thus, a religious may denounce his superior to the promoter of justice for his extravagant administration of community property or for his damaging the religious' good name.[119]

Article 2. The Mandate of the Guardian

Canon Law requires that a procurator be furnished with a special mandate authorizing him to act in judicial matters, before a judge may admit him to represent his client before an ecclesiastical tribunal.[120] The absence of such a mandate would vitiate the

[115] Cf. Roberti, *op. cit.*, I, n. 207, V.

[116] Król, *op cit.*, p. 73; Cf. Noone, *op. cit.*, p. 58.

[117] Cf. pp. 90 ff.

[118] Canon 1652, n. 3. Cf. Woywod-Smith, *A Practical Commentary,* II, n. 1626. Cf. Pichler, *Candidatus,* lib. II, tit. 1, n. 9; Reiffenstuel, *ibid.*, n. 166.

[119] Cf. Roberti, *loc. cit.;* Lega-Bartoccetti, *Commentarius,* I, 317; Noone, *op. cit.*, p. 57. Pichler, *loc. cit.*

[120] Canon 1659, § 1: Procurator ne prius a iudice admittatur quam *speciale mandatum ad lites* . . . apud tribunal deposuerit.

ensuing judicial activity,[121] and render the final sentence irremediably null.[122]

Since it is the function of a guardian to act for, or in the name of his ward, he, too, must be equipped with a legitimate mandate, if the validity of the final sentence is to be ensured. For there can be no doubt that the activity of persons performing the role of guardians falls under the prescription of canon 1892, n. 3, which states in general terms that the sentence is vitiated with irremediable nullity if somebody acted in the name of another without a legitimate mandate.

One may ask, however, whether the guardian has to be supplied with a special mandate, as is the case with procurators. Doheny is of the opinion that the guardian of an insane person needs a special mandate from the court to represent his ward and that if he should act without it the sentence would be vitiated in virtue of irremediable nullity.[123] To support his assertion he cites canon 1659, § 1, article 49, § 1, of the *Instructio,* and canon 1892, n. 3. The first two norms, it must be noted, refer to procurators and are not strictly applicable to guardians.[124] Since the *law* requires that procurators have a *special* mandate (*mandatum speciale ad lites*) to represent his principal in court, it is obvious that the lack of such a mandate would fall under the sanction of canon 1892, n. 3, which mentions a mandate according to law (*legitimo mandato*).[125] The canons which refer to guardians, on the other hand,

[121] Cf. Hogan, *Judicial Advocates and Procurators,* p. 102. In note 2, the author cited refers to several authors who hold the same view.

[122] Canon 1892, n. 3.

[123] Cf. Doheny, *Canonical Procedure in Matrimonial Cases,* I, 26.

[124] The difference between procurators and guardians is briefly stated by Hogan: "Although in many instances a tutor or guardian is for all purposes a procurator, still the distinction must be clearly retained which points to the procurator receiving his mandate directly from the litigant whereas the tutor and guardian may be commissioned by legal authority." —*Op. cit.,* p. 107, note 26. Likewise, Coronata, *De Processibus,* n. 1180: "Differt procurator a curatore et tutore qui negotia agunt nomine alieno, non de mandato domini; sed vel de mandato iuris aut alius tertiae personae, e.g. iudicis."

[125] The phrase *mandatum legitimum* has a wider extension than the phrase *mandatum speciale ad lites.*

seem to imply that a person has the duty (and consequently, the right) to represent his ward in court for the very reason that he is guardian.[126]

Canon 1651, § 1, refers, indeed, to the *consent of the proper ordinary* to be obtained before a civil law guardian be admitted before the ecclesiastical tribunal by the presiding judge; but the canon makes no mention of a *special mandate.* Thus, when a guardian appointed by the proper ecclesiastical authority seeks to act in an ecclesiastical tribunal, the presiding judge may admit him forthwith after ascertaining the fact of his lawful appointment; and when a civil law guardian applies to represent his ward in an ecclesiastical tribunal, the judge may admit him after obtaining the consent of the proper Ordinary.[127] A lawfully appointed guardian, by virtue of his appointment as guardian, possesses the legitimate mandate required by canon 1892, n. 3, to act for his ward.[128] This opinion seems to be more in accord with the prescriptions of Canon Law, which make no mention of a special mandate *ad lites* when referring to guardians, and has the support of an eminent jurist.[129]

The ecclesiastical authority, however, may declare that a person has been appointed guardian in order to act in a judicial process.

---

[126] Cf. canon 1648, § 1.

[127] ". . . non esiste alcuna limitazione circa la abilità processuale o necessità di consensi dell'autorità civile o ecclesiastica o della famiglia; quindi il rappresentante dell' inabile può istituire qualsiasi giudizio, nell' interesse del pupillo, o difenderlo quando è convenuto da altri."—Giustiniani, "De Curatore Dementis," p. 106.

[128] It is a principle accepted by civil law that the general guardian has authority to exercise court action on behalf of his ward. "The protection of the ward's person, the maintenance of his property rights, and the enforcement of his choses in action often require the bringing of a suit; and it is not only the guardian's right, but his duty, to institute and prosecute any litigation which is necessary for those purposes and justified by the exercise of reasonable discretion and judgment."—25 Am. Jur., *Guardian and Ward,* § 147. Statutes generally enumerate actions which the guardian may not exercise on behalf of his ward. Cf. *ibid.*

[129] ". . . tutores, curatores . . . habent mandatum ad agendum et respondendum derivans ex mandato generali administrativo ipsis lege aut peculiari statuto commisso."—Lega-Bartoccetti, *Commentarius,* I, 332.

In such cases there can be no doubt as to the guardian's right to stand in court for his ward[130]

From what has been stated it is apparent that the designation of a guardian is important. Excepting the decree of appointment there is no legal proof that the power of guardianship has been granted or that the person claiming such power is to be recognized as guardian. Should evidence of official appointment not appear in the acts of the case, courts of second or third instance, for example, would be faced with particular difficulty, as they would lack means of ascertaining the legal value of the presumed guardian's activity. Consequently, in order that the acts of the process may bear evident proof of the authorization of a particular person to act as guardian for another, the authentic exemplar of the document of his appointment should be filed in and preserved with the acts of the case.[131] The Ordinary's consent to a civil law guardian to act in the ecclesiastical court may be incorporated in a distinct document introduced into court separately, or it may be attached to, or embodied in, the *libellus* previously drawn up by that guardian.

The Ordinary may ascertain the appointment of a civil law guardian by consulting the court that appointed him, by examining the letters of appointment, or interrogating witnesses, by examining copies of the court record and proceedings instituted to appoint him. He should note whether the proper authority has appointed him, whether the proper procedure has been followed, and whether the period of appointment has already expired.[132] Moreover, he should bear in mind the qualifications of guardians and the possibility of a conflict of interests. The Ordinary will generally

---

[130] Cf. S.R.R., *Decisiones,* XXIV (1932), dec. XLV, n. 2, 4°: "Tutorem seu curatorem, ab Ordinario constitutum, legitimam in iudicio standi personam in causa nullitatis matrimonii ex dementia habere manifesto ex ipso decreto constituentis."

[131] Canon 1660 prescribes: Mandatum *procurationis* asservari debet in actis causae. There is no canonical legislation that presents a similar prescription regarding the guardian's decree of appointment.

[132] At this point, it is well to bear in mind the prescription of canon 1819: Documenta vim probandi in iudicio non habent, nisi originalia sint aut in exemplari authentico exhibita et penes tribunalis cancellariam deposita, exceptis documentis quae publici iuris sunt, ceu leges rite promulgatae.

manifest his consent by issuing a decree, which will then have the force of an appointment to act in the ecclesiastical court.[133]

Pinna offers the following example of a decree appointing a guardian to represent a defendant in a marriage case:

Perusiis die . . . .

> Cum requiratur ut in causa, de qua supra, constituatur curator partis conventae utpote rationis usu destitutae, Nos, hisce litteris, ad norman canonis 1651, §§ 1 et 2, et art. 77 et 78 Instructionis editae a S. Congregatione de Sacramentis die 15 augusti 1936, audita altera parte D.no Martino MARTINI, necnon Defensore vinculi R. D. Henrico Druetti, omnibus perpensis, constitutimus specialem curatorem in hac causa pro D.na Sophia Sofa ac designamus ad hoc munus ipsam eiusdem matrem D.nam Sophiam Sofa-Baner.

✠ N.B. Archiepiscopus
x Cancellarius

(L.S.) . . . . .[134]

It is here suggested that the record of the guardian's appointment should indicate whether the ward is under disability because of insanity or because of mental deficiency, since the measure of incapacity varies in relation to the degree of mental illness,[135] and the presiding judge may proceed differently, or, at least, have

---

[133] Authors speak of a *decretum*. Cf. Aguirre, "De Curatore Dementis," p. 294: "Sufficiet vero ut Ordinarius per decretum consensum praestet."

[134] Pinna, *Praxis Iudicialis Canonica*, p. 32. Doheny offers a briefer form: Auditis Defensore Vinculi et N.N. . . . parte actrici in causa Matrimoniali X, num. prot. . . ., his praesentibus constituitur uti Tutor vel Curator N. . . . ad normam iuris.

N.N. . . . Ordinarius.

N.N. . . . Notarius.

W. J. Doheny, *Practical Manual for Marriage Cases* (Milwaukee: The Bruce Publishing Co., 1938), p. 140.

[135] Cf. above, pp. 46 ff.

reason to proceed differently, depending on the degree of disability.[136]

It may occur that the presiding judge, the Promoter of Justice, the Defender of the Bond, or the opposing party discovers, after the trial has been in progress, that a guardian not duly authorized is acting for a mentally ill person. What action should be taken in such an event? Irregularities in the appointment must be rectified, for if the appointment has not been made according to law, the guardian cannot act validity in the name of his ward, so that his acts as well as the acts which the judge and the adverse party execute in relation to him are invalid.[137] Moreover, in virtue of canon 1682, the judge may declare *ex officio* the nullity of the acts performed by the unauthorized guardian, since the mentally ill are, like minors, under the special tutelage of the Church.[138]

Again, it may happen that the appointment of a guardian to exercise a person's processual rights is a source of injustice or injury to the person placed under guardianship, to his opponent, or to a third party. Given such a situation, what action can the aggrieved person take to ward off his actual or impending injury? The Code does not answer directly. Being a complete legal system, however, it does include remedies to be used against the possible violations of rights, whether those violations are judicial or extrajudicial. Thus, canon 1879 points to the ordinary means available against such violations through judicial sentences: *"Pars quae aliqua sententia se gravatam putat, itemque promotor iustitiae et defensor vinculi in causis in quibus interfuerunt, ius habent a sententia appellandi, idest provocandi ab inferiore iudice qui sententiam tulit, ad superiorem, salvo praescripto can. 1880."*[139]

---

[136] Cf. above, pp. 43 ff. See A. C. Jemolo, *Il Matrimonio nel Diritto Canonico* (Milano: Vallardi, 1941), p. 378, who cites an unpublished decision of the Apostolic Signatura, *Pratensis,* April 29, 1939; Lega-Bartoccetti, *Commentarius,* I, p. 310, n. 4.

[137] Canon 1892, n. 3. Noone, *Nullity in Judicial Acts,* p. 78; Hogan, *Judicial Advocates and Procurators,* p. 102.

[138] Cf. Augustine, *Ecclesiastical Trials,* p. 131; Stitt, *De Promotore Justitiae,* n. 102.

[139] Canon 1880 enumerates sentences which admit of no appeal.

Appeal (*appellatio*), then, seeks to obtain the rectification of an unjust or injurious judicial sentence.[140]

The remedy established by the Code against extrajudicial acts, decrees, dispositions, decisions and transactions of superiors as well as against the extrajudicial decisions of judges is known as recourse (*recursus*). The fundamental norm regarding recourse is contained in canon 1601: *"Contra Ordinariorum decreta non datur appellatio seu recursus ad Sacram Rotam; sed de eiusmodi recursibus exclusive cognoscunt Sacrae Congregationes."*[141] McClunn comments: "Recourses, then, are dealt with by the Roman Congregations only, unless the law makes an exception in some particular case. When a recourse is made, it will be sent to the Congregation which is competent in the matter."[142] Recourse, however, may also originate from a judicial background, i.e., in connection with the non-judicial acts of an ecclesiastical judge.[143] In such cases, "the superior *ad quem* is not the administrative superior of the ordinary, i.e., the Holy See, but the usual court of judicial appeal, i.e., the superior tribunal."[144]

When an appeal or recourse effects the rejection of a particular

---

[140] Cf. canons 1879-1890. T. A. Connolly, (*Appeals,* The Catholic University of America Canon Law Studies, n. 79 [Washington, D.C.: The Catholic University of America, 1932]) offers a complete treatment of the subject.

[141] Cf. also S.R.R., *Decisiones,* XXIV (1932), dec. XLV, pp. 429-433; Lex Propria S.R.R., can. 16—*AAS,* I (1909), 24.

[142] J. D. McClunn, *Administrative Recourse,* The Catholic University of America Canon Law Studies, n. 240 (Washington, D.C.: The Catholic University of America Press, 1946), pp. 76-77.

[143] Pre-Code jurisprudence and doctrine admitted an extra-judicial appeal against the appointment of guardians made by a judge; for the act of appointment was considered as executed by him apart from the use of strictly judicial power. Cf. Pirhing, *Ius Canonicum in V Libros Decretalium Distributum* (5 vols., Dilingae, 1674), lib. II, tit. 28, n. 3; McClunn, *op. cit.,* pp. 3-4, note 14. Another example is presented by McClunn, *op. cit.,* p. 15: "When he rejects a plaintiff's bill of complaint (*libellus*), the party concerned may not make an appeal, for an appeal is referrible to a sentence, and no sentence has been rendered in this case. In rejecting the bill of complaint the judge acts in an administrative way, and consequently the remedy to be invoked against him is that of recourse."

[144] McClunn, *op. cit.,* p. 16.

person as guardian, he loses his right to represent his ward in court, so that the presiding judge may not permit him to exercise the function of guardian. On the other hand, should the guardian consider himself unjustly banished from the ecclesiastical court, he may resort to the remedies of appeal and recourse, as explained.

The guardian ceases to exercise his office, also, because of renunciation or death.

Finally, when a vacancy arises in the post of guardian, the lawsuit remains interrupted until a new guardian has been appointed.[145]

---

[145] Canon 1735. Procuratore aut curatore a munere cessante, tandiu interrupta manet instantia, quandiu pars aut ii ad quos pertinent novum procuratorem vel curatorem nominaverint aut per se ipsi in posterum agere se velle professi fuerint.

CHAPTER VII

The Rights and Duties of Guardians at the Various Periods of the Canonical Trial

Article 1. The Guardian in the Introductory Period

A. *The Formulation of the Bill of Complaint*

The formulation of the introductory bill of complaint is both a duty and a right of the guardian.[1] He may seek the services of a judicial advocate in this task, as counsel, direction, and assistance in this connection is in no way discountenanced by law. On the contrary, the technical nature of the bill of complaint, its juridical form and content,[2] seem to demand an expert's assistance in its formation. Moreover, recourse to such aid lessens the possibility of the rejection of the *libellus* because of some technical defect.[3]

The bill of complaint composed by the guardian must contain the following points: (1) it must state the name of his ward, the name of the judge before whom the case is brought, the object of the petition, and the name of the defendant; (2) it must present, summarily at least, the arguments which tend to prove his claims and his title to redress; and (3) it must be subscribed by the guardian, give the day, month, and year of presentation, the guardian's place of residence or the place at which he may wish to receive communications from the court.[4]

The decree of the guardian's appointment should be joined to the *libellus*. When a civil law guardian wishes to introduce a petition on behalf of his ward, he should petition the consent of the ward's ordinary. The latter may affix the record of his approval

---

1 This duty and right are a logical derivation from the norm contained in canon 1648, § 1.

2 Cf. canons 1706, 1708; *Instructio*, art. 55, 57.

3 Cf. canon 1709, § 2; *Instructio*, art. 62.

4 Cf. canon 1708.

to the *libellus* itself or draw up a separate certified decree. A peculiar situation exists when a mentally ill person has no guardian to act for him. In such cases, any relative or friend may petition the proper authority either personally or through the Promoter of Justice to appoint a guardian.[5]

Finally valuable assistance may be rendered to the court by joining to the bill of complaint documents such as probatory letters and certificates of baptism, marriage, divorce, death, ordination, religious profession, and the like. Similarly, details may be included with reference to the person and location of witnesses, their religious character, probity, and credibility, as well as points upon which they are especially suited to offer testimony. Such documents as require it should be furnished with full legal authentication.

In the event that the *libellus* is rejected by the tribunal, it must be returned to the guardian who may recast it or have recourse within the established period of ten days to the superior court of second instance,[6] or directly to the Tribunal of the Sacred Rota.[7] Kealy remarks that while the finding of the superior court is entirely decisive, there is no legal objection to the submission of another bill of complaint to the tribunal of first instance with regard to the same matter.[8] Moreover, a legal adviser may seek to convince the court to reconsider and readmit the *libellus* which is felt to have been illegitimately rejected.[9]

In the absence of a decree admitting or rejecting the *libellus*

---

[5] Cf. S.R.R., *Decisiones,* XXIV (1932), dec. XLV, p. 429, n. 1, In this particular case, the father denounced his son's matrimony on grounds of lack of consent because of insanity. He petitioned the court to appoint a guardian. The Ordinary granted the petition, issuing the following decree: "1° A Callisto è assegnato un tutore e curatore che agisca nel nome e in luogo di lui avanti ai nostri Tribunali ecclesiastici nella causa di nullità del predetto matrimonio Callisto-Prisoilla; 2° A tutore e curatore del predetto Callisto, nella causa accennata, è nominato l'avv. Virgilio."

[6] Cf. canon 1709, § 3.

[7] *Instructio,* art. 66, § 1.

[8] J. J. Kealy, *The Introductory Libellus in Church Court Procedure,* The Catholic University of America Canon Law Studies, n. 108 (Washington, D.C.: The Catholic University of America, 1937), p. 76.

[9] Kealy, *op. cit.,* p. 68.

within a continuous month,[10] the guardian may act in accordance with canon 1710. Accordingly, he may insist that the judge issue the decree. If the judge is nevertheless silent, the guardian may, on the lapse of five days after his petition to the judge to take action, have recourse to the local Ordinary—if the latter does not act as judge in the case—or to the higher court to petition that the judge be forced to take action, or that another be appointed in his place to try the action.[11]

In the instance that the ordinary himself is negligent, recourse may be directed to the tribunal of the Roman Pontiff[12] or to the court of second instance.[13]

B. *The Formal Summons*

When the defendant is deprived of the use of reason or is weak-minded, the summons must be issued to his or her guardian.[14] There is no difficulty when the mentally ill person is already under the control of a duly appointed guardian.[15] When a guardian has not been legitimately designated to act in the ecclesiastical forum, "the Ordinary should appoint one as early as possible in the course of the preliminary proceedings, at least upon the acceptance of the *libellus*."[16]

If the summons is not legitimately served, both the summons

---

[10] Cf. canons 35, 34, § 3, nn. 1, 3.

[11] Canon 1710. Kealy remarks: "It is more in conformity with ecclesiastical discipline and the hierarchical organization of the Church to direct the recourse to the Ordinary."—*Op. cit.*, p. 78.

[12] Cf. Noval, *De Iudiciis*, pp. 282, 283; Hogan, *Judicial Advocates and Procurators*, p. 140; canons 1625, § 1; 1557, § 1, n. 3. The latter canon involves criminal proceedings against the bishop.

[13] Cf. Roberti, *De Processibus*, I, n. 286; Wernz-Vidal, *De Processibus*, n. 377; Hogan, *op. cit.*, p. 140. Criminal proceedings against a delinquent bishop must be lodged with the tribunal of the Roman Pontiff. Cf. canon 1557, § 1, n. 3.

[14] Cf. *Instructio*, art. 77: Si pars conventa rationis usu sit destituta, vel minus firmae mentis, citatio tutori vel curatori denuncianda est. PCI, 25 Jan. 1943—*AAS*, XXXV (1943), 58, II, 2.

[15] Cf. Torre, *Processus Matrimonialis*, p. 81; Doheny *Canonical Procedure in Matrimionial Cases*, I, 250.

[16] Doheny, *loc. cit.*; Torre, *loc. cit.*

and the subsequent acts of procedure are null and void.[17] Since the summons must be issued to the guardian of the mentally ill person and not to the incapacitated ward himself, it is illegitimately served when issued to the latter, so that canon 1723 operates.[18]

The summons is to be presented to the guardian in written form. It shall express the precept of the judge to the guardian to appear in court. Moreover, it shall state the name of the judge who serves it, indicate the reason why the party is summoned, give the name and surname of the defendant, and mention by whom he is sued and when and where the guardian is to appear to defend his ward. Finally, the summons is to be authenticated with the seal of the court and subscribed by the judge or his auditor and a notary.[19]

On the other hand, when the plaintiff is the incapacitated party, the summons to his adversary should indicate that he will be represented in court according to law; for the defendant has a right to lodge an exception against the personages engaged in the suit,[20] and it is possible that the defendant may have reason to impugn the alleged mental illness of the plaintiff or object to the person of the guardian. It can hardly be contended, however, that the summons is null and void when it omits any mention of representation or indication of the guardian, though the defendant is entitled to know whether the plaintiff may lawfully stand in court.[21]

C. *The Joining of Issues* (*Contestatio Litis*)

In the *contestatio litis* the object of the controversy is clearly and precisely determined. From the fact that the guardian and not

---

[17] Canon 1723.

[18] Hanssen, *De Sanctione Nullitatis,* n. 81: "Si lis moveatur ei qui caret capacitate processuali vel legitimatione ad causam ad normam c. 1648-1654, citatio denuntianda est ei qui eius nomine iudicium suscipere tenetur (c. 1713). Citatio facta ei, qui caret capacitate processuali vel legitimatione ad causam videtur esse nulla. Nam nulla est citatio, quae non fuit legitime intimata (c. 1723), quae sanctio videtur referri etiam ad praescriptum c. 1713."

[19] Cf canon 1715.

[20] Canon 1628, § 1.

[21] Cf. Roberti, *De Processibus,* I, n. 291; Wernz-Vidal, *De Processibus,* n. 386, note 39; Hanssen, *op. cit.,* n. 83.

his incapacitated ward must be cited before the tribunal, it follows that the guardian has the right and obligation to participate in the joining of issues.

When the terms of the controversy have not been clearly indicated or may give way to misunderstanding, the guardian may request the judge to summon the parties to court in order to specify more clearly the paragraphs or counts (*dubia*), so that a precise formulation of the issue may be provided.[22] The entire process is based on the complaint of the plaintiff and the objection of the defendant, and whatever is extraneous to the points raised in the *contestatio litis* is to be excluded from the trial. Indeed, the court may not deviate from the petition, and the sentence must conform to the bill of complaint.[23]

The joining of issues has the following effects: (1) The plaintiff may not change the bill of complaint unless the defendant consents and the judge for good reasons believes that the change should be admitted, but the defendant has always the right to obtain compensation for damages and expenses, if any are due to him. The bill of complaint is not considered changed, if the manner of proof is shortened or altered; if the claim or secondary claims are reduced; if the circumstances of a fact stated in the bill of complaint are illustrated, completed, or amended in such a way that the object of the controversy remains the same; if, instead of the object itself, the price, or interest, or something equivalent is asked.

(2) The judge shall fix an appropriate interval of time within which the parties must procure and complete the proofs of their case. This interval may be prolonged at the discretion of the judge, if the parties request a postponement, but he must see that the trial is not unduly protracted.

(3) The possessor of the property or rights of another ceases to possess in good faith. Consequently, if the case is decided against him, he must restore not only the thing itself, but also the fruits which the thing has produced since the joining of the issues, and

---

[22] Cf. canon 1728. See also canon 1729, §§ 3, 4; *Instructio*, art. 88; *Normae*, art. 77, § 2.

[23] Cf. canon 1873, § 1, n. 1; *Normae*, art. 77, § 1.

he is, moreover, obliged to repair any damages caused since that moment.[24]

At the *contestatio litis,* the guardian must be mindful of his rights and obligations with reference to the question of contumacy.[25]

Before the joining of issues has taken place, the judge shall not, as a rule, proceed with the examination of witnesses or the admission of proofs except in the case of contempt of court. Should the guardian, however, foresee that pertinent information now available will be difficult or impossible to obtain at a later date, he may invoke canon 1730 and request the court to receive testimony or admit the alleged proofs immediately.[26]

Article 2. The Guardian in the Probatory Stage of the Process

A. *Judicial Interrogations*

The judicial interrogation of the parties serves to inform the judge more fully regarding the object of the trial and the attendant facts and circumstances. It is not limited to being merely a sort of preliminary to the probatory period of the trial, but may be resorted to by the tribunal at any stage of the process before the case is closed and under some circustances even after the period for the taking of evidence has been concluded by the decree of the presiding judge.[27]

The guardian, whether acting as plaintiff or defendant, may submit to the judge points or questions which he may desire to propose to the opposing party.[28] He has, however, no legal right

[24] Canon 1731. Cf. Woywod-Smith, *A Practical Commentary,* II, n. 1688.

[25] Cf. canon 1729, § 1; *Instructio,* art. 115.

[26] Canon 1730. Woywod-Smith, *op. cit.,* II, n. 1687; Hogan, *Judicial Advocates and Procurators,* p. 144.

[27] Canons 1742, § 3; 1861. R. B. Clune, *The Judicial Interrogation of the Parties,* The Catholic University of America Canon Law Studies, n. 269 (Washington, D.C.: The Catholic University of America Press, 1948), p. 47.

[28] Cf. canons, 1745, § 1; 1742, § 2. Clune, *op. cit.,* p. 93.

to oppose the judge who modifies or even rejects his proposals,[29] though he may invoke the ruling of canon 1625, § 1.

The Code does not bar the parties and their legal advisers from attending the interrogation of the opposing party. Ordinarily, however, according to some authors, they are not to be admitted.[31]

To the judge's right to propose lawful questions corresponds the parties' obligation to answer such questions.[32] If the party under interrogation refuses to answer or answers falsely, he is liable to punishment. Should he be guilty of perjury, he becomes liable to personal interdict or to suspension.[33] Moreover, refusal to answer to a legitimate question may warrant a personal presumption of admission.[34] On the contrary, the party has a right to object to and refuse to answer an unlawful question,[35] and he is not obliged to answer questions which entail the violation of a professional secret or may occasion grave evils for himself or near relatives.[36]

The questions must be answered orally, so that the deposition

---

29 Cf. Hogan, *op. cit.*, p. 145. Kròl observes that the judge "must exercise extreme care, especially in cases of private interest, lest he impair the right of defense by an arbitrary and undue restriction of questions, or create the impression that he favors one of the litigants."—*The Defendant in Contentious Trials*, p. 128. Cf. also Clune, *op. cit.*, p. 75. The judge may regulate his choice according to the conformity or non-conformity of the proposed questions with the qualities demanded of interrogations by canon 1775.

30 Canon 1625. § 1, declares that judges who do an injustice or cause damage to the contending parties are liable for damages and can be punished by the local Ordinary, or, if the bishop has been guilty, by the Apostolic Sec. The proceedings against the judge may be instituted either at the request of the parties or *ex officio*. Cf. Clune, *op. cit.*, p. 75.

31 Cf. Wernz-Vidal, *De Processibus*, n. 372; Coronata, *De Processibus*, n. 1269, 3°. Canon 1771 expressly forbids the presence of parties at the examination of the witnesses, unless the judge believes that their presence is desirable. Cf. also *Instructio*, art. 128.

32 Cf. Clune, *op. cit.*, p. 113.

33 Cf. canon 1743, §§ 1, 3.

34 Cf. canon 1743, § 2.

35 This statement is the converse of canon 1743, § 1.

36 Cf. canon 1755, § 2. Kròl, *The Defendant in Contentious Trials*, p. 129; Regatillo, *Institutiones Iuris Canonici*, II, n. 542.

may not be read from prepared notes or written statements. An exception is admitted for figures and accounts.[37]

At the conclusion of the interrogation, the deposition as recorded by the notary is read back to the interrogated party, who may correct or change his deposition.[38]

Insane persons are naturally incapable of positing human acts and, consequently, are disqualified absolutely from appearing personally in judgment. The feeble-minded, however, may enjoy enough mental stability to be permitted to appear personally on trial; and canon 1650 accordingly affirms that they may stand trial personally at the order of the judge. It may happen, too, that the degree or nature of mental weakness affecting a party may be such as to disqualify him from standing personally in judgment but not such as to render useless his examination in a judicial interrogation, so that it seems that the judge may issue an order requiring his deposition. Indeed, as Clune observes, "it is quite certain that, unless the nature of the malady renders the examination impossible or useless, the deposition of the party will assist greatly in the search for and the ascertainment of the objective truth of the cause."[39]

B. *The Testimony of Witnesses*

Guardians are debarred from testifying as witnesses in the cases of their wards by canon 1757, § 3, n. 1: Ut incapaces (repulluntur a testimonio ferendo) qui partes sunt in causa, aut partium vice funguntur, veluti tutor in causa pupilli. . . .[40] The Canon indicates the legal reason for the disqualification: guardians really take the place of their wards in a trial. Consequently, just as the parties are debarred from testifying as witnesses, so the guardians may not testify in that capacity. They enjoy the prerogatives of the parties and are bound by the restrictions affecting the parties.[41] Canon

---

[37] Canons 1745, § 2, and 1777.

[38] Canons 1745 § 2 and 1780, § 1.

[39] Clune, *op. cit.*, p. 96, note 20. Such persons should, as a rule, be examined unsworn. Cf. canon 1758 in conjunction with canon 1757, § 1.

[40] Cf. also *Instructio*, art. 119 § 3, n. 1.

[41] Doheny observes that canon 1757, § 3. n. 1, establishes the distinction

1758 allows unfit and suspected persons[42] to testify as witnesses if the judge issues an order stating that he thinks it advisable to do so.[43] No exception, however, is contemplated by law regarding disqualified persons, so that they may not testify as witnesses under any consideration.[44]

Proof through witnesses is admitted in all cases, but the admission of witnesses is subject to the direction of the judge.[45] Since the guardian enjoys the prerogatives of parties, he may introduce witnesses to the court.[46] When engaged in marshalling witnesses, he would do well to regard the legal prescriptions effecting those unfit, suspect, and debarred with reference to the giving of testimony.[47]

At the request of the guardian, witnesses who have already been examined may again be called to the witness stand, if the judge believes it necessary or useful. All danger, however, of collusion or corruption of the witnesses must be absent and they must be cited before the acts or testimonies are made public.[48]

The guardian may also request that witnesses introduced by the opposing party or their testimony be rejected. A just reason, however, for their rejection must be supplied.[49] On the other hand, the guardian may not object to the admission of a witness whom

---

between the depositions of the parties and the testimony of witnesses because they are evaluated according to different norms. "The depositions of the parties are evaluated according to the norms enunciated in Canons 1750-1752 and Articles 116 and 117; whereas, the testimony of witnesses is evaluated according to the norms established in Canons 1789-1791." *Canonical Procedure in Matrimonial Cases,* I, 353.

[42] Cf. canon 1757, §§ 1, 2.

[43] Their testimony is accepted as an indication and support of proof and they are examined unsworn. Cf. canon 1758.

[44] Doheny, *loc. cit.;* Roberti, *De Processibus,* I, n. 337: "Testes incapaces numquam possunt vocari ad testandum: si vocentur, non tenentur respondere; si respondeant, eorum testimonium non attenditur." Cf. Regatillo, *Institutiones Iuris Canonici,* II, n. 569; Coronata, *De Processibus,* n. 1287.

[45] Canon 1754.

[46] Canon 1759, § 1.

[47] Cf. canon 1757.

[48] Canon 1781. Cf. also canon 1786.

[49] Canon 1764, § 2; 1783, § 2.

he himself presented, unless a new reason for objecting to him arises after he has been introduced. He may, however, object to the witness's testimony.[50] The objection to a witness must be raised within three days after the names of the witnesses summoned have been communicated to the guardian.[51] Objections made at a later date are not heard unless the party can prove or at least affirms under oath that he was not aware of the defect of the witness.[52]

Moreover, the guardian has the right to be notified in the event that following the publication of the testimony previous witnesses are recalled for examination on questions already examined or new witnesses are admitted.[53]

Before giving testimony, a witness must ordinarily take the oath that he will state the whole truth and nothing but the truth.[54] The guardian has the right to be present as witnesses take the required oath.[55] Unless the judge believes that his presence is desirable, the guardian may not be present at the examination of the witnesses.[56] When present at the said examination and desirous to put new questions to a witness, he may not do so directly but must propose the questions to the judge or the person taking his place, who is to put them to the witness.[57]

After the publication of the testimony,[58] the guardian no longer has the right to reject a witness, unless he proves or asserts under oath that he had no knowledge of the defect of the witness previous to the publication;[59] but he retains the right to object to the manner of the examination or to the depositions themselves.[60]

---

[50] Canon 1764, § 3.

[51] Canon 1764, § 4.

[52] Canon 1764, § 4.

[53] Canon 1786.

[54] Canon 1767, § 1. *Ordinarily,* for the unfit and suspected are examined unsworn. Cf. canon 1758.

[55] Canon 1767, § 2. This canon does not run counter to the exceptional case contemplated in canon 1763.

[56] Canon 1771.

[57] Canon 1773, § 2.

[58] Canon 1782.

[59] Canons, 1783, n. 1, and 1764, § 4.

[60] Canon 1783, § 2.

C. *Documents*

Private and public documents are admissible as evidence in every kind of trial.[61] They have no force of proof in court, however, unless they are presented in the original or in duly authenticated copies; and they are to be deposited with the chancery of the court before the conclusion of the case is decreed.[62]

If the guardian himself is unable to secure the necessary documents, he may request the judge to secure public documents for him, to compel the opposing party to restore the documents which he had obtained from him by force or stealth, and to oblige his opponent to exhibit the private documents which are common to both parties. When in court as the defendant in the case, he may also ask the judge to compel the plaintiff to exhibit private documents which exclusively belong to the plaintiff and to compel a third party to yield documents which he deems necessary for his defense.[63]

Neither he, however, nor his opponent is obliged to exhibit documents which may not be furnished without danger of damage mentioned in canon 1755, § 2, n. 2, or without imperiling the violation of a secret which must be kept.[64] If, however, a part of the document which is of interest to one of the parties can be extracted and presented in authenticated copy without such danger, the judge may decree the presentation of the part.[65]

---

[61] Canons 1812, 1813.

[62] Canons 1819; 1861, § 1. They may be presented after the conclusion of the case only if they were previously unavailable (canon 1861, § 1) or if the nature of the case admits of their admission after that time (cf. canon 1905, § 2, n. 2). Cf. Król, *The Defendant in Contentious Trials*, p. 139.

[63] Cf. canons 1822-1824; Król, *op. cit.*, p. 139; Roberti, *De Processibus*, II, n. 374; Coronata, *De Processibus*, n. 1355. Król adds: "Though the defendant can also be compelled to exhibit documents, authors commonly maintain that, unlike the plaintiff, he cannot be compelled to exhibit the private documents which belong to him rightfully and exclusively, unless of course such are necessary to sustain his own averments."—*Op. cit.*, pp. 139-140. Cf. Noval, *De Iudiciis*, n. 556; Wernz-Vidal, *De Processibus*, n. 512; Coronata, *op. cit.*, n. 1355.

[64] Canon 1823, § 1.

[65] Canon 1823, § 2. Thus the judge may secretly read the document to

Lastly, the guardian may "challenge and refute documents concerning which he has reason to maintain that they are defective with regard to their authenticity, genuineness, integrity or content inasmuch as they contain statements which are probably erroneous."[66]

D. *Judicial Experts*

If special proficiency in the subject of inquiry is required to formulate a correct judgment upon it, the guardian may petition recourse to the aid of experts.[67] In cases of private interest he may propose the names of the experts whom he desires to have appointed, but the appointment itself pertains to the judge.[68] Canon 1796, § 1, empowers him to take exception to experts for the same reasons and in the same circumstances that he can challenge witnesses.

He may be present when the experts take the oath that they will faithfully perform their office, as well as during the exercise of their office, unless the nature of the case, the sense of propriety, the law, or an order of the judge forbid his presence.[69]

The guardian may propose points to which the experts should pay particular attention,[70] and must be consulted by the judge when the period within which the experts were to present their findings and opinion is to be prolonged.[71]

After the experts report their findings, the guardian may object that they failed to carry out their instructions or that their findings are contradictory or can be disproved by contrary arguments.[72]

---

verify the fact of the alleged dangers and to select pertinent parts which may be exhibited without danger. Cf. Król, *op. cit.*, p. 140.

[66] Król, *op. cit.*, p. 140. ". . . if the sentence is based on a document which is found to be false, the remedy of appeal or of *restitutio in integrum* is available against it." Cf. canon 1905, §§ 1, 2, n. 1.

[67] Canon 1793, § 2.

[68] Canon 1793, § 1.

[69] Canon 1797, § 2.

[70] Canon 1799, § 1.

[71] Canon 1799, § 2.

[72] Cf. Wernz-Vidal, *De Processibus*, n. 494; Roberti, *De Processibus*, II, n. 362; Król, *op. cit.*, p. 141.

If the guardian feels that the judge has been unfair in fixing the expenses and fees of the experts, he may within ten days raise an objection before the same judge, who can then reconsider the matter and correct or change the ruling on the charge.[73]

E. *Judicial Access and Inspection*

When the judge believes that judicial access and inspection of the object of controversy are necessary for the correct understanding and just definition of the case, he may issue a decree ordering such access and inspection. He must, however, consult the guardian before issuing the decree.[74] If he considers the inspection superfluous and an occasion of excessive expenditure, the guardian may oppose it in cases of private interest.[75]

He may be present at the judicial inspection, unless the judge forbids him because of danger of quarrels and disturbances.[76] When present, he may make appropriate remarks to insure his defense.[77]

F. *Presumptions*

A presumption is a probable conjecture about an uncertain affair and is twofold—viz., either a legal presumption (when it is stated in the law itself) or a personal presumption (which the judge conjectures for himself).[78] Legal presumptions may be rebuttable (*praesumptio iuris simpliciter*) or irrebutable (*praesumptio iuris et de iure*).[79] Rebuttable presumptions admit direct as well as indirect contrary proofs, while irrebuttable presumptions can be attacked by indirect arguments alone.[80]

---

73 Canons 1805, and 1913, § 1.

74 Canon 1806.

75 Cf. Król, *op. cit.*, p. 142. Król adds: ". . . if both parties object, the judge must decide the case on the basis of proof adduced in court, and in accord with the rule, "*actore non probante reus absolvitur.*" Cf. canons 1619, § 1 and 1748, § 2.

76 Canon 1809.

77 Król, *op. cit.*, p. 142.

78 Cf. canon 1825, § 1.

79 Canon 1825, § 2.

80 Canon 1826. Woywod-Smith state: a) against a rebuttable presumption: a person who violates the law is generally presumed to have known

A guardian can greatly aid his ward's cause by providing the court with facts from which the judge may conjecture presumptions in favor of his client's position. The Code, however, though it recognizes, does not encourage the use of personal presumptions as a method of proof, so that the guardian must propose certain and specific facts directly related to the fact in controversy.[81]

The probative force of presumptions is well set forth by Król: "If a thing is presumed merely because it occasionally results or simply because it can be deduced incidentally from the circumstantial evidence, the presumption is rash and lacks probative force. If a thing is presumed because it ordinarily results or because it normally can be deduced from the circumstantial evidence, then the presumption is grave, but nevertheless, lacks sufficient probative force to resolve a controversy. If a thing is presumed because any result or deduction from the certain and specific established facts other than that presumed would be unlikely, the presumption is compelling (*violenta-gravissima*).

"In contentious cases in which complete direct proof is unavailable, only a compelling presumption can warrant a sentence adverse to the defendant.[82] Consequently, unless the presumption is entirely consistent with the facts and circumstances shown, and absolutely inconsistent with any other reasonable presumption derivable from the same facts and circumstances, moral certainly is lacking, and the rule *"actore non probante reus absolvitur"* must be applied."[83]

---

the law, but proof that he actually was ignorant of the law is admitted; b) against an irrebuttable presumption: Canon 1904 establishes an absolute presumption in favor of a judicial sentence which has become a *res judicata*, so that the justice or truth of the sentence can never be directly attacked, though one may prove that there had been no foundation for the lawsuit which was based on contract, because no contract had existed between the parties.—Cf. *A Practical Commentary,* II, n. 1755.

[81] Król, *op. cit.,* p. 143; canon 1828.

[82] Lega-Bartoccetti, *Commentarius,* II, 821; Roberti, *De Processibus,* II, n. 378; Augustine, *Ecclesiastical Trials,* p. 272; Wernz-Vidal, *De Processibus,* n. 520.

[83] Król, *op. cit.,* p. 143.

G. *Probatory Oaths*

Probatory oaths may be conceived as substitute means of proof. Though their use is infrequent, it may be to the advantage of a party to promote the use of one or other of these oaths, of which the Code considers three types: the supplementary, the estimatory, and the decisive oath.[84]

a) The supplementary oath is used to complement partial or incomplete proofs, when there are no further means available to strengthen the proof.[85] It may be demanded by the judge *ex officio* or at the request of one of the parties, as well as at the request of the promotor of justice or of the defender of the bond when these officials take part in the trial.[86] As a rule, it is tendered to the party who has produced more complete proof or more convincing evidence in his favor.[87] The judge shall decide by decree whether and when the circumstances are such as to warrant or necessitate the use of this oath, but he shall abstain from admitting its use in criminal cases and in civil cases in which the disputed right or object is of great value or in which the fact involved is of great moment.[88] When asked to take the supplementary oath in affairs which do not pertain to his civil or religious status, the party may for a just reason refuse to take the oath or request that his opponent take it. The judge is to decide the implications of a refusal to take the oath. Lastly, the oath taken by one of the parties may be challenged by his opponent.[89]

b) The estimatory oath is used to determine the amount of indemnity due to a party who has established his right to compensation, when otherwise the amount cannot be calculated with

---

[84] Canons 1829, 1832, 1834. For an extensive treatment of this subject, cf. E. J. Moriarity, *Oaths in Ecclesiastical Courts,* The Catholic University of America Canon Law Studies, n. 110 (Washington, D.C.: The Catholic University of America, 1937). See also Król, *op. cit.,* pp. 143-146; Woywod-Smith, *op. cit.,* II, nn. 1757-1763.

[85] Canon 1829.

[86] Canon 1830, § 3.

[87] Canon 1830, § 4.

[88] Canon 1830, §§ 2, 5.

[89] Canon 1831, §§ 1-3.

certainty.[90] The party who suffered damage must state under oath what goods or property were lost to him by the malice of his opponent and assess the value thereof according to a reasonable estimate.[91] If the estimate seems excessive to the judge, he should reduce it to an equitable amount, summoning, if necessary, experts to assist him in arriving at a true and just appraisal.[92] The defendant also may impugn the estimate and, as a last resort, appeal from the sentence based on the unjust evaluation.[93]

c) The decisive oath, administered under the conditions required by canons 1834 and 1835, produces the effect of settling the controversy, be it the principal action or an incidental question. This oath must be requested by one of the contestants and must be approved of by the judge.[94] The judge shall permit the parties to settle the dispute by oath only under the following conditions, enumerated in canon 1835: 1) The object of the oath must admit of cession and transaction,[95] and it must not be of very great importance or value to the litigants; 2) The party who demands that it be tendered must be capable of ceding the rights involved or of making a private settlement concerning them; 3) The party of whom it is demanded must likewise be capable of such cession and transaction and must not already have full proof in his favor;[96] 4)The oath must concern the mere knowledge of a fact or a fact personal to the party who is to take the oath.

The party who has requested that the decivise oath be tendered

---

[90] Canon 1832.

[91] Canon 1833, n. 1. This estimate should be based "on the objective value of the goods or property taken or destroyed and the consequent damages and loss of profit, and not on the subjective or sentimental values attached to such articles or property."—Król, *op. cit.*, p. 146; Moriarity, *op. cit.*, pp. 82-85.

[92] Canon 1833, n. 2.

[93] Cf. Moriarity, *op. cit.*, p. 84.

[94] Canon 1834.

[95] Canon 1927, §§ 1, 2, determines such objects positively and negatively.

[96] Should he have full proof in his favor, he cannot be asked to take this oath, as he already has a right to a favorable sentence. Cf. Woywod-Smith, *op. cit.*, II, n. 1762.

to his opponent may recall his demand at any time before it has been taken.[97] *A fortiori,* he may request a change in the formula of the oath. His opponent is free to comply with the demand and take the oath, or to refuse to take it, or finally to retender it to the proposer. The latter must then take it. The judge is to estimate the implications of the refusal of the parties to take the oath. When the oath is taken, the controversy is settled according to the sworn formula, which the judge merely confirms with a sentence or decree.[98]

Article 3. The Guardian in the Definitive Stage of the Trial

A. *The Publication of the Process*

Publication of the process is effected when the parties and their attorneys are permitted to examine a copy of the complete proceedings, viz., the acts of procedure as well as the acts of evidence, including the evidence which to the present has remained secret.[99]

The parties have a strict right to examine and possess a copy of the acts; for the litigants have a right to defend themselves and their defense measures would prove inadequate should they not possess a thorough knowledge of the evidence marshalled against them. Such knowledge, it is obvious, is obtained not from a passing examination of the acts but rather from a continued study of them.[100]

Per se, the right to possess and inspect the acts cannot be denied the litigants. Should one, however, seriously threaten to abuse this right by divulging information capable of causing serious harm to his opponent or to the Church, he must be considered as having forfeited that right and the party would not be in a position to invoke canon 1859 in his favor.[101] A guardian who would thus

[97] Canon 1836, § 1.

[98] Canon 1836, §§ 1-3.

[99] Canons 1858, 1859.

[100] Cf. Król, *op. cit.*, p. 147; Hogan, *Judicial Advocates and Procurators*, pp. 154-155.

[101] Cf. F. Cappello, "Quaestio Canonica," *Periodica,* XIX (1930) 71-73; Hogan, *op. cit.*, p. 155; Król, *op. cit.*, pp. 147-148.

jeopardize his ward's case would show himself unworthy of the trust placed in him and could be substituted by the judge with a guardian *ad litem;* for, if a guardian may be removed and a substitute named when a conflict arises between his and his ward's rights,[102] all the more it seems to the writer, should a substitute be named when he reveals himself uncooperative and ready to abuse his rights and obligations.

The Instruction of 1936 states explicitly what can be deduced from the prescriptions of canons 1858, 1859 and 1860, namely: When publishing the process, the judge should grant to the parties an equitable period of time within which to submit documents and to propose arguments with which they may support, explain, and supplement the proofs and contentions which they have adduced.[103] New witnesses may also be introduced by the parties provided that all danger of fraud and subornation is removed and that the opposing litigant and tribunal officials are consulted.[104] Finally, if the period allotted for the examination of the acts and the accumulation of further proofs is insufficient, the parties may petition the court for an extension of time.[105]

B. *The Conclusion of the Process*

When activity relative to the producing of evidence has ceased, the tribunal shall proceed to the conclusion of the case (*conclusio in causa*). Ordinarily the case is concluded upon the expiration of the term designated by the tribunal for the presentation of evidence. The judge, however, may issue the decree after obtaining a declaration from the parties that their evidence is exhausted or after declaring himself sufficiently informed in the case.[106]

After this formal declaration that the evidence is exhausted, the admission of further proof is, as a rule, prohibited; exceptions to this rule are admitted in cases which never become irrevocably

---

[102] Cf. canon 1648, § 2.

[103] *Instructio,* art. 175, § 3. Cf. Wernz-Vidal, *De Processibus,* n. 577.

[104] Cf. *Instructio,* art. 175, § 4, together with art. 135. See also canons 1786, 1983.

[105] Canon 1634, § 2. Cf. Król, *op. cit.,* p. 149; Hogán, *op. cit.,* p. 154

[106] Cf. canon 1860.

adjudged[107] and to allow for the presentation of newly discovered documents or for the introduction of witnesses who because of some lawful obstacle could not be brought before the court within the proper time.[108]

In the event that the judge admits such new evidence, he must allow the other litigant sufficient time to examine the new evidence and to prepare contrary proofs.[109] The latter may not be denied the opportunity to study and prepare a defense against the new evidence. This right of defense is protected by the invalidating clause of the cited canon (*aliter iudicium nullius est momenti*) which declares the nullity of the entire trial should that right be violated.

On the other hand, when the judge issues a decree rejecting the introduction of new evidence, the party may make recourse to the collegiate tribunal as a whole.[110]

C. *The Discussion of the Case*

After the formal closing of the case, each party must be granted sufficient time to prepare his defense and present to the court a brief containing his views on, and his arguments against, the evidence produced by his opponent.[111] The amount of time to be allotted is left to the discretion of the judge,[112] who may do well to consider the intricacies inherent in the case and the amount of evidence produced.[113] The judge may prolong the interval at the request of one party, provided the other party is granted a hearing; and with the consent of both parties he may even shorten the period.[114]

---

[107] Cf. canon 1903. Numquam transeunt in rem iudicatam causae de statu personarum . . . Very likely the Code alludes to the three states induced by marriage, by sacred ordination, and by religious profession. Cf. Woywod-Smith, *A Practical Commentary,* II, n. 1821.

[108] Canon 1861, § 1.

[109] Canon 1861, § 2.

[110] *Instructio,* art. 178, § 2.

[111] Canon 1862, § 1.

[112] Canon 1862, § 1.

[113] Cf. Król, *The Defendant in Contentious Trials,* p. 151.

[114] Canon 1862, § 2.

If the parties fail to submit their defense within the allotted time or if they commit the matter to the knowledge and conscience of the judge, the latter may pronounce sentence on the day set for the defense,[115] provided the acts and proofs of the case furnish him full knowledge of the controversy.[116] The court should exercise special care to safeguard the rights of a ward when his guardian is negligent in his duty to furnish an adequate defense. The guardian should be admonished by the court in such cases. A guardian's defective defense should be corrected or supplemented *ex officio* by the judge or by the promoter of justice.[117]

The final discussion of the case is regularly effected by submitting one's defense in writing;[118] but the parties may request an oral discussion of the case,[119] and the judge may permit such a discussion in extraordinary circumstances, if it appears advisable.[120]

D. *The Formulation and Publication of the Sentence*

Though he must be allowed sufficient time for a diligent study of the evidence adduced in the case,[121] the judge may not unreasonably delay the pronouncement of the final sentence. An unreasonable delay could well be attributed to negligence, and in virtue of canon 1625, § 1, the parties could seek redress against the guilty judge. Moreover, in virtue of the same canon, a party has a right to indemnification for the losses caused by the unreasonable delay.

The sentence must settle the controversy as it was proposed to the court in the bill of complaint and determined in the joinder of issue. It must resolve appropriately each of the points of the controversy, and absolve or condemn the defendant in reference

---

115 Cf. Woywod-Smith, *op. cit.*, II, n. 1790.

116 Canon 1867.

117 Canons 1618 and 1619 seem to justify this affirmation, as the adequate defense of a ward is of interest to the public good.

118 Canon 1863, § 3.

119 The petition must be presented in writing and indicate the points of discussion.——Canon 1866, § 3.

120 Canon 1866, § 2.

121 Canon 1870. "Three days should normally suffice to deliberate on an ordinary case and, except in the more difficult marriage cases, the postponement should not exceed fifteen days."—Król, *op. cit.*, p. 153.

to the charges or claims registered against him. Furthermore, as far as the nature of the case permits, the sentence must determine clearly and specifically: a) what the condemned party must do, or refrain from doing, the indemnity he must make, the nature and extent of the penalty he must suffer; and b) the time, place, and manner in accordance with which the provisions of the sentence must be fulfilled. Finally, it must contain the legal and factual motivation of the decision and settle the question of judicial expenses.[122]

After the sentence has been properly drawn up,[123] it should be published as soon as possible.[124] Canon 1877 indicates the three ways in which the publication of the sentence may be made: 1. by summoning the parties to hear the sentence solemnly read by the judge who should be seated while reading; 2. by notifying the parties that the sentence is at the chancery of the tribunal and they may read it there or secure a copy of it; or 3. by forwarding a copy of the sentence to the parties by registered mail.

On January 25, 1943, the Pontifical Commission for the Authentic Interpretation of the Code clearly affirmed that, in cases wherein the parties are insane or feeble-minded, the communication of the sentence must be directed to their legally appointed guardians, and not to the parties themselves.[125] The norm is a

---

[122] Canon 1873, § 1, nn. 1-4.

[123] Cf. canons 1584; 1642, §§ 1, 2; 1872; 1894, nn. 2, 3, 4: From these canons is deduced the manner in which the sentence is to be framed: It must be drawn up in writing and contain: a) an invocation of the Divine Name; b) the names of the judge or judges, the names and domiciles of the plaintiff, defendant, and procurators, the names of the promoter of justice and of the defender of the bond, if either took part in the trial; c) a brief statement of the case, the claims made by the parties, and the decisive part of the sentence prefaced by the reasons on which it is based. It shall conclude with the indication of the place and time of issuance and be subscribed by the judge, or judges, and by the notary.

[124] Canon 1876.

[125] *AAS*, XXXV (1943), 58, II, 2: "Utrum denuntiatio citationis et communicatio sententiae, de quibus in canonibus 1712 et 1877, fieri debeant ipsi rationis usu destituto aut mente infirmo, an eorundem curatori legitime constituto. R. Negative ad primam partem; affirmative ad secundam."

logical deduction from the principles of law governing the cases of the mentally ill.[126]

Article 4. The Guardian and Legal Redress Against the Sentence

The Code safeguards the right of parties to seek legal redress against a sentence which is a source of injury to them by placing at their disposal a number of remedies against the sentence. These remedies are available to them from the moment of the publication of the sentence.

A. *The Correction of Material Errors*

Material errors prejudicial to a party may occur in the transcription of the decisive part of the sentence, in the restatement of the facts or of the petitions of the parties, in calculations of numbers, and the like.[127] At the request of the aggrieved party, the judge shall make the desired correction by issuing a decree to that effect. If, however, the other litigant objects to the proposed correction, the issue is treated as an incidental question.[128]

The party may also join his request for the correction of material errors to an appeal lodged against the trial or sentence because of a formal error.[129]

B. *The Right of Appeal*

An appeal against a sentence is the ordinary remedy against a valid but unjust sentence. This remedy consists in the right to a

[126] Cf. Giustiniani, "De Curatore Dementis," p. 12; Doheny, *Canonical Procedure in Matrimonial Cases,* I, p. 490; canons 1648, § 1; 1650; 1735.

[127] Canon 1878, § 1. The enumeration of errors contained in this canon seems to be intended as an exemplification and not as an all—inclusive list of the possible material errors whose correction may be requested by the parties. Cf. Król, *op. cit.,* p. 165, note 2; Roberti, *De Processibus,* II, n. 464; Lega-Bartoccetti, *Commentarius,* II, 971.

[128] Canon 1878, §§ 2-3. The incidental question is to be settled without the formalities of a trial by a decree of the judge. The decree shall be added at the foot of the corrected sentence.

[129] Cf. Król, *op. cit.,* p. 166; Roberti, *loc. cit.;* Lega-Bartoccetti, *op. cit.,* II, 973.

new investigation of the suit by a superior tribunal.[130] Its purpose is to correct possible errors committed by the inferior court and thus secure a more perfect administration of justice.[131] An appeal is permitted by law to any and all parties interested in a suit if the sentence pronounced by the judge on the cause in question is not considered to be in accordance with the requirement of justice.[132] Accordingly, the plaintiff, the defendant, and those associated in juridic interest with either party in the trial may lodge an appeal against the sentence. Thus, guardians of the mentally ill because of their association with the parties may exercise this right.[133] Moreover, since the defender of the bond and the promoter of justice may also have a just complaint to make against a judicial sentence, each is permitted to file an appeal when acting in his official capacity and when convinced that the public welfare has not been sufficiently protected.[134]

Man has a natural right to protect and defend himself and his lawful interests from aggression and injustice. The rules of positive law but determine the species of defense, prescribing that the natural right be actualized in a given manner and according to specified norms. The remedy of appeal is a determined species of defense, envisaged by the positive law of the Church and regulated in its application by the Code.[135] There is no appeal in the following cases:[136]

1. From a sentence of the Supreme Pontiff or of the Apostolic Signatura. For there is no judge superior to the former and no tribunal higher than the latter, so that the very nature of the remedy of appeal makes it inadmissible in the given cases. The aggrieved party, however, may request of the Supreme Pontiff a *beneficium*

---

[130] Canon 1879.

[131] Cf. Król. *op. cit.*, p. 166; Wernz-Vidal, *De Processibus*, n. 600.

[132] Cf. canon 1879.

[133] Wernz-Vidal, *op. cit.*, n. 602.

[134] Canons 1879; 1986; 1987; 1991; 1998, § 2. Cf. Roberti, *op. cit.*, II, n. 468; Blat, *De Processibus*, n. 409; Coronata, *De Processibus*, n. 1409.

[135] The restrictions placed on the application of the remedy of appeal are inspired by principles of natural equity and are directed to safeguard the public good as well as the rights of the opposing litigants.

[136] Cf. canon 1880, nn. 1-9.

novae audientiae—namely, the favor of a new hearing;[137] and the Signatura may admit an appeal from sentences which it issues in criminal cases against judges of the Roman Rota.[138]

2. From a sentence of a judge delegated by the Holy See to judge a case with an appended clause barring appeal (*appellatione remota*).[139]

3. From a sentence vitiated by an invalidating defect.[140]

4. From a sentence which has become a *res iudicata.*[141]

5. From a final sentence based on a decisory oath.[142]

6. From a decree of the judge or from an interlocutory sentence which does not have the force of a final decree or sentence. To the appeal from the final sentence, however, one may also adjoin an appeal against an interlocutory sentence or decree.

7. From a sentence in a case in which the law ordains that the matter be speedily settled.[143]

8. From a sentence against a party guilty of contempt of court, when he fails to clear himself of contumacy before the sentence is pronounced. The guilty party may petition the judge to reinstate him in the right of appeal; and if his request is granted, he may then lodge his appeal.[144]

9. From a sentence against a person who has expressly stated in writing that he renounced the right to appeal.[145]

---

[137] Coronata, *op. cit.,* n. 1409; Roberti, *op. cit.,* II n. 469; Wernz-Vidal, *op. cit.,* nn. 604, 606.

[138] Canon 1604, § 1.

[139] Roberti observes: "S. Sedes rarius iudices delegat, rarissime cum dicta clausula."—*De Processibus,* II, n. 469.

[140] The proper remedy against a sentence so vitiated is the complaint of nullity. Cf. canons 1892; 1894.

[141] Cf. canon 1902.

[142] Cf. canons 1834-1836. Canon 1905, § 2, n. 3, provides the remedy of *restitutio in integrum* against perjury in connection with the decisory oath.

[143] Cf., e.g., canons 1616; 1709, §3; 1856, § 2. The prescription of a speedy settlement must be explicitly stated in the law. Cf. Król, *op cit.,* p. 170.

[144] Cf. canon 1847.

[145] Król offers further considerations on the prescriptions of canon 1880.—Cf., *op. cit.,* pp. 167-171.

The party who intends to do so may lodge an appeal orally before the judge when the latter reads the sentence publicly, or he may, within ten days from the notice of the publication of the sentence, file a written appeal with the court that rendered the sentence.[146] Unless the judge to whom the appeal is presented extends the period of time, the appeal must be prosecuted within a month from the date of its lodging.[147] The *tempus utile* in both cases is not only interrupted but entirely abated when during the specified periods of time the guardian who was representing a party in court ceases to exercise the function of guardianship.[148] The succeeding guardian must then be notified of the sentence or of the pendency of the appeal, and a new period of ten days or of one month begins to lapse from the date of notification.[149] Since the guardian must seek the best interests of the ward, he must appeal against the sentence when those interests so require. This obligation of the guardian, it seems, can be derived as an *a fortiori* consequence of the guardian's function to protect and defend his ward from injury and injustice to his person and property. The guardian is obliged by law to institute court proceedings in the name of his ward in order to safeguard the latter's rights.[150] In like manner must he perform the judicial acts conducive to that end. Appeal is a legal means to achieve a just sentence, so that negligence in filing an appeal would be no less serious than negligence in instituting proceedings or in placing judicial acts during the course of the trial.[151]

---

[146] Canons 1882, 1881.

[147] Canon 1883. Canons 34, §§ 1 and 3, n. 3, and 1635 are applied in the computing of the time element.

[148] Cf. canon 1733; canon 1885, §§ 1 and 2. Cf. Connolly, *Appeals*, p. 109.

[149] Canon 1885, §§ 1 and 2. See also Król, *op. cit.*, p. 172, note 41.

[150] Cf. canons 1648, § 1; 1650.

[151] Canon 1664, § 2, establishes the right and obligation of the procurator to appeal against an adverse sentence. Hogan comments: "In declaring that the procurator has a right to appeal, the Code indicates that this official, commissioned to place any and all legitimate judicial acts conducive to the best interests of his client, can employ this legal means of safeguarding those rights to the ultimate stages provided by law. Furthermore,

C. *The Complaint of Nullity*

A sentence may be invalid owing to some extrinsic defect, so that the guardian should be mindful of the irregularities which render a sentence irremediably or remediably null.[152] In these cases he has the right and, in consideration of the purpose of his activity, the duty of presenting to the court which issued the sentence a formal complaint of nullity.[153]

Against a sentence that is irremediably null the remedy may be proposed as an action or as an exception. In the first case, it must be presented before the judge who issued the sentence within thirty years from the date of publication of the sentence; as an exception, however, the plaint of nullity may be brought before any tribunal and is perpetual.[154] A complaint of nullity against a remediaby null sentence may be proposed together with an appeal within ten days from the date of publication of the sentence, or it may within three months from the day on which the sentence was published be presented separately before the judge who issued the sentence.[155]

Authors are not agreed as to whether the enumeration of nullities in canons 1892 and 1894 is or is not all-inclusive. Roberti,[156]

---

states the Code, he has a duty to do this. So intimately is the legal remedy of appeal associated with the sentence that negligence in this regard would be no less serious than delinquency during the course of the trial. Lega points out that he who neglects to apply a remedy to a legal set-back sustained is at fault in equal measure with the one who culpably failed to prevent the reverse."—*Judicial Advocates and Procurators,* p. 163. Cf. Lega-Bartoccetti, *Commentarius,* I, 348.

[152] Cf. canons 1892 and 1894.

[153] Canon 1897, § 1.

[154] Canon 1893. Cf. Coyle, *Judicial Exceptions,* p. 62.

[155] Canon 1895.

[156] *De Processibus,* II, 491-494; "Circa limites querelae nullitatis et restitutionis in integrum," *Apollinaris,* I (1928), 476-483; "De nullitate sententiae ob defectum habilitatis ad accusandum matrimonium," *Apollinaris,* XII (1939); 415-416; "De nullitate sententiae," *Apollinaris,* II (1929), 76-78.

Lemieux,[157] and Hogan,[158] for instance, maintain that the list is not all-inclusive.[159]

On the other hand, a greater number of authors, among whom are found D'Angelo,[160] Wernz-Vidal,[161] Feeney,[162] and Noone,[163] favor and defend the strict interpretation, limiting the plaint of nullity to the cases listed in canons 1892 and 1894.[164] Though the jurisprudence of the Sacred Roman Rota favors the strict interpretation,[165] the judge is free to adopt either of the conflicting opinions, since even a precedent established by the Rota has not the force of law, and the Pontifical Commission for the Interpretation of the Code has not rendered a decision on the issue. As for

---

157 *The Sentence in Ecclesiastical Procedure,* p. 99.

158 *Judicial Advocates and Procurators,* p. 169.

159 Noone offers a clear presentation of this "liberal interpretation." Cf. *Nullity in Judicial Acts,* pp. 107-109. "The principal argument," he writes, "for the extensive interpretation of canons 1892 and 1894 is based on canon 1680, § 2, which implies that an act is invalid if it depends on an invalid act. In the law on processes there are many formalities which are required under sanction of nullity of the acts of the case. Consequently the sentence is, in virtue of canon 1680, § 2, invalid because of a derived nullity if it depends on an act which is invalid because of the violation of such a formality. It matters not whether the cause of the invalidity comes under one of the causes of nullity enumerated in canons 1892 and 1894.—*Op. cit.,* pp. 107-108.

160 Cf. "De restitutione in integrum iuxta canonem 1905, § 2, 4°," *Periodica,* XVIII (1929), 37*-62*; "Un caso di 'restitutio in integrum' nella vigente disciplina canonica," *Ephemerides Theologicae Lovanienses,* III (1926), 355-365.

161 *De Processibus,* n. 623.

162 *Restitutio in Integrum,* pp. 111-130.

163 *Nullity in Judicial Acts,* pp. 106-120, *passim.*

164 Cf. Noone, *op. cit.,* pp. 109-120, for the substance of the arguments presented by authors and for arguments based on Rota decisions. Against the principal argument proposed by the advocates of the "liberal interpretation" Noone cites, for instance, S.R.R., *Matriten* (Nullitatis Actorum et Sententiae) 3 iul. 1933, coram R.P.D. Francisco Parrillo, dec. *XLVII,* n. 2: ". . . acta quidem sunt nulla (can. 1587, § 2) haud vero semper sententia, quae super his actis nullis fuerit forte prolata."—S.R.R., *Decisiones,* XXV (1933), 421.

165 Cf. Noone, *op. cit.,* p. 106, note 27, for a list of decisions in which the tendency of the Rota jurisprudence is manifest.

a party who wishes to obtain legal redress against injury resulting from the violation of procedural laws not embraced in canons 1892 and 1894, he would do well to "petition for the application of the extraordinary remedy of *restitutio in integrum,* with the added request that if this remedy does not apply to the case, a declaration of nullity should be issued against the sentence."[166]

The party making the plea of nullity may avail himself of the provision of canon 1896, when he fears prejudice on the part of the judge who pronounced the sentence which he means to impugn. The law allows the party an objection of suspicion and enables the party to demand that another judge in the same tribunal be substituted to hear the complaint.[167]

The judge, too, may revoke *ex officio* a sentence that he has issued and correct it within the period of time prescribed by law.[168] This disposition of the Code is in accord with canon 1618 as regards procedure in criminal trials and in affairs that concern the public good of the Church or the salvation of souls. Lega-Bartoccetti maintain that the provisions of canon 1897, § 2, do not apply to the judge in causes that involve private interests alone. This position can hardly be defended, as that canon does not restrict the activity of the judge as does canon 1618. Moreover, the validity of the sentence always concerns the public good, since the sentence is essential to the proper administration of justice.[169] Lastly, considerations of natural justice dictate that one retract acts of his which bring injury on others, as long as he can make good his fault.[170] The judge, however, cannot compel the parties to renew the trial with the purpose of rectifying the sentence in cases of merely private interest.[171]

---

[166] Coyle, *op. cit.*, pp. 60-61; cf. also, Hogan, *op. cit.*, p. 170.

[167] See also *Instructio,* art. 211, § 4.

[168] Canon 1897, § 2. Cf. also canons 1893 and 1894.

[169] Cf. Coyle, *op. cit.*, p. 61.

[170] Cf. Roberti, *De Processibus,* II, n. 498; Coronata, *De Processibus,* n. 1420; Wernz-Vidal, *De Processibus,* n. 620.

[171] Cf. Roberti, *loc. cit.* "Volenti non fit iniuria," "ad agendum nemo cogi potest," are principles applicable to cases of merely private interest.

D. *Restitutio in Integrum*

If the ordinary remedy of appeal or the complaint of nullity is not available against a sentence which is manifestly unjust, the party may still under certain limitations recur to the extraordinary remedy of *restitutio in integrum* to avoid the damage consequent to an unjust sentence.[172] When granted, this remedy restores the parties to the status which they enjoyed before incurring the protested injustice or damage.[173]

This remedy is granted only when it is established that the sentence issued is evidently unjust. The injustice is manifest when: 1) the sentence was based on documents which were found to be false; 2) new documents were found which peremptorily prove new facts and which demand a contrary decision; 3) the sentence was issued because of the fraud of one party to the detriment of the other;[174] and 4) a precept of law was evidently neglected.

---

[172] Canon 1905, § 1.

[173] Canon 1689. In virtue of this same canon, those rights acquired by others in good faith before the petition for *restitutio in integrum* remain undisturbed.

[174] Canon 1905, § 2. Cf. Woywod-Smith, *A Practical Commentary,* II, n. 1823. Does the neglect of a merely formal procedural law which inflicts serious damage on a litigant suffice to allow the granting of the *restitutio in integrum?* Authors do not agree. The controversy regarding the extension of canon 1905, § 2, n. 4, is related to the dispute about the enumeration of nullities in canons 1892 and 1894; and the exponents of the restrictive interpretation in the latter dispute espouse the extensive interpretation in the former and vice versa. Cf. Roberti, *De Processibus,* II, n. 520-523; "Circa limites querelae nullitatis et restitutionis in integrum," *Apollinaris,* I (1928), 476-483; Lemieux, *The Sentence in Ecclesiastical Procedure,* pp. 99, 102. These authors defend the restrictive interpretation against the following: D'Angelo, "De restitutione in integrum," *Periodica,* XVIII (1929), 37*-62*; Wernz-Vidal, *De Processibus,* n. 639; Coronata, *De Processibus,* n. 1427, b; Vermeersch-Creusen, *Epitome,* III, n. 246; Feeney, *Restitutio in Integrum,* p. 129; Król observes: "The crux of this dispute is not whether a remedy is available, but which of the two remedies (he refers to *querela nullitatis* and *restitutio in integrum*) is the proper one. With particular reference to the defendant, the dispute is of concern only inasmuch as it presents a problem in procedure for the defendant who has suffered grave damage from a sentence which terminated a process in

Justinian decreed that in the causes of minors and of other persons subject to legal disability, when the guardian entered suit on behalf of his ward and then through neglect of duty lost the right of action, the damage resulting from such neglect was to be charged to the guardian or his surety or even his heirs, and that when the guardian's property was not sufficient to cover the damage, the ward was entitled by law to the benefit of complete restitution for all the loss which he had suffered.[175] The Code obliges guardians of the mentally ill to exercise court action on behalf of their wards. Now, a guardian's negligence must not be allowed to injure his ward's condition, so that the court should proceed to admonish the guardian or to remove him if he proves uncooperative and when necessary, the judge may grant the ward the benefit of *restitutio in integrum* either *ex officio* or at the instance of the promoter of justice.[176]

The petition for this remedy suspends the execution of the sentence, if the execution has not yet commenced. The judge may, however, order that the sentence be executed if he has good reason to suspect that the petition was made simply to delay the execution; but in this event the petitioner must be given sufficient security that he will be indemnified if he is granted the *restitutio in integrum*.[177]

---

which a formal procedural law has been violated. It is certain that a remedy is available. The problem merely concerns the use of the proper remedy." —*The Defendant in Contentious Trials,* p. 180.

[175] Cf. C. (3, 1) 13.

[176] Canon 1688, § 2.

[177] Canon 1907, §§ 1-2.

CONCLUSIONS

The following statements present, in summary form, some of the conclusions arrived at in the course of the composition of this dissertation.

1) Historically there appears very little canonical legislation concerning the subject of guardians, as the institute of guardianship was considered of particular concern to the civil authorities. Moreover, the prescriptions of the Roman Law of guardianship were considered adequate and were referred to consistently in canonical writings up to the publication of the Code.

2) The scattered norms and references regarding guardianship found in ecclesiastical writings reveal the interest of the Church in the legal protection of the immature, of the weak, and of the incapacitated.

3) The two terms, *tutor* and *curator,* employed by the Code to denote guardians, do not imply any substantial difference in the functions performed by the persons designated. The terms are frequently interchanged in ecclesiastical documents.

4) The jurist is not chiefly concerned with the causes, the nature, or the distinctive characteristics of mental diseases, but rather with their existence in a particular case and their consequences as to the performance of juridical acts.

5) Generally speaking, a person is qualified to act as guardian in an ecclesiastical lawsuit if he is competent personally to exercise court action and is not otherwise unsuitable or disqualified.

6) To act validly as guardians of major persons in ecclesiastical trials parents must be designated as such by the competent authorities.

7) The guardian may be a layman or a cleric, a man or a woman, a Catholic or a non-Catholic.

8) The law of the Church does not require judicial proceedings to declare a person's disability before placing him under guardianship. If, however, a person's incompetency and his guardian's

appointment are contested, it may be advisable to resort to a formal judicial process.

9) The prior adjudication of insanity or feeble-mindedness by civil courts may be followed by the ecclesiastical authorities. Nevertheless, the mere fact that a person has been confined in an asylum for the insane does not, of itself, constitute full proof of insanity.

10) A guardian appointed for a person by the civil authority requires the consent of the incompetent person's proper Ordinary before being admitted to stand for his ward in a canonical process. As a rule, the guardian appointed by the civil authority should be accepted.

11) If a guardian who has not been properly appointed represents an incompetent person in a trial, the sentence is vitiated by an irremediable nullity.

12) A record of appointment of the guardian should be kept among the acts of the cause.

13. Guardians enjoy all the prerogatives of the parties in law and are bound by all the restrictions binding the same.

14) If a guardian ceases to act for his ward, the process remains interrupted until the proper authority has appointed a new guardian.

BIBLIOGRAPHY

Sources

Acta Apostolicae Sedis, Commentarium Officiale, Romae, 1909—.

Acta et Decreta Concilii Plenarii Baltimorensis Tertii (1884), Baltimore: John Murphy, 1886.

Acta et Decreta Sacrorum Conciliorum Recentiorum, Collectio Lacensis, 7 vols., Friburgi Brisgoviae: Herder & Co., 1870-1890.

Bouscaren, T. L., *The Canon Law Digest,* Officially Published Documents Affecting the Code of Canon Law, 3 vols., Milwaukee: The Bruce Publishing Company, 1934-1943-1954.

Bruns, C. G., *Fontes Iuris Romani Antiqui,* Tubingae: Mohr, 1909.

Codex Iuris Canonici Pii X Pontificis Maximi iussu digestus Benedicti Papae XV auctoritate promulgatus, Praefatione, Fontium annotatione et Indice Analytico-Alphabetico ab Emo. Petro Card. Gasparri Auctus, Romae: Typis Polyglottis Vaticanis, 1917.

Codex Theodosianus, ed. P. Krueger, T. Mommsen, 3 vols., Berolini, 1905.

Codicis Iuris Canonici Fontes, cura Emi Petri Card. Gasparri editi, 9 vols., Romae (Civitate Vaticana): Typis Polyglottis Vaticanis, 1923-1939. (Vols. VII-IX ed. cura et studio Emi. Iustiniani Card. Serédi).

Concilii Plenarii Baltimorensis II., in Ecclesia Metropolitana Baltimorensi, a die VII ad diem XXI Octobris, (1866), et a Sede Apostolica Recogniti, Acta et Decreta, ed. altera, Baltimorae: Ioannes Murphy, 1894.

Corpus Iuris Canonici, 2. ed., Lipsiensis, post Aemilii Ludovici Richteri curas instruxit Aemilius Friedberg, 2 vols., Lipsiae: Tauchnitz, 1879-1881.

Corpus Iuris Civilis, Vol. I, *Institutiones*—recognovit P. Krueger; *Digesta*—recognovit T. Mommsen, retractavit P. Krueger; Vol. II, *Codex Iustinianus*—recognovit et retractavit P. Krueger; Vol. III, *Novellae Constitutiones*—recognovit R. Schoell; opus Schoellii morte interceptum absolvit G. Kroll, Berolini, 1928-1929.

Decretales Gregorii IX, una cum Glossis Restitutae, Romae, 1582

Fontes Iuris Romani Antejustiniani, editio altera aucta et emendata: Pars Prima: *Leges* (Riccobono), 1941; Pars Altera: *Auctores* (Baviera), *Liber Syro-Romanus* (Furlani), 1940; Pars Tertia: *Negotia* (Arangio-Ruiz), 1943, Florentiae: Barbera, 1940-1941-1943.

Jaffé, P., *Regesta Pontificum Romanorum ab condita Ecclesia ad annum post Christum natum 1198,* 2. ed. correctam et auctam auspiciis Gulielmi Wattenbach curaverunt, F. Kaltenbrunner, P. Ewald, S. Loewenfeld, 2 vols., Lipsiae, 1885-1888.

Liber Sextus Decretalium, una cum Clementinis et Extravagantibus earumque glossis restitutis, Romae, 1582.

Mansi, Joannes, *Sacrorum Conciliorum Nova et Amplissima Collectio,* 53 vols., Paris, 1901-1927.

Monumenta Germaniae Historica, Legum Sectio I, *Epistolae,* Tomus I et II, *Gregorii I Papae Registrum Epistolarum,* edd. Paulus Ewald et Ludovicus M. Hartmann, Berolini, 1891-1899.

Potthast, A., *Regesta Pontificum Romanorum inde ab anno post Christum natum 1198 ad annum 1304,* 2 vols., Berolini, 1874-1875.

Sacrae Romanae Rotae Decisiones seu Sententiae (ab anno 1909), Romae: Typis Vaticanis, 1912—.

Sartori, C., *Enchiridion Canonicum seu Sanctae Sedis Responsiones,* 8. ed., Romae: Pontificium Athenaeum Antonianum, 1947.

Reference Works

Altimarus, Blasius, *Tractatus de Nullitatibus in XIV Rubricas Divisus,* Neapoli, 1678.

American Jurisprudence: a text treatise of American case law, supported by references to the leading decisions of the courts, 58 vols. and indices, San Francisco: Bancroft-Whitney Co., 1935-1952.

Arangio-Ruiz, Vincenzo, *Istituzioni di Diritto Romano,* 10. ed., Napoli: Jovene, 1949.

Augustine, Charles, *A Commentary on the New Code of Canon Law,* 8 vols., Vol. VII, 3. ed., 1930, St. Louis, Mo.: B. Herder & Co.

Beste, Udalricus, *Introductio in Codicem,* 3. ed., Collegeville, Minn.: St. John's Abbey Press, 1946.

Black, Henry C., *A Law Dictionary,* 2. ed., St. Paul, Minn.: West Publishing Co., 1910.

Blat, Albertus, *Commentarium Textus Codicis Iuris Canonici, Liber IV, De Processibus,* Romae: Collegio Angelico, 1927.

Bonfante, Pietro, *Corso di Diritto Romano,* Roma, 1925.

Bouix, D., *Tractatus de Judiciis Ecclesiasticis,* 3. ed., 2 vols., Paris, 1883.

Brugi, Biagio, *Istituzioni di Diritto Romano (Diritto Privato Giustinianeo),* 3. ed., Torino: Unione Tipografico—Editrice Torinese, 1926.

Brunini, Joseph B., *The Clerical Obligations of Canons 139 and 142,* The Catholic University of America Canon Law Studies, n. 103, Washington, D.C.: The Catholic University of America, 1937.

Buckland, William W., *A Manual of Roman Private Law,* Cambridge: Cambridge University Press, 1925.

Burdick, William L., *The Principles of Roman Law and Their Relation to Modern Law,* Rochester: The Lawyers Co-operative Publishing Co., 1938.

Bussi, Emilio, *La Formazione dei Dogmi di Diritto Privato nel Diritto Comune (Contratti, Successioni, Diritti di Famiglia)*, Padova: Cedam, 1939.

Butera, Antonio, *Il Codice Civile Italiano commentato secondo l'ordine degli articoli,* Torino: Unione Tipografico-Editrice Torinese, 1939.

Calisse, Carlo, *Diritto Ecclesiastico e Diritto Longobardo,* Roma, 1888.

Cappello, Felix M., *Praxis Processualis ad Norman Codicis et Peculiarem Sanctae Sedis Instructionem,* editio altera emendata et aucta, Romae: Marietti, 1948.

———, *Summa Iuris Canonici,* 3. ed., 3 vols., Romae: Apud Aedes Universitatis Gregorianae, 1938-1948.

Cassola, Ovidio, *La Recezione del Diritto Civile nel Diritto Canonico,* Tortona: Tipografia San Giuseppe, 1941.

Catholic Encyclopedia, The, 15 vols., Index and 2 Supplements, New York, 1907-1922.

Chelodi, Ioannes, *Ius Canonicum de Personis,* 3. ed., curavit P. Ciprotti, Trento: Libreria Moderna Editrice, 1942.

Ciprotti, P., *Contributo alla Teoria della Canonizzazione delle Leggi Civili,* Roma: Università Civile, 1941.

———, *Le Nuove Norme per i Processi di Nullità di Matrimonio Presso i Tribunali Diocesani,* Roma, 1937.

Claeys Bouuaert, F., et Simenon, G., *Manuale Iuris Canonici ad Usum Seminariorum,* Vols. I & III, 3. ed.; Vol. II, 1. ed., Gandae et Leodii, 1930-1931.

Clark, E. C., *History of Roman Private Law,* 4 vols., Cambridge: University Press, 1906-1919.

Cocchi, Guidus, *Commentarium in Codicem Iuris Canonici,* 8 vols., Vol. II, *De Personis,* 3. ed., 1948, Vol. VII, *De Processibus,* 3. ed., 1940, Taurinorum Augustae: Marietti.

Connolly, Thomas A., *Appeals,* The Catholic University of America Canon Law Studies, n. 79, Washington, D.C.: The Catholic University of America, 1932.

Coronata, Matthaeus Conte, a, *Institutiones Iuris Canonici,* 3 ed., 5 vols., Taurini: Marietti, 1947-1948.

———, *Institutiones Iuris Canonici, De Sacramentis,* 2. ed., 3 vols., Taurini: Marietti, 1948-1949.

Costello, John M., *Domicile and Quasi-Domicile,* The Catholic University of America Canon Law Studies, n. 60, Washington, D.C.: The Catholic University of America, 1930.

Coyle, Paul R., *Judicial Exceptions,* The Catholic University of America Canon Law Studies, n. 193, Washington, D.C.: The Catholic University of America Press, 1944.

Cuq, Edouard, *Institutions Juridiques des Romains,* 2 vols., Paris, 1891-1892.

D'Angelo, Sosio, *Ius Digestorum,* Romae: Apollinaris, 1927-1928.

D'Annibale, Joseph, *Summula Theologiae Moralis,* 5. ed., 3 vols., Romae, 1908.

D'Avack, Pietro A., *Cause di Nullità e di Divorzio nel Diritto Matrimoniale Canonico,* Vol. 1, Firenze: Casa Editrice del Dott. Carlo Cya, 1952.

Della Rocca, Fernando, *Istituzioni di Diritto Processuale Canonico,* Torino: Tip. Torinese, 1946.

De Meester, *Juris Canonici et Juris Canonico-Civilis Compendium,* 3 vols. in 4, Brugis: Desclée, 1921-1928.

Devoti, Joannes, *Ius Canonicum Universum et Privatum,* 3 vols., Romae, 1803.

Doheny, William J., *Canonical Procedure in Matrimonial Cases,* Vol. I, *Formal Judicial Procedure,* 2. ed., Milwaukee: The Bruce Publishing Co., 1948.

———, *Practical Manual for Marriage Cases,* Milwaukee: The Bruce Publishing Co., 1938.

Dolan, John L., *The Defensor Vinculi, His Rights and Duties,* The Catholic University of America Canon Law Studies, n. 85, Washington, D.C.: The Catholic University of America, 1934.

Durandus (Durantis), Gulielmus, *Speculum Iuris,* 3 vols., Venetiis, 1577.

Encyclopaedia Britannica, 23 vols., Chicago: Encyclopaedia Britannica, Inc., 1944.

Enciclopedia Italiana di Scienze, Lettere ed Arti, 36 vols. and Appendix, Roma: Istituto Giovanni Treccani, 1929-1939.

Farren, Neil, *Domicile and Quasi-Domicile,* Dublin: Gill and Son, 1920.

Feeney, Thomas J., *Restitutio in Integrum,* The Catholic University of America Canon Law Studies, n. 129, Washington, D.C.: The Catholic University of America Press, 1941.

Ferraris, Lucius, *Prompta Bibliotheca Canonica, Iuridica, Moralis, Theologica, necnon Ascetica, Polemica, Rubricistica, Historica,* ed. noviss., 9 vols., Romae, 1885-1899.

Ferreres, Ioannes B., *Institutiones Canonicae iuxta Novissimum Codicem Pii X,* 2. ed., 2 vols., Barcinone, 1920.

Gibbons, Marion L., *Domicile of the Wife Unlawfully Separated from Her Husband,* The Catholic University of America Canon Law Studies, n. 249, Washington, D.C.: The Catholic University of America Press, 1947.

Glynn, John C., *The Promoter of Justice,* The Catholic University of America Canon Law Studies, n. 101, Washington, D.C.: The Catholic University of America, 1936.

Goyeneche, Servus, *De Processibus,* Vol. I, *De Iudiciis in Genere,* Pro manuscripto (Romae: S. Joannis Lat.).

Gutierrez, Joannes, *Tractatus Novus de Tutelis et Curis,* Francofurti: Impensis Wolfgangi Endteri, 1650.

Hanssen, Antonius, *De Sanctione Nullitatis in Processu Canonico,* Romae: Apollinaris, 1939.

Hogan, James J., *Judicial Advocates and Procurators,* The Catholic University of America Canon Law Studies, n. 133, Washington, D.C.: The Catholic University of America Press, 1941.

Jemolo, A. C., *Il Matrimonio nel Diritto Canonico,* Milano: Vallardi, 1941.

Jolowicz, Herbert F., *Historical Introduction to the Study of Roman Law,* 2. ed., Cambridge: University Press, 1952.

Karlowa, Otto, *Römische Rechtsgeschichte,* 2 vols., Leipzig: Veit and Co., 1885-1901.

Kealy, John J., *The Introductory Libellus in Church Court Procedure,* The Catholic University of America Canon Law Studies, n. 108, Washington, D.C.: The Catholic University of America, 1937.

Król, John J., *The Defendant in Contentious Trials,* The Catholic University of America Canon Law Studies, n. 146, Washington, D.C.: The Catholic University of America Press, 1942.

Larousse du XXe Siècle, 6 vols., publié sous la direction de Paul Auge, Paris: Librairie Larousse, 1929.

Leage, R. W., *Roman Private Law,* 2. ed. by C. H. Ziegler, London: Macmillan and Co., 1948.

Lega, Michael, *Praelectiones de Iudiciis Ecclesiasticis,* 4 vols., Romae, 1896-1901.

———, *Commentarius in Iudicia Ecclesiastica iuxta Codicem Iuris Canonici, curante Victorio Bartoccetti,* 3 vols., Romae: Anonima Libreria Cattolica Italiana, 1939-1941.

Lemieux, Delisle A., *The Sentence in Ecclesiastical Procedure,* The Catholic University of America Canon Law Studies, n. 87, Washington, D. C.: The Catholic University of America, 1934.

Longo, C.—Scherillo, G., *Storia del Diritto Romano,* Milano: Giuffre, 1944.

Maroto, Philippus, *Institutiones Iuris Canonici ad Norman Novi Codicis,* 2 vols., Romae: Vol. I, 3. ed., 1921; Vol. II, 1919, Apud Commentarium pro Religiosis.

McBride, James T., *Incardination and Excardination of Seculars,* The Catholic University of America Canon Law Studies, n. 145, Washington, D. C.: The Catholic University of America Press, 1941.

McCloskey, Joseph A., *The Subject of Ecclesiastical Law According to Canon 12,* The Catholic University of America Canon Law Studies, n. 165, Washington, D.C.: The Catholic University of America Press, 1943.

McClunn, Justin D., *Administrative Recourse,* The Catholic University of America Canon Law Studies, n. 240, Washington, D. C.: The Catholic University of America Press, 1946.

Michiels, Gommarus, *Normae Generales Juris Canonici,* editio altera, 2 vols., Tournai: Desclée & Co., 1949.

———, *Principia Generalia de Personis in Ecclesia,* Lublin: Universitas Catholica, 1932.

Migne, J. P., *Patrologiae Cursus Completus—Series Graeca,* 161 vols. Parisiis, 1857-1866.

———, *Patrologiae Cursus Completus—Series Latina,* 221 vols., Parisiis, 1844-1864.

Moore, Thomas V., *The Nature and Treatment of Mental Disorders,* New York: Grune and Stratton, 1944.

Moriarity, Eugene J., *Oaths in Ecclesiastical Courts,* The Catholic University of America Canon Law Studies, n. 110, Washington, D.C.: The Catholic University of America, 1937.

Muirhead, James, *Historical Introduction to the Private Law of Rome,* revised and edited by Henry Goudy, 3. ed. revised and edited by Alexander Grant, London: Black, 1916.

———, *Roman Law,* London, 1899.

Muñiz, T., *Procedimientos Eclesiasticos,* 2. ed., 3 vols., Sevilla: Lib. de Sobrino de Isquierdo, 1926.

Noone, John J., *Nullity in Judicial Acts,* The Catholic University of America Canon Law Studies, n. 297, Washington, D. C.: The Catholic University of America Press, 1950.

Noval, Joseph, *Commentarium Codicis Iuris Canonici,* Lib. IV, *De Processibus,* Pars I, *De Iudiciis,* Augustae Taurinorum: Marietti, 1920.

O'Donnell, Cletus, F., *The Marriage of Minors,* The Catholic University of America Canon Law Studies, Washington, D. C.: The Catholic University of America Press, 1945.

Ojetti, B., *Commentarium in Codicem Iuris Canonici,* 4 vols., Romae: Apud Aedes Universitatis Gregorianae, 1927-1931.

Olivero, Giuseppe, *Le Parti nel Giudizio Canonico,* Milano: Giuffre, 1941.

Ottaviani, Alaphridus, *Institutiones Iuris Publici Ecclesiastici,* 2 vols., Vol. I, *Ius Publicum Internum,* 3. ed., Civitas Vaticana: Typis Polyglottis Vaticanis, 1947.

Pacchioni, Giovanni, *Corso di Diritto Romano,* 2 vols., Torino, 1918.

Palmieri, Vincenzo M., *Medicina Legale Canonistica,* Bari, 1946.

Panormitanus (Nicolaus de Tudeschis), *Commentaria in Quinque Libros Decretalium,* 8 vols., Venetiis, 1588.

Passerini, P., *Commentaria in Sextum Librum Decretalium,* 2 vols., Romae: 1667-1670.

Perozzi, Silvio, *Istituzioni di Diritto Romano,* 2 ed., 2 vols., Roma: Athenaeum, 1928.

Pertile, Antonio, *Storia del Diritto Italiano, dalla caduta dell'Impero romano alla codificazione,* 2. ed., 6 vols., Torino: Unione Tipografico-Editrice, 1892-1902.

Perugini, A., *Concordata Vigentia, Notis Historicis et Iuridicis Declarata,* Romae: Apud Custodiam Librariam Pont. Instituti Utriusque Iuris, 1934.

Pickett, R. C., *Mental Affliction and Church Law,* Ottawa, Ontario: The University of Ottawa Press, 1952.

———, *Roman Law and the Insane,* Ottawa, Ontario: The University of Ottawa Press, 1949.

Pichler, Vitus, *Candidatus Jurisprudentiae Sacrae seu Juris Canonici, Secundum Gregorii Papae IX Decretalium Titulos Explicati,* 3. ed., Sumptibus G. Schluter & M. Happach, 1726-1728.

Pignatelli, J., *Consultationes Canonicae,* 11 vols. in 5, Coloniae Allobrogum, 1700-1711.

Pinna, Joannes M., *Praxis Judicialis Canonica,* Romae: Catholic Book Agency, 1952.

Regatillo, Eduardus F., *Institutiones Iuris Canonici,* 3. ed., 2 vols., Santander: Sal Terrae, 1949.

Reiffenstuel, Anacletus, *Jus Canonicum Universum,* 5 vols. in 6, Romae, 1831-1834.

Reinhardt, Marion J., *The Rogatory Commission,* The Catholic University of America Canon Law Studies, Washington, D. C.: The Catholic University of America Press, 1949.

Rivier, A., *Précis du Droit de Famille Romain,* Paris: Rousseau, 1891.

Roberti, Franciscus, *Codex Iuris Canonici Schemata,* Lib. IV, *De Processibus,* Romae: Typis Polyglottis Vaticanis, 1940.

———, *De Delictis et Poenis,* Vol. I, Partes I et II, Romae: Apud Custodiam Librariam Pontificii Instituti Utriusque Iuris, 1938.

———, *De Processibus,* 2 vols., Vol. I, 2. ed., Romae: Apud Custodiam Librariam Pontificii Instituti Utriusque Iuris, 1941.

———, *Iuris Processualis Compendium,* Vol. I, Romae: Apud Custodiam Librariam Pontificii Instituti Utriusque Iuris.

Robinson, James J., *Selections from the Public and Private Law of the Romans,* New York: American Book Company, 1905.

Roby, Henry J., *An Introduction to the Study of Justinian's Digest,* Cambridge: Cambridge University Press, 1886.

Sanchez, Thomas, *Disputationum de Sancto Matrimonii Sacramento Tomi Tres,* Antverpiae, 1607.

Sanfilippo, Cesare, *Istituzioni di Diritto Romano,* 2. ed., Napoli: Humus, 1946.

Schmalzgrueber, Franciscus, *Jus Ecclesiasticum Universum,* 5 vols. in 12, Romae, 1843-1845.

Schroeder, H. J., *Disciplinary Decrees of the General Councils,* St. Louis: Herder, 1937.

Schulz, Fritz, *Classical Roman Law,* Oxford: Clarendon Press, 1951.

———, *Principles of Roman Law,* Oxford: Clarendon Press, 1936.

Sherman, Charles P., *Roman Law in the Modern World,* 2. ed., 3 vols., New York: Baker, Voorhis & Co., 1924.

Sipos, Stephanus, *Enchiridion Iuris Canonici,* ed. altera, Pecs, 1936.

Sohm, Rudolf, *The Institutes of Roman Law,* translated by James C. Ledlie, 3. ed., Oxford: Clarendon Press, 1907.

Stickler, Alphonsus M., *Historia Iuris Canonici Latini,* Vol. I, *Historia Fontium,* Augustae Taurinorum: Apud Custodiam Librariam Pontif. Athenaei Salesiani, 1950.

Stitt, Archibaldus M., *De Promotore Justitiae Ejusque Munere in Curia Dioecesana,* Dissertatio ad Lauream in Facultate Juris Canonici Pontificiae Universitatis Gregorianae, Romae: Ed. Scientifica Internazionale, 1939.

Strecker, Edward A., *Fundamentals of Psychiatry,* 4. ed., Philadelphia: Lippincott, 1947.

Tobin, Thomas, *De Officiali Curiae Dioecesanae,* Romae: Apud Aedes Pontificiae Universitatis Gregorianae, 1936.

Torre, Joannes, *Processus Matrimonialis,* Neapoli: M. D'Auria, 1947.

Traité di Droit Canonique, sous la direction de Raoul Naz, 4 vols., Paris: Letouzey et Ané, 1948-1949.

Vaughan, William Edward, *Constitutions for Diocesan Courts,* The Catholic University of America Canon Law Studies, n. 210, Washington, D. C.: The Catholic University of America Press, 1944.

Van der Veldt, James H. and Odenwald, Robert P., *Psychiatry and Catholicism,* New York: McGraw-Hill Book Company, Inc., 1952.

Van Hove, A., *Commentarium Lovaniense in Codicem Iuris Canonici,* Vol. I, Tom. I, *Prolegomena,* 2. ed., Mechliniae et Romae: H. Dessain, 1945.

Vermeersch, Arthurus-Creusen, Josephus, *Epitome Iuris Canonici,* 3 vols., 6. ed., Mechliniae-Romae: H. Dessain, 1937-1946.

Vantius, Sebastianus, *Tractatus de Nullitatibus Processuum et Sententiarum,* Venetiis: Apud Jacobum Cornettum, 1588.

Wernz, Franciscus, *Ius Decretalium,* 6 vols., Romae: 1898-1914.

Wernz, Franciscus X.-Vidal, Petrus, *Ius Canonicum,* 7 toms. in 8 vols., Romae: *Apud Aedes Universitatis Gregorianae,* Vol. II, *De Personis,* 3. ed., 1943, Vol. VI, *De Processibus,* 1927, Vol. VII, *Ius Poenale,* 1937.

Woywod, Stanislaus, *A Practical Commentary on the Code of Canon Law,* Revised by Callistus Smith, 2 vols., New York: Joseph F. Wagner, Inc., 1945.

Zacchia, Paulus, *Quaestiones Medico-Legales,* 4. ed., 6 vols., Venetiis: 1789.

PERIODICALS

Apollinaris, Romae, 1928—

Canoniste, Le, Paris, 1924-1926 (originally *Le Canoniste Contemporain,* Paris, 45 vols., 1878-1922).

Diritto Ecclesiastico, Il, Roma, 1890—

Homiletic and Pastoral Review, The, New York, 1900—

Jurist, The, Washington, 1941—

Ius Pontificium, Romae, 1921-1940.

Monitore Ecclesiastico, Il, Roma, 1876-1948.

Perfice Munus, Torino, 1926—

Periodica de Re Canonica et Morali, Brugis, 1905; ab anno 1927: *Periodica de Re Canonica, Morali, Liturgica.*

Salesianum, Torino, 1939—

ARTICLES

Aguirre, Philippus, "Annotationes: II. Decuratore dementis," *Periodica,* XXXII (1943), 294-296.

Allers, Rudolf, "Annulment of marriage by lack of consent because of insanity," *AER,* LI (1939), 33.

Amanieu, A., "Aliénation mentale en matière de nullité de marriage," *DDC,* Paris: Librairie Letouzey et Ané, 1935, Tome I, coll. 417-440.

Cappello, Felix, "De acatholicorum incapacitate agendi in foro ecclesiastico," *Miscellanea Vermeersch,* 2 vols., Romae: Pontificia Universitas Gregoriana, 1935, I, 393-402.

———, "Quaestio Canonica," *Periodica,* XIX (1930), 71.

Couly, August, "L'Officialité: Les Parties en cause," *Le Canoniste,* XLVIII (1926), 347-357, 381-391.

Crnica, A., "De Lacunis Legis Supplendis ad Norman Codicis J. C.," *Jus Pontificium,* XVI (1936), 193-196.

D'Angelo, Sosio, "De Restitutione in Integrum iuxta canonem 1905, § 2, n. 4," *Periodica,* XVIII (1929), 37*-62*.

———, "Un caso di 'restitutio in integrum' nella vigente disciplina canonica," *Ephemerides Theologicae Lovanienses,* III (1926), 355-365.

Del Corpo, Aegidius, "De iure agendi in iudiciis ecclesiasticis communistarum aliorumque acatholicorum," *Monitor Ecclesiasticus,* LXXV (1950), 97-102.

De Visscher, Fernand, "Potestas et Cura," *Studi Perozzi,* Palermo: Castiglia, 1925, 399-406.

Giustiniani, Roberto, "De curatore dementis," *Il Diritto Ecclesiaastico,* LIV (1943), 105-108.

Joddard, H. G.-X (anonymous), "Feeble-mindedness," *Encyclopaedia Britannica,* Chicago: Encyclopaedia Britannica, Inc., 1944, Vol. XII, 392-393.

Lefebvre, Ch., "Debilité mentale," *DDC,* Paris; Librairie Letouzey et Ané, 1949, Tome IV, coll. 1043-1051.

Noval, Joseph, "De semi-amentibus et semi-imputabilitati obnoxiis," *Jus Pontificium,* IV (1924), 76-85.

Pugliese, Agostino, "La necessitá del curatore canonico e dell'avvocato d'ufficio per le persone deboli di mente nelle cause matrimoniali ecclesiastiche," *Salesianum,* VI (1944), 183-188.

Read, C. Stanford, "Insanity," *Encyclopaedia Britannica,* Chicago: Encyclopaedia Britannica, Inc., 1944, Vol. XII, 383-389.

Renier, E., "Observations de la terminologie de l'aliénation mentale," *Revue Internationale des Droits de l'Antiquité,* V (1950), 429-455.

Roberti, F., "Animadversiones," *Apollinaris,* I (1928), 214-219.

———, "Circa limites querelae nullitatis et restitutionis in integrum." *Apollinaris,* I (1928), 476-483.

———, "De nullitate sententiae ob defectum habilitatis ad accusandum matrimonium," *Apollinaris,* XII (1939), 415-416.

———, "De nullitate sententiae," *Apollinaris,* II (1929), 76-78.

Roberti, Melchiorre, "Cristianesimo e collezione giustinianee," *Cristianesimo e Diritto Romano,* Milano: Vita e Pensiero, 1935, 1-64.

Schmidt, John R., "The juridic value of the *Instructio* provided by the Motu Proprio 'Cum Iuris Canonici' September 15, 1917," The Jurist, I (1941), 289-316.

Staffa, Dinus, "De constitutione curatoris pro mente infirmis in jure canonico," *Apollinaris,* XVI (1943), 63-81.

Toso, Albertus, "De constitutione curatoris in foro ecclesiastico," *Jus Pontificium,* XIX (1939), 115-119.

Tuttle, Charles H., "Insanity in Law (United States)", *Encyclopaedia Britannica,* Chicago: Encyclopaedia Britannica, Inc., 1944, Vol. XII, 392-393.

Woywod, Stanislaus, "Procurators, advocates and exceptions," *HPR,* XXXI (1931), 607-614.

Abbreviations

AAS—*Acta Apostolicae Sedis.*
AER—*American Ecclesiastical Review, The,.*
Am. Jur.—*American Jurisprudence.*
C.—Codex Iustinianus, or Causa.
c.—canon or caput.
Coll. Lac.—*Collectio Lacensis.*
D.—Digesta.
DDC—*Dictionnaire de Droit Canonique.*
ER—*Ecclesiastical Review, The*
Fontes—*Codicis Iuris Canonici Fontes* cura . . . Gasparri editi.
HPR—*Homiletic and Pastoral Review.*
Inst.—Institutiones
Jaffé—*Regesta Pontificum Romanorum ad annum MCXCVIII* (edited by Kaltenbrunner, Ewald, Loewenfeld).
Mansi—*Sacrorum Conciliorum Nova et Amplissima Collectio.*
MGH—*Monumenta Germaniae Historica.*
MPG—Migne, *Patrologia Graeca.*
MPL—Migne, *Patrologia Latina.*
N.—Novellae.
PCI—Pontifical Commission for the Authentic Interpretation of the Code.
Potthast—*Regesta Pontificum Romanorum ab anno MCXVIII ad annum MCCCIV.*
S.R.R.—Sacra Romana Rota.

ALPHABETICAL INDEX

Access, judicial, 143
Administrative procedure, 74
Adgnati, 63, 65
Alexander Severus, 52
Ambrose, Saint, 171
Amentes, 16, 38, 39
Amentia, 35, 39
Appeal, 128, 152
Apostates, 118
Aquilius Gallus, 31

Baldus de Ubaldis, 20
Bouix, 16
Brief, 149
Brumini, 60

Capacitas partis, 103
Capacity, jural, in Roman law, 11
  jural, in Church, 109
  natural, 43, 45, 111
Chiovenda, 68
Citation, 133
Clerics, as guardians, 17, 53, 60
Clune, 138
Complaint of nullity, 156
Conclusion of the process, 148
Contentious trials, 72
Contestatio litis, 134
Contumacy, 136
Corpus iuris civilis, 6, 22, 31, 67
Council of,
  III Carthage, 17
  IV Chalcedon, 18
  Lyons, 116
  IV Toledo, 19
Criminal cases, 105
  and infidels, 113
  and non-Catholics, 119
Cura, 6, 31, 65, 66
  ad certam rem, 11
  bonorum, 11
  debilium, 10, 43
  furiosi, 8, 10
  legitima, 64
  minorum, 10
  prodigi, 10
  ventris, 11

Curator, legitimus, 30
  in Roman law, 6, 8, 13, 14
  term in Ecclesiastical law, 30

D'Angelo, 157
D'Annibale, 39
D'Avack, 58
Decretum Gratiani, 21
Dementes, 38, 39
Dementia, description of, 37
Digest, of Justinian, 5, 14
Discussion of case, 149
Disqualification, see incapacity to act
  effects of, 49
Documents, 132, 141
Doheny, 57, 61, 80
Domicile, loss of, 93, 95
  of feeble-minded, 84, 96
  of insane, 84, 91, 94, 95
  necessary, 91
  voluntary, 90

Exception, against apostates, 119
  against guardian, 55, 57
  against heretics, 119
  against infidels, 113
  against participants in trial, 130, 134
  against schismatics, 119
  of excommunication, 117
Excommunicates, 103, 110, 114, 117
Experts, 142

Feeble-minded (feeble-mindedness),
  see *Mentis debilitas* (*debilis*)
  may be interrogated, 138
Feeney, 157
Ferraris, 58
Furiosi, 3, 12, 13, 16, 32, 34
  see also *cura furiosi*

Gaius, 5, 9
Gasparri, 40
Gentiles, 62
Giustiniani, 57
Gratian, 21
Guardian, *ad litem,* 97, 148
  appointment of, 62, 89, 97
  approval of civil guardian, 82

cleric as, 17, 53, 60
Defensor Vinculi as, 61
exception against, 55, 57
moral person as, 61
necessity of, 45
orphanage as, 53
parents as, 58
persons disqualified or unsuitable as, 55, 56
Promotor iustitiae as, 61
qualifications of, 52
removal of, 53, 54, 148
Guardianship, in Code of Canon Law, 23
development in Church law and doctrine, 15
development in Roman law, 3, 13, 23, 65
function in Church law, 29
function in modern civil law, 15, 82
function in Roman law, 13, 65
terminology in Code, 30
terminology in Roman law, 6, 7
treatment of by Roman jurists, 5, 10
see also *cura, tutela*
Guilelmus Durantis, 19

Heretics, 110, 118
Hogan, 157
Holy Office and non-Catholics in matrimonial cases, 111, 118

Incapacity to act, of blind, deaf-mutes, 48
of excommunicated, 114
of feeble-minded, 47
of infidels, 109
of insane, 46
of non-Catholics, 118
of religious, 119
Infidels, disqualifications of, 109
Insane, criminal liability, 40
incapacity to act, 46
notion, 37
Insanity, 33
Inspection, judicial, 143
Institutes, of Justinian, 5, 14
Instructio, 47, 74, 76
Interrogation, of insane and feeble-minded, 138
of parties, 130
Interruption of instance, 130

Jemolo, 74
Joannes Andreae, 20
Joining of issues, the, 134
Judge, appoints guardian, 97
and civil law guardian, 82
Jus novum, 19
Justinian, 160

Kealy, 132
Król, 144

Lega, 43, 59, 74
Legitimatio, ad causam, 105
ad processum, 106
Lemieux, 157
Libellus, 131
Litis contestatio, 134
Lucid intervals, in canonical jurisprudence, 40
and capacity to act, 47
and Roman doctors, 34

Mandate, effect of illegitimate, 88, 123
guardian's, 108, 123
Maroto, 71
McClunn, 129
Mental diseases, attitude of jurists towards, 35, 36
degree of, 79
see *dementia*
description of, 37
and psychiatrists, 36, 37
terms denoting, 31, 32, 35, 37
Mentally ill, and Code, 37
in ecclesiastical trials, 31
incapacity to act, 33, 35, 43, 47
interdiction of, 67
and Roman jurists, 31
terms denoting, 31, 32
Mentis debilitas (*debiles*), incapacity to act, 47
notion, 41
Minors, 27
Monomaniacs, 38

Napoleonic Code, 67, 68
Nomocanones, 21
Non-Catholics, as guardians, 56
as procurators, 56
Noone, 58, 75, 157
Novices, 120
Nullity, of court action, 49, 124, 128
of sentence, 50, 62, 124

Oaths, 145
Ordinary, appoints guardian before summons, 133
consent of and civil law guardian, 83, 86, 132
meaning of term, 85
proper, 84, 85, 90, 96

Paterfamilias, and guardianship, 4, 8, 53
and jural capacity, 12
and *potestas*, 8, 12
Paul, Saint, 17
Persona standi in iudicio, 49, 102, 107
Pope, Boniface VIII, 61
Gelasius I, 18
Innocent IV, 116
John VIII, 21
Lucius II, 22
Pius XI, 86
Poste, 13
Presumptions, 143
Puberty, in Roman law, 7
Publication, of process, 147
of sentence, 150

Quasi-domicile, of feeble-minded, 85, 96
of insane, 94, 95
loss of, 93
necessary, 92
voluntary, 90
Querela nullitatis, 156

Recourse, 129
Religious, domicile of, 92
as guardians, 60
proper Ordinary of, 96
and *persona standi in judicio*, 119
Restitutio in integrum, 159
Roberti, 59, 75, 156
Roman law, and canon law, 16, 19, 20
and Code, 22
and guardianship, see guardianship

Sanchez, 38
Schismatics, 118
Sentence, correction of, 152
formulation and publication of, 150
Servius Sulpicius, 14
Severus, 66
Staffa, 73, 76
Status, in Roman law, 11
Summons, formal, 133
Synod of Pavia, 27

Testimony of witnesses, 138
Torre, 71
Toso, 74
Tutela, of clerics, 19
definition of by Sulpicius, 14
impuberum, 7, 9, 17
mulierum, 7, 9
Tutor, in Roman law, 5, 6, 8
term in Ecclesiastical law, 30
Twelve Tables, and guardianship, 3, 8, 13, 62

Ulpian, 32, 63, 64

Van der Veldt-Odenwald, 39
Vicar-general, power to appoint guardian of, 78, 85

Wach, 68
Wernz-Vidal, 157
Witnesses, guardians as, 138
right to introduce, 139
right to reject, 139

Zacchia, 37

CANON LAW STUDIES*

358. Sesto, Rev. Gennaro J., S.D.B., A.B., S.T.L., J.C.L., Guardians of the mentally ill in ecclesiastical trials.
359. Carroll, Rev. James J., A.B., J.C.L., The bishop's quinquennial report.
360. Curtin, Rev. William Thomas, A.B., J.C.L., The plaint of nullity against the sentence.
361. Ganter, Rev. Bernard J., J.C.L., Clerical attire.
362. Goertz, Rev. Victor M., J.C.L., The judicial summons.
363. Heintschel, Rev. Donald E., A.B., J.C.L., The mediaeval concept of an ecclesiastical office.
364. Kelliher, Rev. Jeremiah Francis, S.A., A.B., S.T.L., J.C.L., Loss of privileges.
365. Mock, Rev. Timothy, C.M.M., J.C.L., Disqualification of electors in ecclesiastical elections.
366. Smyer, Rev. Francis Anthony, A.B., J.C.L., Canonical regulations regarding exposition of the Blessed Sacrament according to canons 1274 and 1275.
367. Wiggins, Rev. Urban C., A.B., J.C.L., Property laws of the State of Ohio affecting the Church.

* For a complete list of the available numbers of this series apply to the Catholic University of America Press, 620 Michigan Ave., N.E., Washington 17, D.C., for a general catalogue.

BIOGRAPHICAL NOTE

Gennaro J. Sesto was born on August 1, 1921, in Biddeford, Maine. He attended the North School in Portland, Maine, before entering the Don Bosco Juniorate at Newton, New Jersey, in the fall of 1935. After completing his high school studies there, he entered the novitiate house of the Salesians of Don Bosco. He was admitted to the religious profession, which he made on September 8, 1940. Having received the Bachelor of Arts degree from Don Bosco College, where he made his philosophical studies, he was assigned to teach at the Salesian High School in New Rochelle, New York, from September, 1943, to June, 1946. In October, 1946, he entered the Pontificium Athenaeum Salesianum, Turin, Italy. There he received the Licentiate in Sacred Theology in June, 1950. On July 2 of that year he was ordained to the priesthood. In the fall of 1950 he was enrolled in the School of Canon Law of the same Pontifical University, where he received the Baccalaureate Degree in Canon Law in June, 1951, and the Licentiate Degree in June, 1952. He was admitted to the School of Canon Law at the Catholic University of America in the fall of 1952.

www.ingramcontent.com/pod-product-compliance
Lightning Source LLC
LaVergne TN
LVHW050233080826
844660LV00012B/525